Introduction to Programming
with **Greenfoot**

Object-Oriented Programming in Java
With Games and Simulations

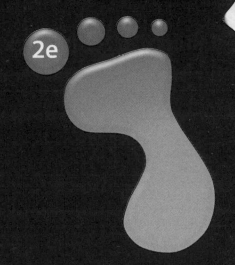

2e

Introduction to Programming
with Greenfoot

Object-Oriented Programming in Java
With Games and Simulations

Michael Kölling

PEARSON

Boston   Columbus   Indianapolis   New York   San Francisco   Hoboken
Amsterdam   Cape Town   Dubai   London   Madrid   Milan   Munich   Paris   Montréal   Toronto
Delhi   Mexico City   São Paulo   Sydney   Hong Kong   Seoul   Singapore   Taipei   Tokyo

Editorial Director: *Marcia Horton*
Executive Editor: *Tracy Johnson*
Editorial Assistant: *Kelsey Loanes*
VP of Marketing: *Christy Lesko*
Director of Field Marketing: *Tim Galligan*
Product Marketing Manager: *Bram van Kempen*
Field Marketing Manager: *Demetrius Hall*
Marketing Assistant: *Jon Bryant*
Director of Product Management: *Erin Gregg*
Team Lead Product Management: *Scott Disanno*
Program Manager: *Carole Snyder*
Production Project Manager: *Camille Trentacoste*
Procurement Manager: *Mary Fischer*
Senior Specialist, Program Planning and Support: *Maura Zaldivar-Garcia*
Manager, Rights Management: *Rachel Youdelman*
Senior Project Manager, Rights Management: *Timothy Nicholls*
Cover Designer: *Black Horse Designs*
Cover Art: *Ivan kmit/Fotolia*

Library of Congress Cataloging-in-Publication Data on File

Kölling, Michael.
    Introduction to programming with greenfoot object-oriented programming in java with games and simulations / Michael Kölling. — 2nd edition.
        pages cm
    Includes bibliographical references and index.
    ISBN 978-0-13-405429-2 — ISBN 0-13-405429-6   1. Greenfoot (Electronic resource)   2. Object-oriented programming (Computer science)—Study and teaching.   3. Java (Computer program language)   4. Computer games—Programming.   I. Title.
    QA76.64.K657 2016
    794.8'1526—dc23

                                                                                    2015000976

10 9 8 7 6 5 4 3 2 1

ISBN-13: 978-0-13-405429-2
ISBN-10:   0-13-405429-6

To my darling girl.

Contents

List of scenarios discussed in this book

Leaves and Wombats   (Chapter 1)

This is a simple example showing wombats moving around on screen, occasionally eating leaves. The scenario has no specific purpose other than illustrating some important object-oriented concepts and Greenfoot interactions.

Asteroids 1   (Chapter 1)

This is a simple version of a classic arcade game. You fly a spaceship through space and try to avoid being hit by asteroids. At this stage, we only use the scenario to make some small changes and illustrate how to edit source code to change program behavior.

Little Crab   (Chapters 2, 3, 4)

This is our first full development. Starting from almost nothing, we develop a simple game slowly, adding things such as movement, keyboard control, sound, and many other elements of typical games.

Fat Cat   (Chapter 2)

This is a small scenario serving as a basis for exercises with methods calls and simple statements. Make the cat perform while you practice your Java.

Stickman   (Chapter 3)

Another small exercise scenario. This does not do much to start with, and we use it to do some exercises with if-statements at the end of the chapter.

White Blood Cell (WBC)   (Chapter 5)

A typical side-scrolling game. We develop it from a very primitive, rudimentary start to a full, playable game. You steer a white blood cell through an artery to catch and neutralize bacteria.

Piano   (Chapter 6)

An on-screen piano that you can really play.

Bubbles   (Chapter 6)

A small scenario serving as a platform to practice writing some loops.

Autumn   (Chapter 7)

This scenario shows leaves floating in the air, occasionally blown around. It is not a game, or any completed project in any sense, but it gives a good first look at collision detection and lists.

Newton's Lab   (Chapter 8)

Newton's Lab is a simulation of the motion of stars and planets in space. Gravity plays a central role here. We also make a variant of this that combines gravity with making music, ending up with musical output triggered by objects under gravitational movement.

Asteroids 2   (Chapter 9)

We come back to the asteroids example from Chapter 2. This time, we investigate more fully how to implement it and add some more game elements.

Loop Practice   (Chapter 9)

As the name suggests: a scenario with the sole purpose of reinforcing the use of loops. This scenario could also be used much earlier for similar exercises.

Greeps   (Interlude 2)

Alien creatures land on earth to collect tomatoes. This scenario is a competition: Program the *greeps* so that they collect as many tomatoes in a limited time.

Color Chart   (Chapter 10)

A small scenario just to display a chart of RGB colors.

Smoke   (Chapter 10)

This scenario demonstrated a visual effect: smoke trailing a moving ball. In general, it serves to discuss dynamic drawing, to create more interesting visuals.

Path Follower   (Chapter 10)

A small scenario demonstrating a creature following a colored path on the ground. This example is used to practice more work with color.

Foxes and Rabbits   (Chapter 11)

A predator/prey simulation. This scenario is fairly complete, and we use it to make some experiments and gain some understanding about the nature of simulations.

Ants   (Chapter 11)

A simulation of ant colonies searching for food, communicating via drops of phero-mones left on the ground.

Simple Camera   (Chapter 12)

Showing a camera image on screen, using the Microsoft Kinect.

Greenscreen   (Chapter 12)

Using Kinect input to create a greenscreen effect (placing a user in front of a fixed background image).

Stick Figure (Chapter 12)

A demonstration of skeleton tracking with the Microsoft Kinect.

Body Paint (Chapter 12)

We extend the skeleton tracking to allow multiple users to paint on screen by waving their hands in the air. Again, making use of the Microsoft Kinect.

Kinect Pong (Chapter 12)

A very simple game, but this time with gesture input instead of keyboard control.

Fred With Radio (Chapter 12)

A last demo scenario for the Microsoft Kinect. We do not discuss this scenario in the chapter, but it serves as a model demo for studying how a cartoon character could be controlled by gestures.

The following scenarios are presented in Chapter 13, and selected aspects of them briefly discussed. They are intended as inspiration for further projects.

Marbles

A simulation of a marble board game. Marbles have to be cleared of the board within a limited number of moves. Contains simple physics.

Lifts

A start of a lift simulation. Incomplete at this stage—can be used as a start of a project.

Boids

A demo showing flocking behavior: A flock of birds flies across the screen, aiming to stick together while avoiding obstacles.

Explosion

A demo of a more sophisticated explosion effect.

Breakout

This is the start of an implementation of the classic Breakout game. Very incomplete, but with an interesting visual effect.

Platform jumper

A demo of a partial implementation of an ever-popular genre of games: platform jumpers.

Wave

This scenario is a simple demonstration of a physical effect: the propagation of a wave on a string.

Map

A scenario showing use of live data from the Internet, in this case Google maps.

About the companion website

Additional material and resources for this book can be found at
http://www.greenfoot.org/book/

For students:

- The Greenfoot software

- The scenarios discussed in this book

- The Greenfoot Gallery—a scenario showcase

- Tutorial videos

- A discussion forum

- Technical support

For Instructors:

- The "Greenroom," a free, instructor-only community site containing many teaching resources, worksheets, project ideas, and a discussion forum. Sign up here and talk to thousands of other instructors who are using Greenfoot. **http://greenroom.greenfoot.org**

- Scenarios are available to qualified instructors. Contact your Pearson representative or visit the Pearson Instructor Resource Center. **http://www.pearsonhighered.com/irc**

Acknowledgments

This book is the tip of an iceberg. It is an introduction to programming with Java, but this kind of approach would not be possible without the Greenfoot ecosystem. This book builds on many years of work by several people who have helped build Greenfoot.

The book rests first and foremost on the software itself—Greenfoot—but this is not the whole story. Much time and effort has gone into the design of websites (the Greenfoot community website, the Greenroom), development of material, building and supporting a user community, workshops and outreach, and a number of people have played very important roles in this.

Poul Henriksen was the first person to join me in this project. He started the Greenfoot implementation as part of his Masters thesis and was the main contributor to the software for many of the early years. Davin McCall, Bruce Quig, and Neil Brown are the next wave of designers and developers who have worked on Greenfoot for many years and shaped large parts of the design and implementation of the system as it is today. It is not easy to maintain a software system of this size with such few people and resources, but all are outstanding programmers and have managed to develop a system that has survived for almost ten years so far and runs with few problems on millions of computers around the world. This is an outstanding achievement, and I have been very lucky to have these people on my team.

Other important contributions to the ecosystem were by Ian Utting and our more recent team members, Amjad Altadmri and Fabio Hedayioglu. A wide variety of activities has helped to make the Greenfoot community what it is today.

The development of Greenfoot is being supported by Oracle Inc., through charitable donations over many years. Their consistent and ongoing support have allowed us to maintain our group; without this, Greenfoot would not exist. We are very grateful for their commitment and substantial contribution to the education community.

The people at Pearson Education have struggled on bravely in the face of the many delays caused by my missing of every possible deadline for sending in this manuscript. Tracy Johnson has worked with me on this book from the very beginning, through the first edition, and now the second one. She has been consistently positive, excited and encouraging, and her support has made a huge difference. Camille Trentacoste and Carole Snyder have done a lot of the important detail work to get this book produced, and I am grateful for their input and help.

The first edition of this book was reviewed by a number of people who have provided very detailed, thoughtful and useful feedback. They are Carolyn Oates, Damianne President, Detlef Rick, Gunnar Johannesmeyer, Josh Fishburn, Mark Hayes, Marla Parker, Matt Jadud, Todd O'Bryan, Lael Grant, Jason Green, Mark Lewis, Rodney Hoffman, and Michael Kadri. They helped spotting many errors and pointed out many opportunities for improvement. Josh Buhl and Adrienne Decker made a number of very useful suggestions after the publication of the first edition that have helped improve the examples for the second edition.

I am very grateful to Kerstin Wachholz for her expert proofreading—she found and fixed many of my errors and removed the warts of my language—, and to my good friend Michael Caspersen for providing encouragement very early in the project that was very important to me, partly because it helped improve the book, but most importantly because it encouraged me to believe that the idea of the Greenfoot system itself might be interesting to teachers and worthwhile completing.

About the 2nd edition

This is the second edition of this book. It tries to stick with what worked well the first time around, and to improve the parts that were not as smooth as they could have been.

We maintain the overall style of the book: the hands-on presentation of programming projects, the practical work interspersed with discussion and explanation, and the general tone. This has worked very well.

However, there were points in the first edition where readers found progression challenging when the pace picked up in the second half of the book. We have now added two chapters to introduce some concepts more slowly and gradually, and to provide more practice with the most difficult concepts. We have also added a significant amount of exercises to each chapter to provide much more practice and reinforcement of the concepts covered. This includes the presentation and use of many more practice scenarios.

We have also added a chapter about programming Greenfoot with the Microsoft Kinect. While not every reader can make use of this (because it requires having the hardware available), the level of enthusiasm and excitement that these examples have generated when we presented them in workshops justify, in our view, inclusion here. There is so much potential.

And, of course, the book has been updated to make use of new features of more recent versions of the Greenfoot software. We have adapted Greenfoot to make some popular tasks possible or easier and to illustrate some concepts better. The book incorporates this in the new scenarios.

Overall, we hope that the added material serves to make your path through the maze that is the learning of programming even more smooth and more interesting.

Introduction

Welcome to Greenfoot! In this book, we will discuss how to program graphical computer programs, such as simulations and games, using the Java Programming Language and the Greenfoot environment.

There are several goals in doing this: one is to learn programming, another is to have fun along the way. While the examples we discuss in this book are specific to the Greenfoot environment, the concepts are general: working through this book will teach you general programming principles in a modern, object-oriented programming language. However, it will also show you how to make your own computer game, a biology simulation, or an on-screen piano.

This book is very practically oriented. Chapters and exercises are structured around real, hands-on development tasks. First, there is a problem that we need to solve, then we look at language constructs and strategies that help us solve the problem. This is quite different from many introductory programming textbooks that are often structured around programming language constructs.

As a result, this book starts with less theory, and more practical activity than most programming books. This is also the reason we use Greenfoot: It is the Greenfoot environment that makes this possible. Greenfoot allows us to play. And that does not only mean playing computer games; it means playing with programming: we can create objects, move them around on screen, call their methods, and observe what they do, all interactively and easily. This leads to a more hands-on approach to programming than what would be possible without such an environment.

A more practical approach does not mean that the book does not cover the necessary theory and principles as well. It's just that the order is changed. Instead of introducing a concept theoretically first and then doing some exercises with it, we often jump right in and use a construct, initially explaining only as much as necessary to solve the task at hand, then come back to the theoretical background later. We typically follow a spiral approach: we introduce some aspects of a concept when we first encounter it, then revisit it later in another context, and gradually deepen our understanding.

The emphasis throughout is to make the work we do interesting, relevant, and enjoyable. There is no reason why computer programming has to be dry, formal, or boring. Having fun along the way is okay. We think we can manage to make the experience interesting and pedagogically sound at the same time.

This book can be used both as a self-study book or as a textbook in a programming course. Exercises are worked into the text throughout the book—if you do them all, you will come out of this as a fairly competent programmer.

The projects discussed in this book are easy enough that they can be managed by high school students, but they are also open and extendable enough that even seasoned programmers can find interesting and challenging aspects to do. While Greenfoot is an educational environment, Java is not a toy language. Since Java is our language of choice for this book, the projects discussed here (and others you may want to create in Greenfoot) can be made as complex and challenging as you like.

While it is possible to create simple games quickly and easily in Greenfoot, it is equally possible to build highly sophisticated simulations of complex systems, possibly using artificial intelligence algorithms, agent technology, database connectivity, network communication, or anything else you can think of. Java is a very rich language that opens the whole world of programming, and Greenfoot imposes no restrictions as to which aspects of the language you can use.

In other words: Greenfoot scales well. It allows easy entry for young beginners, but experienced programmers can also implement interesting, sophisticated scenarios.

Programming is a creative discipline, and Greenfoot is a tool that helps you build what you invent.

1 Getting to know Greenfoot

topics:	the Greenfoot interface, interacting with objects, invoking methods, running a scenario
concepts:	object, class, method call, parameter, return value

This book will show you how to develop computer games and simulations with Greenfoot, a development environment. In this chapter, we shall take a look at Greenfoot itself and see what it can do and how to use it. We do this by trying out some existing programs.

Once we are comfortable with using Greenfoot, we shall jump right into writing a game ourselves.

The best way to read this chapter (and indeed the whole book) is by sitting at your computer with Greenfoot open on your screen and the book open on your desk. We will regularly ask you to do things in Greenfoot while you read. Some of the tasks you can skip; however, you will have to do some in order to progress in the chapter. In any case, you will learn most if you follow along and do them.

At this stage, we assume that you have already installed the Greenfoot software and the book scenarios (described in Appendix A). If not, read through the appendix first.

1.1 Getting started

Start Greenfoot and open the scenario *leaves-and-wombats* from the *Greenfoot book scenarios* folder. You can do this by choosing *Scenario–Open*[1] from the menu.

---

[1] We use this notation to tell you to select functions from the menu. Scenario–Open refers to the *Open* item in the *Scenario* menu.

Figure 1.1

The Greenfoot main
window

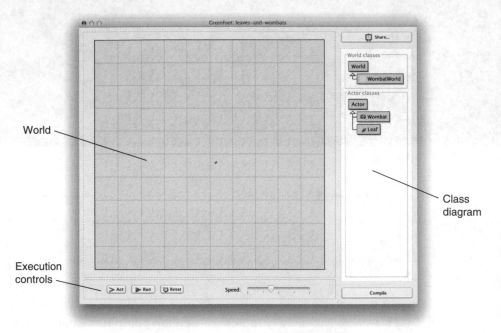

World

Class
diagram

Execution
controls

You will now see the Greenfoot main window, with the scenario open, looking similar
to Figure 1.1.

The main window consists of three main areas and a couple of extra buttons. The
main areas are:

■ The *world*. The largest area covering most of the screen (a sand-colored grid in this
case) is called the world. This is where the program will run and we will see things
happen.

■ The *class diagram*. The area on the right with the beige-colored boxes and arrows is
the class diagram. We shall discuss this in more detail shortly.

■ The *execution controls*. The *Act*, *Run*, and *Reset* buttons and the speed slider at the
bottom are the execution controls. We'll come back to them in a little while, too.

1.2   Objects and classes

We shall discuss the class diagram first. The class diagram shows us the classes involved
in this scenario. In this case, they are `World`, `WombatWorld`, `Actor`, `Wombat`, and `Leaf`.

Concept

Greenfoot
scenarios consist
of a set of
classes.

We shall be using the Java programming language for our projects. Java is an *object-
oriented* language. The concepts of classes and objects are fundamental in object
orientation.

Let us start by looking at the `Wombat` class. The class `Wombat` stands for the general
concept of a wombat—it describes all wombats. Once we have a class in Greenfoot, we

can create *objects* from it. (Objects are also often referred to as *instances* in programming—the two terms are synonyms.)

A wombat, by the way, is an Australian marsupial (Figure 1.2). If you want to find out more about them, do a Web search—it should give you plenty of results.

Right-click[3] on the Wombat class, and you will see the *class menu* pop up (Figure 1.3a). The first option in that menu, *new Wombat( )*, lets us create new wombat objects. Try it out.

You will see that this gives you a small picture of a wombat object, which you can move on screen with your mouse (Figure 1.3b). Place the wombat into the world by clicking anywhere in the world (Figure 1.3c).

Figure 1.2
A wombat[2]

Figure 1.3
a) The class menu
b) Dragging a
new object
c) Placing the object

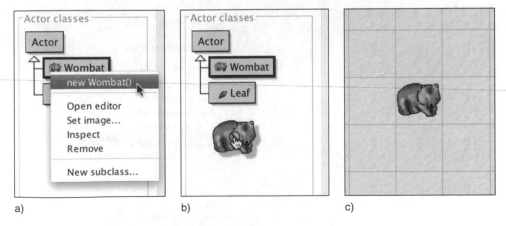

[2] Image source: Marco Tomasini/Fotolia
[3] On Mac OS, use ctrl-click instead of right-click if you have a one-button mouse.

> **Concept**
>
> Many **objects** can be created from a **class**.

Once you have a class in Greenfoot, you can create as many objects from it as you like.

> **Exercise 1.1** Create some more wombats in the world. Create some leaves.

Currently, only the Wombat and Leaf classes are of interest to us. We shall discuss the other classes later.

1.3 Interacting with objects

> **Concept**
>
> Objects have **methods**. Invoking these performs an action.

Once we have placed some objects into the world, we can interact with these objects by right-clicking them. This will pop up the *object menu* (Figure 1.4). The object menu shows us all the operations this specific object can perform. For example, a wombat's object menu shows us what this wombat can do (plus two additional functions, *Inspect* and *Remove*, which we shall discuss later).

In Java, these operations are called *methods*. It cannot hurt to get used to standard terminology straight away, so we shall also call them methods from now on. We can *invoke* a method by selecting it from the menu.

> **Exercise 1.2** Invoke the move() method on a wombat. What does it do? Try it several times. Invoke the turnLeft() method. Place two wombats into your world and make them face each other.

Figure 1.4

The wombat's object menu

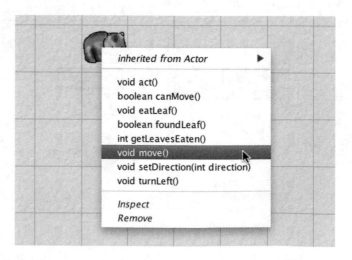

In short: we can start to make things happen by creating objects from one of the classes provided, and we can give commands to the objects by invoking their methods.

Let us have a closer look at the object menu. The *move* and *turnLeft* methods are listed as:

```
void move()
void turnLeft()
```

We can see that the method names are not the only thing shown. There is also the word *void* at the beginning and a pair of parentheses at the end. These two cryptic bits of information tell us what data goes into the method call, and what data comes back from it.

1.4 Return types

> **Concept**
>
> The **return type** of a method specifies what a method call will return.

The word at the beginning is called the *return type*. It tells us what the method returns to us when we invoke it. The word `void` means "nothing" in this context: methods with a `void` return type do not return any information. They just carry out their action, and then stop.

Any word other than `void` tells us that the method returns some information when invoked, and of what type that information is. In the wombat's menu (Figure 1.4), we can also see the words `int` and `boolean`. The word `int` is short for "integer" and refers to whole numbers (numbers without a decimal point). Examples of integer numbers are 3, 42, –3, and 12000000.

> **Concept**
>
> A method with a **void** return type does not return a value.

The type `boolean` has only two possible values: `true` and `false`. A method that returns a `boolean` will return either the value `true` or the value `false` to us.

Methods with `void` return types are like commands for our wombat. If we invoke the `turnLeft` method, the wombat obeys and turns left. Methods with non-void return types are like questions. Consider the `canMove` method:

```
boolean canMove()
```

When we invoke this method, we see a result similar to that shown in Figure 1.5, displayed in a dialog box. The important information here is the word "true," which

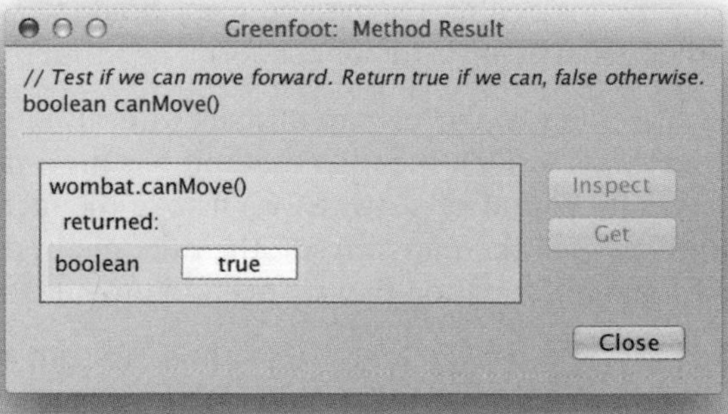

Figure 1.5

A method result

was returned by this method call. In effect, we have just asked the wombat "*Can you move?*", and the wombat has answered by saying "*Yes!*" (true).

> **Exercise 1.3** Invoke the `canMove()` method on your wombat. Does it always return *true*? Or can you find situations in which it returns *false*?

Try out another method with a return value:

```
int getLeavesEaten()
```

Using this method, we can get the information how many leaves this wombat has eaten.

> **Exercise 1.4** Using a newly created wombat, the `getLeavesEaten()` method will always return zero. Can you create a situation in which the result of this method is not zero? (In other words: can you make your wombat eat some leaves?)

Methods with non-void return types usually just tell us something about the object (*Can it move? How many leaves has it eaten?*), but do not change the object. The wombat is just as it was before we asked it about the leaves. Methods with void return types are usually commands to the objects that make it do something.

1.5 Parameters

The other bit in the method menu that we have not yet discussed is the parentheses after the method name.

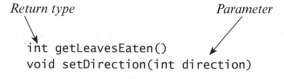

```
int getLeavesEaten()
void setDirection(int direction)
```

Return type   *Parameter*

The parentheses after the method name hold the *parameter list*. This tells us whether the method requires any additional information to run, and if so, what kind of information.

If we see only a pair of parentheses without anything else between it (as we have in all methods so far), then the method has an *empty parameter list*. In other words, it expects no parameters—when we invoke the method, it will just run. If there is anything between the parentheses, then the method expects one or more parameters— additional information that we need to provide.

Let us try out the *setDirection* method. We can see that it has the words *int direction* written in its parameter list. When we invoke it, we see a dialog box similar to the one shown in Figure 1.6.

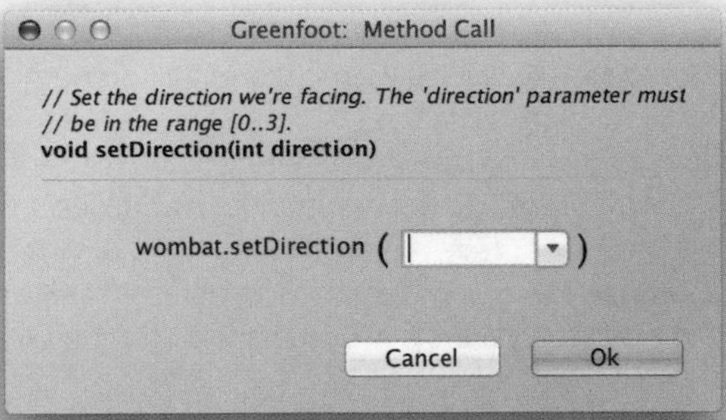

Figure 1.6
A method call dialog

The words *int direction* tell us that this method expects one parameter of type *int*, which specifies a *direction*. A parameter is an additional bit of data we must provide for this method to run. Every parameter is defined by two words: first the parameter type (here: *int*) and then a name, which gives us a hint what this parameter is used for. If a method has a parameter, then we must provide this additional information when we invoke the method.

In this case, the type *int* tells us that we now should provide a whole number, and the name suggests that this number somehow specifies the direction to turn to.

At the top of the dialog is a comment that tells us a little more: the direction parameter should be between 0 and 3.

> **Exercise 1.5** Invoke the `setDirection(int direction)` method. Provide a parameter value and see what happens. Which number corresponds to which direction? Write them down. What happens when you type in a number greater than 3? What happens if you provide input that is not a whole number, such as a decimal number (2.5) or a word (three)?

Concept

The specification of a method, which shows its return type, name, and parameters is called its **signature**.

The `setDirection` method expects only a single parameter. Later, we shall see cases where methods expect more than one parameter. In that case, the method will list all the parameters it expects between the parentheses.

The description of each method shown in the object menu, including the return type, method name, and parameter list, is called the *method signature*.

We have now reached a point where you can do the main interactions with Greenfoot objects. You can create objects from classes, interpret the method signatures, and invoke methods (with and without parameters).

1.6 Greenfoot execution

There is one other way of interacting with Greenfoot objects: The execution controls.

Tip

You can place objects into the world more quickly by selecting a class in the class diagram, and then shift-clicking in the world.

Exercise 1.6 Place a wombat and a good number of leaves into the world, and then invoke a wombat's `act()` method several times. What does this method do? How does it differ from the move method? Make sure to try different situations, for example, the wombat facing the edge of the world, or sitting on a leaf.

Exercise 1.7 Still with a wombat and some leaves in the world, click the *Act* button in the execution controls near the bottom of the Greenfoot window. What does this do?

Exercise 1.8 What is the difference between clicking the *Act* button and invoking the `act()` method? (Try with several wombats in the world.)

Exercise 1.9 Click the *Run* button. What does it do?

The `act` method is a very fundamental method of Greenfoot objects. We shall encounter it regularly in all the following chapters. All objects in a Greenfoot world have this `act` method. Invoking `act` is essentially giving the object the instruction "*Do whatever you want to do now.*" If you tried it out for our wombat, you will have seen that the wombat's `act` does something like the following:

- If we're sitting on a leaf, eat the leaf.
- Otherwise, if we can move forward, move forward.
- Otherwise, turn left.

Concept

Objects that can be placed into the world are known as **actors**.

The experiments in the exercises above should also have shown you that the *Act* button in the execution controls simply calls the `act` method of the actors in the world. The only difference to invoking the method via the object menu is that the *Act* button invokes the `act` method of all objects in the world, while using the object menu affects only the one chosen object.

The *Run* button just calls `act` over and over again for all objects, until you click *Pause*.

Let us try out what we have discussed in the context of another scenario.

1.7 A second example

Open another scenario, named *asteroids1*, from the *chapter01* folder of the book scenarios. It should look similar to Figure 1.7 (except that you will not see the rocket or the asteroids on your screen yet).

1.8 Understanding the class diagram

Let us first have a closer look at the class diagram (Figure 1.8). At the top, you see the two classes called `World` and `Space`, connected by an arrow.

Figure 1.7
The asteroids1 scenario

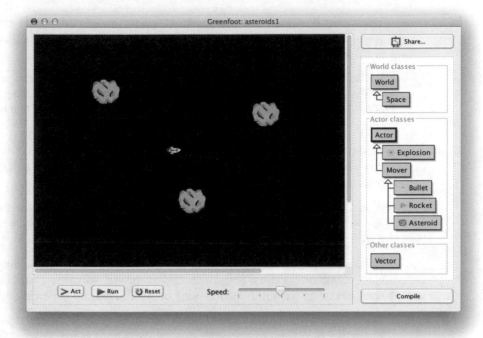

Figure 1.8
A class diagram

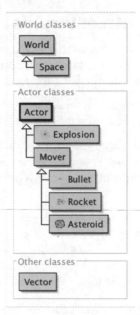

The World class is always there in all Greenfoot scenarios—it is built into Greenfoot. The class under it, Space in this case, represents the specific world for this particular scenario. Its name can be different in each scenario, but every scenario will have a specific world here.

The arrow shows an *is-a* relationship: `Space` *is a* `World` (in the sense of Greenfoot worlds: `Space`, here, is a specific Greenfoot world). We also sometimes say that `Space` is a *subclass* of `World`.

We do not usually need to create objects of world classes—Greenfoot does that for us. When we open a scenario, Greenfoot automatically creates an object of the world subclass. The object is then shown on the main part of the screen. (The big black image of space is an object of the `Space` class.)

Below this, we see another group of six classes, linked by arrows. Each class represents its own objects. Reading from the bottom, we see that we have asteroids, rockets, and bullets, which are all "movers," while movers and explosions are actors.

Again, we have subclass relationships: `Rocket`, for example, is a subclass of `Mover`, and `Mover` and `Explosion` are subclasses of `Actor`. (Conversely, we say that `Mover` is a *superclass* of `Rocket` and `Actor` is a *superclass* of `Explosion`.)

Subclass relationships can go over several levels: `Rocket`, for example, is also a subclass of `Actor` (because it is a subclass of `Mover`, which is a subclass of `Actor`). We shall discuss more about the meaning of subclasses and superclasses later.

The class `Vector`, shown at the bottom of the diagram under the heading *Other classes* is a helper class used by the other classes. We cannot place objects of it into the world.

1.9   Playing with asteroids

We can start playing with this scenario by creating some actor objects (objects of subclasses of `Actor`) and placing them into the world. Here, we create objects only of the classes that have no further subclasses: `Rocket`, `Bullet`, `Asteroid`, and `Explosion`.

Let us start by placing a rocket and two asteroids into space. (Remember: you can create objects by right-clicking on the class, or selecting the class and shift-clicking into the world.)

When you have placed your objects, click the *Run* button. You can then control the spaceship with the arrow keys on your keyboard, and you can fire a shot by using the space bar. Try getting rid of the asteroids before you crash into them.

Exercise 1.10 If you have played this game for a bit, you will have noticed that you cannot fire very quickly. Let us tweak our spaceship firing software a bit so that we can shoot more quickly. (That should make getting rid of the asteroids a bit easier!) Place a rocket into the world, then invoke its **setGunReloadTime** method (through the object menu), and set the reload time to 5. Play again (with at least two asteroids) to try it out.

Exercise 1.11 Once you have managed to remove all asteroids (or at any other point in the game) stop the execution (press *Pause*) and find out how many shots you have fired. You can do this using a method from the rocket's object menu. (Try destroying two asteroids with as few shots as possible.)

Exercise 1.12 You will have noticed that the rocket moves a bit as soon as you place it into the world. What is its initial speed?

Exercise 1.13 Asteroids have an inherent *stability*. Each time they get hit by a bullet, their stability decreases. When it reaches zero, they break up. What is their initial stability value after you create them? By how much does the stability decrease from a single hit by a bullet? (Hint: Just shoot an asteroid once, and then check the stability again. Another hint: To shoot the asteroid, you must run the game. To use the object menu, you must pause the game first.)

Exercise 1.14 Make a very big asteroid.

1.10 Source code

> **Concept**
>
> Every class is defined by **source code**. This code defines what objects of this class can do. We can look at the source code by opening the class's editor.

The behavior of each object is defined by its class. The way we can specify this behavior is by writing *source code* in the Java programming language. The source code of a class is the code that specifies all the details about the class and its objects. Selecting *Open editor* from the class's menu will show us an editor window (Figure 1.9) that contains the class's source code.

The source code for this class is fairly complex, and we do not need to understand it all at this stage. However, if you study the rest of this book and program your own games or simulations, you will learn over time how to write this code.

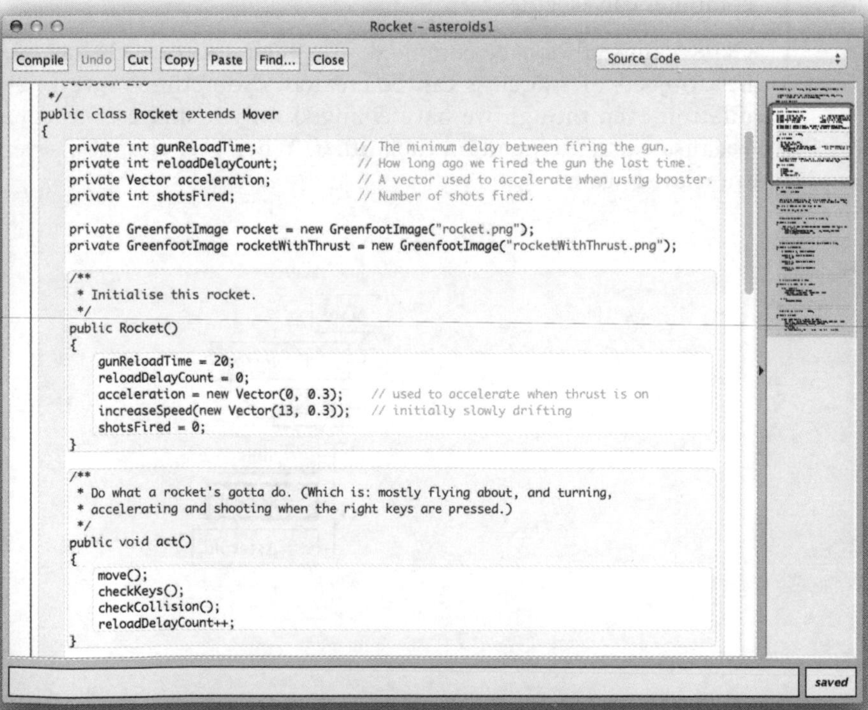

Figure 1.9
The editor window of class Rocket

At this point, it is only important to understand that we can change the behavior of the objects by changing the class's source code. Let us try this out.

We have seen before that the default firing speed of the rocket was fairly slow. We could change this for every rocket individually by invoking a method on each new rocket, but we would have to do this over and over again, every time we start playing. Instead, we can change the code of the rocket so that its initial firing speed is changed (say, to 5), so that all rockets in the future start with this improved behavior.

Open the editor for the Rocket class. About 25 lines from the top, you should find a line that reads

```
gunReloadTime = 20;
```

This is where the initial gun reloading time gets set. Change this line so that it reads

```
gunReloadTime = 5;
```

Be sure to change nothing else. You will notice very soon that programming systems are very fussy. A single incorrect or missing character can lead to errors. If, for example, you remove the semicolon at the end of the line, you would run into an error fairly soon.

Close the editor window (our change is complete) and look at the class diagram again. It has changed: The Rocket class now appears striped (Figure 1.10). The striped look indicates that a class has been edited and now must be *compiled*. Compilation is a translation process: the class's source code is translated into a machine code that your computer can execute.

Classes must always be compiled after their source code has been changed, before new objects of the class can be created. (Sometimes several classes need recompilation even though we have changed only a single class. This may be the case because classes depend on each other. When one changes, several may need to be translated again.)

Figure 1.10

Classes after editing

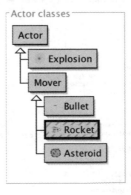

We can compile the classes by clicking the *Compile* button in the bottom right corner of Greenfoot's main window. Once the classes have been compiled, the stripes disappear, and we can create objects again.

> **Exercise 1.15** Make the change to the **Rocket** class source code as described above. Close the editor, and compile the classes. Try it out: Rockets should now be able to fire quickly right from the start.

We shall come back to the asteroids game in Chapter 7, where we will discuss how to write this game.

Summary

In this chapter, we have seen what Greenfoot scenarios can look like, and how to interact with them. We have seen how to create objects, and how to communicate with these objects by invoking their methods. Some methods were commands to the object, while other methods returned information about the object. Parameters are used to provide additional information to methods, while return values pass information back to the caller.

Objects were created from their classes, and source code controls the definition of the class (and with this, the behavior and characteristics of all the class's objects).

We have seen that we can change the source code using an editor to make changes. After editing the source, classes need to be recompiled.

We will spend most of the rest of the book discussing how to write Java source code to create scenarios that do interesting things.

Concept summary

- Greenfoot scenarios consist of a set of **classes**.
- Many **objects** can be created from a **class**.
- Objects have **methods**. Invoking these performs an action.
- The **return type** of a method specifies what a method call will return.
- A method with a **void** return type does not return a value.
- Methods with void return types represent **commands**; methods with non-void return types represent **questions**.

- A **parameter** is a mechanism to pass additional data to a method.

- Parameters and return values have **types**. Examples of types are **int** for numbers, and **boolean** for true/false values.

- The specification of a method, which shows its return type, name, and parameters, is called its **signature**.

- Objects that can be placed into the world are known as **actors**.

- A **subclass** is a class that represents a specialization of another. In Greenfoot, this is shown with an arrow in the class diagram.

- Every class is defined by **source code**. This code defines what objects of this class can do. We can look at the source code by opening the class's editor.

- Computers do not understand source code. It needs to be translated to machine code before it can be executed. This is called **compilation**.

2

The first program: Little Crab

> **topics:** writing code: movement, turning, reacting to the screen edges
>
> **concepts:** source code, method call, parameter, sequence, if-statement

In the previous chapter, we discussed how to use existing Greenfoot scenarios: We created objects, invoked methods, and played a game.

Now we want to start to make our own game.

2.1 The Little Crab scenario

The scenario we use for this chapter is called *little-crab*. You will find this scenario in the *book-scenarios* folder.

The scenario you see should look similar to Figure 2.1.

> **Exercise 2.1** Start Greenfoot and open the *little-crab* scenario. Place a crab into the world and run the program (click the *Run* button). What do you observe? (Remember: If the class icons on the right appear striped, you have to compile the project first.)

On the right you see the classes in this scenario (Figure 2.2). We notice that there are the usual Greenfoot `Actor` and `World` classes, and subclasses called `CrabWorld` and `Crab`.

The hierarchy (denoted by the arrows) indicates an *is-a* relationship (also called *inheritance*): A crab *is an* actor, and the `CrabWorld` *is a* world.

Initially, we will work only with the `Crab` class. We will talk a little more about the `CrabWorld` and `Actor` classes later on.

If you have just done the exercise above, then you know the answer to the question "What do you observe?" It is: "nothing."

Figure 2.1

The Little Crab scenario

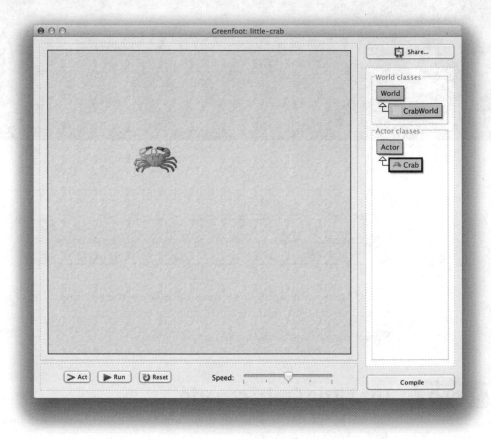

Figure 2.2

The Little Crab classes

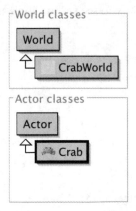

The crab does not do anything when Greenfoot runs. This is because there is no source code in the definition of the Crab class that specifies what the crab should do.

In this chapter, we shall work on changing this. The first thing we will do is to make the crab move.

2.2 Making the crab move

Let us have a look at the source code of class `Crab`. Open the editor to display the `Crab` source. (You can do this by selecting the *Open editor* function from the class's popup menu, or you can just double-click the class.)

The source code you see is shown in Code 2.1.

Code 2.1

The original version of the "Crab" class

```java
import greenfoot.*;

/**
 * This class defines a crab. Crabs live on the beach.
 */
public class Crab extends Actor
{
    public void act()
    {
        // Add your action code here
    }
}
```

This is a standard Java class definition. That is, this text defines what the crab can do.

You will notice the different colored backgrounds: The whole class definition is enclosed in a green box and, within it, every method definition is in a separate box with yellowish background. (There is also a separate statement at the top, before the class definition, on white background.)

We will look at this in more detail later. For now we will concentrate on getting the crab to move.

Within the class definition, we can see what is called the *act method* (the bit in the yellow box). It looks like this[1]:

```java
public void act()
{
    // Add your action code here.
}
```

The first line is the *signature* of the method. The last three lines—the two curly brackets and anything between them—are called the *body* of the method. Here we can add some code that determines the actions of the crab. We can replace the grey text in the middle with a command. One such command is

```java
move(5);
```

---

[1] In this book, when we show code inline in the text, we do not show the background colors. Don't worry about this: the colors do not alter the meaning of the code. They just help you read and write your code when you are in Greenfoot.

Note that it has to be written exactly as shown, including the parentheses and the semicolon. The act method should then look like this:

```
public void act()
{
    move(5);
}
```

> **Exercise 2.2** Change the *act* method in your crab class to include the **move(5)**; instruction, as shown above. Compile the scenario (by clicking the *Compile* button) and place a crab into the world. Try clicking the *Act* and *Run* buttons.
>
> **Exercise 2.3** Change the number 5 to a different number. Try larger and smaller numbers. What do you think the number means?
>
> **Exercise 2.4** Place multiple crabs into the world. Run the scenario. What do you observe?

Concept

A **method call** is an instruction that tells an object to perform an action. The action is defined by a method of the object.

You will see that the crab can now move across the screen. The move(5) instruction makes the crab move a little bit to the right.

When we click the *Act* button in the Greenfoot main window, the act method is executed once. That is, the instruction that we have written inside the act method (move(5)) executes. The number 5 in the instruction defines how far the crab moves in each step: In every act step, the crab moves five pixels to the right.

Clicking the *Run* button is just like clicking the *Act* button repeatedly, very quickly. The act method is executed over and over again, until we click *Pause*.

> **Exercise 2.5** Can you find a way to make the crab move backwards (to the left)?

Terminology

The instruction *move(5)* is called a **method call**. A **method** is an action that an object knows how to do (here, the object is the crab) and a **method call** is an instruction telling the crab to do it. The parentheses and number within them are part of the method call. Instructions like this are ended with a semicolon.

2.3 Turning

Let us see what other instruction we can use. The crab also understands a *turn* instruction. Here is what it looks like:

```
turn(3);
```

Concept

Additional information can be passed to some methods within the parentheses. The value passed is called a **parameter**.

The number 3 in the instruction specifies how many degrees the crab should turn. This is called a *parameter*. (The number 5 used for the move call above is also a parameter.)

We could also use other numbers, for example:

```
turn(23);
```

The degree value is specified out of 360 degrees, so any value between 0 and 359 can be used. (Turning 360 degrees would turn all the way around, so it is the same as turning 0 degrees, or not turning at all.)

If we want to turn instead of moving, we can replace the move(5) instruction with a turn(3) instruction. (The parameter values, 5 and 3 in this case, are picked somewhat arbitrarily; you can also use different values.) The act method then looks like this:

```
public void act()
{
    turn(3);
}
```

Concept

Multiple instructions are executed **in sequence**, one after the other, in the order in which they are written.

Exercise 2.6 Replace move(5) with turn(3) in your scenario. Try it out. Also, try values other than 3 and see what it looks like. Remember: every time after you change your source code, you must compile again.

Exercise 2.7 How can you make the crab turn left?

The next thing we can try is to both move and turn. The act method can hold more than one instruction—we can just write multiple instructions in a row.

Code 2.2 shows the complete Crab class, as it looks when we move and turn. In this case, at every act step, the crab will move and then turn (but this will happen so quickly after each other that it appears as if it happens at the same time).

Code 2.2

Making the crab move and turn

```
import greenfoot.*;

/**
 * This class defines a crab. Crabs live on the beach.
 */
public class Crab extends Actor
{
    public void act()
    {
        move(5);
        turn(3);
    }
}
```

Exercise 2.8 Try it out: use a `move(N)` and `turn(M)` instruction in your crab's act method. Try different values for N and M.

Terminology

The number between the parentheses in the turn instruction—i.e., the 5 in *turn(5)*—is called a **parameter**. A parameter is an additional bit of information that we have to provide when we call some methods.

Some methods do not expect any parameters. We write those by writing the method name, the parentheses, and nothing in-between, for example *stop()*. Other methods, such as *turn* and *move*, want more information: *How much should I turn? How far should I move?* In this case, we have to provide that information in the form of a parameter value between the parentheses, for instance *turn(17)*.

Side note: Errors

Concept

When a class is compiled, the compiler checks to see whether there are any errors. If an error is found, an **error message** is displayed.

When we write source code, we have to be very careful: every single character counts. Getting one small thing wrong will result in our program not working. Usually, it will not compile.

This will happen to us regularly: when we write programs, we inevitably make mistakes, and then we have to correct them. Let us try that out now.

If, for example, we forget to write the semicolon after the `move(5)` instruction, we will be told about it when we try to compile.

Exercise 2.9 Open your editor to show the crab's source code, and remove the semicolon after `move(5)`. Then compile. Also experiment with other errors, such as misspelling **move** or making other random changes to the code. Make sure to change it all back after this exercise.

Exercise 2.10 Make various changes to cause different error messages. Find at least five different error messages. Write down each error message and what change you introduced to provoke this error.

Tip

When an error message appears at the bottom of the editor window, a question mark button appears to the right of it. Clicking this button displays some additional information about the error message.

As we can see with this exercise, if we get one small detail wrong, Greenfoot will open the editor, highlight a line, and display a message at the bottom of the editor window. This message attempts to explain the error. The messages, however, vary considerably in their accuracy and usefulness. Sometimes they tell us fairly accurately what the problem is, but sometimes they are cryptic and hard to understand. The line that is highlighted is often the line where the problem is, but sometimes it is the line after the problem. When you see, for example, a "; expected" message, it is possible that the semicolon is in fact missing on the line above the highlighted line.

We will learn to read these messages a little better over time. For now, if you get a message and you are unsure what it means, look very carefully at your code and check that you have typed everything correctly.

2.4 Dealing with screen edges

When we made the crabs move and turn in the previous sections, they got stuck when they reached the edge of the screen. (Greenfoot is designed so that actors cannot leave the world and fall off its edge.)

Now we shall improve this behavior so that the crab notices that it has reached the world edge and turns around. The question is: How can we do that?

Above, we have used the `move` and `turn` methods, so there might also be a method that helps us with our new goal. (In fact, there is.) But how do we find out what methods we have got available?

The `move` and `turn` methods we have used so far, come from the `Actor` class. A crab is an actor (signified by the arrow that goes from `Crab` to `Actor` in the class diagram); therefore it can do whatever an actor can do. Our `Actor` class knows how to move and turn—that is why our crab can also do it. This is called *inheritance*: the `Crab` class inherits all the abilities (methods) from the `Actor` class.

The question now is: what else can our actors do?

To investigate this, we can open the `Actor` class. You will notice when you open (double-click) the `Actor` class, it does not open in a text editor like the `Crab` class, but shows some documentation in a Web browser instead (Figure 2.3). This is because the

Concept

A subclass **inherits** all the methods from its superclass. That means that it has and can use all methods that its superclass defines.

Figure 2.3

Documentation of the Actor class

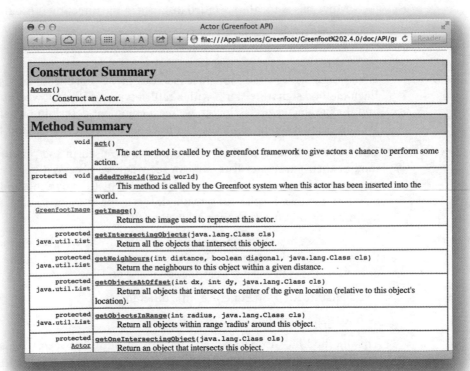

Constructor Summary	
`Actor()` Construct an Actor.	

Method Summary	
void	`act()` The act method is called by the greenfoot framework to give actors a chance to perform some action.
protected void	`addedToWorld(World world)` This method is called by the Greenfoot system when this actor has been inserted into the world.
GreenfootImage	`getImage()` Returns the image used to represent this actor.
protected java.util.List	`getIntersectingObjects(java.lang.Class cls)` Return all the objects that intersect this object.
protected java.util.List	`getNeighbours(int distance, boolean diagonal, java.lang.Class cls)` Return the neighbours to this object within a given distance.
protected java.util.List	`getObjectsAtOffset(int dx, int dy, java.lang.Class cls)` Return all objects that intersect the center of the given location (relative to this object's location).
protected java.util.List	`getObjectsInRange(int radius, java.lang.Class cls)` Return all objects within range 'radius' around this object.
protected Actor	`getOneIntersectingObject(java.lang.Class cls)` Return an object that intersects this object.

Actor class is built-in in Greenfoot; it cannot be edited. But we can still use the Actor's methods to call them. This documentation tells us what methods exist, what parameters they have, and what they do. (We can also look at the documentation of our other classes by switching the editor view from "Source Code" to "Documentation", using the pop-up control in the top right of each editor window. But for Actor, there is only the documentation view.)

> **Exercise 2.11** Open the documentation for the Actor class. Find the list of methods for this class (the "Method Summary"). How many methods does this class have?
>
> **Exercise 2.12** Look through the list of methods available. Can you find one that sounds like it might be useful to check whether we are at the edge of the world?

If we look at the method summary, we can see all the methods that the Actor class provides. Among them are three methods that are especially interesting to us at the moment. They are:

```
boolean isAtEdge()
```
Detect whether the actor has reached the edge of the world.

```
void move(int distance)
```
Move this actor the specified distance in the direction it is currently facing.

```
void turn(int amount)
```
Turn this actor by the specified amount (in degrees).

Here we see the signatures for three methods, as we first encountered them in Chapter 1. Each method signature starts with a return type, and is followed by the method name and the parameter list. Below it, we see a comment describing what the method does. We can see that the three method names are isAtEdge, move, and turn.

The move and turn methods are the ones we used in the previous sections. If we look at their parameter lists, we can see what we observed before: they each expect one parameter of type *int* (a whole number). For the move method, this specifies the distance to move; for the turn method, this is the amount to turn. (Read Section 1.5 again if you are unsure about parameter lists.)

We can also see that the move and turn methods have void as their return type. This means that neither method returns a value. We are commanding or instructing the object to move, or to turn. The crab will just obey the command and not respond with an answer to us.

The signature for isAtEdge is a little different. It is

```
boolean isAtEdge()
```

This method has no parameters (there is nothing between the parentheses), but it specifies a return value: boolean. We have briefly encountered the boolean type in Section 1.4—it is a type that can hold two possible values: *true* or *false*.

Calling methods that have return values (where the return type is not *void*) is not like issuing a command, but asking a question. If we use the `isAtEdge()` method, the method will respond with either *true* (Yes!) or *false* (No!). Thus, we can use this method to check whether we are at the edge of the world.

> **Exercise 2.13** Create a crab. Right-click it, and find the `boolean isAtEdge()` method. (It is in the "inherited from Actor" submenu, since the crab inherited this method from the `Actor` class). Call this method. What does it return?
>
> **Exercise 2.14** Let the crab run to the edge of the screen (or move it there manually), and then call the `isAtEdge()` method again. What does it return now?

We can now combine this method with an *if-statement* to write the code shown in Code 2.3.

Code 2.3
Turning around
at the edge of the
world

```java
import greenfoot.*;

/**
 * This class defines a crab. Crabs live on the beach.
 */
public class Crab extends Actor
{
    public void act()
    {
        if ( isAtEdge() )
        {
            turn(17);
        }
        move(5);
    }
}
```

The if-statement is part of the Java language that makes it possible to execute commands only if some condition is true. For example, here we want to turn only if we are at the edge of the world. The code we have written is:

```java
if ( isAtEdge() )
{
    turn(17);
}
move(5);
```

The general form of an *if-statement* is this:

```java
if ( condition )
{
    instruction;
    instruction;
    ...
}
```

Tip

In the Greenfoot editor, when you place the cursor behind an opening or closing bracket, Greenfoot will mark the matching closing or opening bracket. This can be used to check whether your brackets match up as they should.

In place of the *condition* can be any expression that is either true or false (such as our isAtEdge() method call), and the *instructions* will only be executed if the condition is true. There can be one or more instructions.

If the condition is false, the instructions are just skipped, and execution continues under the closing curly bracket of the if-statement.

Note that our move(5) method call is outside the if-statement, so it will be executed in any case. In other words: If we are at the edge of the world, we turn and then move; if we are not at the edge of the world, we just move.

> **Exercise 2.15** Try it out! Type in the code discussed above, and see if you can make your crabs turn at the edge of the screen. Pay close attention to the opening and closing brackets—it is easy to miss one or have too many.
>
> **Exercise 2.16** Experiment with different values for the parameter to the turn method. Find one that looks good.
>
> **Exercise 2.17** Place the move(5) statement into the if statement, rather than behind it. Test—what is the effect? Explain the behavior you observe. (Then fix it again by moving it back where it was.)

Side note: Scope coloring and indentation

When you look at source code in Greenfoot or in the code examples in this book (for instance, Code 2.3), you will notice the colored boxes used for the background. These are called *scopes*. A scope is the extent of a given Java construct. In Greenfoot, different kinds of construct have been given different colors: a class is green, for example, a method is yellow, and an if-statement is a purplish-grey. You see that these scopes can be *nested*: an if-statement is inside a method, a method is inside a class.

Paying attention to these colored scopes pays off over time; they can help you avoid some common errors. Scopes are usually defined in your code by a pair of curly brackets (usually with a header above the opening bracket that defines what kind of scope we are looking at). It can happen very easily to get the curly brackets out of balance—to have more opening than closing ones, or vice versa. If this happens, your program will not compile.

Scope coloring helps you detect such a problem. You will get used to what the scopes should look like quite quickly, and you will notice that it just looks wrong when a bracket is mismatched.

Hand-in-hand with scope colors goes indentation.

In all the code examples you have seen so far, you may have noticed some careful indentation being used. Every time a curly bracket opens, the following lines are indented one level more than the previous ones. When a curly bracket closes, the indentation goes back one level, so that the closing curly bracket is directly below the matching opening bracket. This makes it easy to find the matching bracket.

We use four spaces for one level of indentation. The TAB key will insert spaces in your editor for one level of indentation. Greenfoot can also help you should your indentation get too messy: the editor has an `Auto-Layout` function in its `Edit` menu, which will try to fix your indentation for the whole class.

Taking care with indentation in your own code is very important. If you do not indent carefully, the scope coloring will look messy, become useless, and some errors (particularly misplaced or mismatched curly brackets) are very hard to spot. Proper indentation makes code much easier to read, and thus avoids potential errors.

> **Exercise 2.18** Open the source code for your **Crab** class. Remove various opening or closing curly brackets and observe the change in scope coloring. In each case, can you explain the change in color? Also experiment with changing the indentation of brackets and other code and observe how it affects the look. At the end, fix the brackets and indentation so that the code looks nice again.

Summary of programming techniques

In this book, we are discussing programming from a very example-driven perspective. We introduce general programming techniques as we need them to improve our scenarios. So from now on, we shall summarize the important programming techniques at the end of each chapter, to make it clear what you really need to take away from the discussion to be able to progress well.

In this chapter, we have seen how to call methods (such as `move(5)` or `isAtEdge()`), with and without parameters. This will form the basis for all further Java programming. We have also learnt to identify the body of the act method—this is where we start writing our instructions.

You have encountered some error messages. This will continue throughout all your programming endeavors. We all make mistakes, and we all encounter error messages. This is not a sign of a bad programmer—it is a normal part of programming.

We have encountered a first glimpse of inheritance: Classes inherit the methods from their superclasses. The documentation of a class gives us a summary of the methods available.

And, very importantly, we have seen how to make decisions: We have used an if-statement for conditional execution. This went hand in hand with the appearance of the type *boolean*, a value that can be *true* or *false*.

Concept summary

- A **method call** is an instruction that tells an object to perform an action. The action is defined by a method of the object.

- Additional information can be passed to some methods within the parentheses. The value passed is called a **parameter**.

- Multiple instructions are executed **in sequence**, one after the other, in the order in which they are written.

- When a class is compiled, the compiler checks to see whether there are any errors. If an error is found, an **error message** is displayed.

- A subclass **inherits** all the methods from its superclass. That means that it has, and can use, all methods that its superclass defines.

- Calling a method with a **void return type** issues a command. Calling a method with a **non-void return type** asks a question.

- An **if-statement** can be used to write instructions that are only executed when a certain condition is true.

Drill and practice

Some of the chapters include "Drill and practice" sections at the end. These sections introduce no new material but give you a chance to practice an important concept that has been introduced in this chapter in another context, and to deepen your understanding.

The two most important constructs we have encountered in this chapter are method calls and if-statements. Here we do some more exercises with these two constructs. (See Figure 2.4.)

Figure 2.4

Fat Cat

Method signatures

Exercise 2.19 Look at the following method signatures:

```
public void play();

public void addAmount(int amount);

public boolean hasWings();

public void compare(int x, int y, int z);

public boolean isGreater (int number);
```

For each of these signatures, answer the following questions (in writing):

a) What is the method name?
b) Does the method return a value? If yes, what is the type of the return value?
c) How many parameters does the method have?

Exercise 2.20 Write a method signature for a method named "go." The method has no parameters, and it does not return a value.

Exercise 2.21 Write a method signature for a method named "process." The method has a parameter of type "int" that is called "number", and it returns a value of type "int."

Exercise 2.22 Write a method signature for a method named "isOpen." This method has no parameters and returns a value of type "boolean."

Exercise 2.23 On paper, write a method call (note: this is a method call, not a signature) for the "play" method from Exercise 2.19. Write another method call for the "addAmount" method from Exercise 2.19. And finally, write a method call for the "compare" method from the same exercise.

Reading documentation

All the following exercises are intended to be implemented in the Greenfoot scenario "fatcat." Open the scenario in Greenfoot before continuing.

Exercise 2.24 Open the editor for class **Cat**. Change the view of the editor from "Source Code" to "Documentation" view using the control in the top right of the editor window. How many methods does the class **Cat** have?

Exercise 2.25 How many of the **Cat**'s methods return a value?

Exercise 2.26 How many parameters does the **sleep** method have?

Writing method calls (with and without parameters)

Exercise 2.27 Try calling some of your cat's methods interactively, by using the cat's popup menu. The interesting methods are all "inherited from Cat."

Exercise 2.28 Is the cat bored? How can you make it not bored?

Exercise 2.29 Open the editor for class **MyCat**. (This is where you will write the code for all the following exercises.)

Exercise 2.30 Make the cat eat when it acts. (That is, in the **act** method, write a call to the **eat** method.) Compile. Test by pressing the Act button in the execution controls.

Exercise 2.31 Make the cat dance. (Don't do this interactively—write code in the act method to do this. When done, click the Act button in the execution controls.)

Exercise 2.32 Make the cat sleep.

Exercise 2.33 Make the cat do a routine of your choice, consisting of a number of the available actions in sequence.

If-statements

Exercise 2.34 Change the **act** method of your cat so that, when you click Act, if the cat is tired, it sleeps a bit. If it is not tired, it doesn't do anything.

Exercise 2.35 Change the **act** method of your cat so that it dances if it is bored. (But only if it is bored.)

Exercise 2.36 Change the **act** method of your cat so that it eats if it is hungry.

Exercise 2.37 Change the **act** method of your cat to the following: If the cat is tired, it sleeps a bit, and then it shouts hooray. If it is not tired, it just shouts hooray. (For testing, make the cat tired by calling some methods interactively. How can you make the cat tired?)

Exercise 2.38 Write code in the **act** method to do the following: If your cat is alone, let it sleep. If it is not alone, make it shout "Hooray." Test by placing a second cat into the world before clicking Act.

3 Improving the crab: more sophisticated programming

> topics: random behavior, keyboard control, sound
>
> concepts: dot notation, random numbers, defining methods, comments

In the previous chapter, we looked at the basics of starting to program our first game. There were many new things that we had to look at. Now, we will add more interesting behavior. Adding code will get a little easier from now on, since we have seen many of the fundamental concepts.

The first thing we will do is add some random behavior.

3.1 Adding random behavior

In our current implementation, the crab can walk across the screen, and it can turn at the edge of our world. But when it walks, it always walks exactly straight. That is what we want to change now. Crabs don't always go in an exact straight line, so let us add a little random behavior: the crab should go roughly straight, but every now and then it should turn a little off course.

<div class="concept">

Concept

When a method we wish to call is not in our own class or inherited, we need to specify the class or object that has the method before the method name, followed by a dot. This is called **dot notation**.

</div>

We can achieve this in Greenfoot by using random numbers: the Greenfoot environment itself has a method to give us a random number. This method, called getRandomNumber, expects a parameter that specifies the limit of the number. It will then return a random number between 0 (zero) and the limit. For example,

```
Greenfoot.getRandomNumber(20)
```

will give us a random number between 0 and 20. The limit—20—is excluded, so the number is actually in the range 0 to 19.

The notation used here is called *dot notation*. When we called methods that were defined in our own class or inherited, it was enough to write the method name and parameter list. When the method is defined in another class, we need to specify the class or object that has the method, followed by a period (dot), followed by the method name and parameter. Since the `getRandomNumber` method is not in the `Crab` or `Actor` class, but in a class called `Greenfoot`, we have to write "`Greenfoot.`" in front of the method call.

<table>
<tr><td>

Concept

Methods that belong to classes (as opposed to objects) are marked with the keyword **static** in their signature. They are also called **class methods**.

</td><td>

Note: Static methods

Methods may belong to objects or classes. When methods belong to a class, we write

```
class-name.method-name (parameters);
```

to call the method. When a method belongs to an object, we write

```
object.method-name (parameters);
```

to call it.

Both kinds of methods are defined in a class. The method signature tells us whether a given method belongs to objects of that class, or to the class itself.

Methods that belong to the class itself are marked with the keyword **static** at the beginning of the method signature. For example, the signature of Greenfoot's *getRandomNumber* method is

```
static int getRandomNumber(int limit);
```

This tells us that we must write the name of the class itself (Greenfoot) before the dot in the method call.

We will encounter calls to methods that belong to other objects in a later chapter.

</td></tr>
</table>

Let us say we want to program our crab so that there is a 10 percent chance at every step that the crab turns a little bit off course. We can do the main part of this with an if-statement:

```
if ( something-is-true )
{
    turn(5);
}
```

Now we have to find an expression to put in place of *something-is-true* that returns true in exactly 10 percent of the cases.

We can do this using a random number (using the `Greenfoot.getRandomNumber` method) and a less-than operator. The less-than operator compares two numbers and returns true if the first is less than the second. "Less-than" is written using the symbol "<." For example:

```
2 < 33
```

is true, while

```
162 < 42
```

is false.

> **Exercise 3.1** Before reading on, try to write down, on paper, an expression using the `getRandomNumber` method and the less-than operator that, when executed, is true exactly 10 percent of the time.
>
> **Exercise 3.2** Write down another expression that is true 7 percent of the time.

Note

Java has a number of operators to compare two values. They are:

<	less than	>=	greater than or equal
>	greater than	==	equal
<=	less than or equal	!=	not equal

If we want to express the chance in percent, it is easiest to deal with random numbers out of 100. An expression that is true 10 percent of the time, for example, could be

```
Greenfoot.getRandomNumber(100) < 10
```

Since the call to `Greenfoot.getRandomNumber(100)` gives us a new random number between 0 and 99 every time we call it, and since these numbers are evenly distributed, they will be below 10 in 10 percent of all cases.

We can now use this to make our crab turn a little in 10 percent of its steps (Code 3.1).

Code 3.1
Random course changes—first try

```java
import greenfoot.*;  // (World, Actor, GreenfootImage, and Greenfoot)

/**
 * This class defines a crab. Crabs live on the beach.
 */
public class Crab extends Actor
{
    public void act()
    {
        if ( isAtEdge() )
        {
            turn(17);
        }

        if ( Greenfoot.getRandomNumber(100) < 10 )
        {
            turn(4);
        }

        move(5);
    }
}
```

Exercise 3.3 Try out the random course changes shown above in your own version. Experiment with different probabilities for turning.

This is a pretty good start, but it is not quite perfect yet. First of all, if the crab turns, it always turns the same amount (four degrees), and secondly, it always turns right, never left. What we would really like to see is that the crab turns a small but random amount to either its left or its right. (We will discuss this now. If you feel confident enough, try to implement this on your own before reading on.)

The simple trick to the first problem—always turning the same amount, in our case 4 degrees—is to replace the fixed number 4 in our code with another random number, like this:

```
if ( Greenfoot.getRandomNumber(100) < 10 )
{
    turn( Greenfoot.getRandomNumber(45) );
}
```

In this example, the crab still turns in 10 percent of its steps. And when it turns, it will turn a random amount, between 0 and 44 degrees.

Exercise 3.4 Try out the code shown above. What do you observe? Does the crab turn different amounts when it turns?

Exercise 3.5 We still have the problem that the crab turns right only. That's not normal behavior for a crab, so let's fix this. Modify your code so that the crab turns either right or left by up to 45 degrees each time it turns.

Exercise 3.6 Try running your scenario with multiple crabs in the world. Do they all turn at the same time, or independently? Why?

Exercise 3.5 is not easy at first if you have never seen anything like this before and probably deserves a hint. There is a temptation at first to perhaps use an if-statement to deal with the two directions, but there is actually a much simpler solution.

Think about it this way: Greenfoot.getRandomNumber only gives us numbers with a lower bound of zero. We want numbers from −45 to 45. That means we want (roughly) 90 different numbers. We can get a range of 90 numbers using Greenfoot.getRandomNumber(90), but this gives us 0–90. How can we get from 0–90 to −45–45?

The answer is: we can just get random numbers out of 90, and then subtract 45. Figure 3.1 attempts to illustrate this. (Note that this is actually out by 1: the range of the random number is actually 0–89, so after subtracting 45 we end up with −45–44. But since we don't care about accuracy with our random turns, that is okay.)

Figure 3.1

a) Random angle 0–90 degrees b) Random angle -45–45 degrees

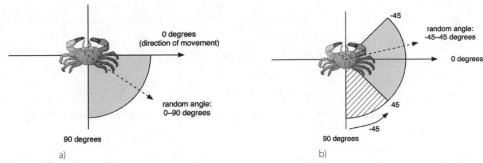

Try solving this exercise yourself. The project *little-crab-2* (included with this book) shows an implementation of what we have done so far, including the last exercises.

3.2 Adding worms

Let us make our world a little more interesting by adding another kind of animal.

Crabs like to eat worms. (Well, that is not true for all kinds of crab in the real world, but there are some that do. Let's just say our crab is one of those that like to eat worms.) So let us now add a class for worms.

We can add new actor classes to a Greenfoot scenario by selecting *New subclass* from one of the existing actor classes (Figure 3.2). In this case, our new class `Worm` is a subclass of class `Actor`. (Remember, being a subclass is an *is-a* relationship: a worm *is an* actor.)

When we are creating a new subclass, we are prompted to enter a name for the class and to select an image (Figure 3.3).

In our case, we name the class "Worm." By convention, class names in Java should always start with a capital letter. They should also describe what kind of object they represent, so "Worm" is the obvious name for our purpose.

Figure 3.2

Creating new subclasses

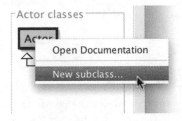

Figure 3.3

Creating a new class

Then, we should assign an image to the class. There are some images associated with the scenario, and a whole library of generic images to choose from. In this case, we have prepared a worm image and made it available in the scenario images, so we can just select the image named *worm.png*.

Once done, we can click *Ok*. The class is now added to our scenario, and we can compile and then add worms to our world.

> **Exercise 3.7** Add some worms to your world. Also add some crabs. Run the scenario. What do you observe? What do the worms do? What happens when a crab meets a worm?

We now know how to add new classes to our scenario. The next task is to make these classes interact.

3.3 Eating worms

We now want to add new behavior to the crab: when a crab runs into a worm, it eats it. Again, we first check what methods we have already inherited from the Actor class. When we open the documentation for class Actor again, we can see the following two methods:

```
boolean isTouching (java.lang.Class cls)
```
Check whether this actor is touching any other objects of the given class.

```
void removeTouching (java.lang.Class cls)
```
Remove one object of the given class that this actor is currently touching (if any exist).

Using these methods, we can implement this behavior. The first method checks whether the crab touches a worm. This method returns a boolean—*true* or *false*—so we can use it in an if-statement.

The second method removes a worm. Both methods expect a parameter of type `java.lang.Class`. This means that we are expected to specify one of our classes from our scenario. Here is some sample code:

```
if ( isTouching(Worm.class) )
{
    removeTouching(Worm.class);
}
```

In this case, we specify `Worm.class` as the parameter to both method calls (the `isTouching` method and the `removeTouching` method). This declares which kind of object we are looking for, and which kind of object we want to remove. Our complete act method at this stage is shown in Code 3.2.

Code 3.2

First version of eating a worm

```
public void act()
{
    if (isAtEdge() )
    {
        turn(17);
    }

    if ( Greenfoot.getRandomNumber(100) < 10 )
    {
        turn(Greenfoot.getRandomNumber(90)-45);
    }

    move(5);

    if ( isTouching(Worm.class) )
    {
        removeTouching(Worm.class);
    }
}
```

Try this out. Place a number of worms into the world (remember: shift-clicking into the world is a shortcut for quickly placing several actors), place a few crabs, run the scenario, and see what happens.

Advanced note: Packages

(The notes labeled "Advanced note" are inserted for deeper information for those readers really interested in the details. They are not crucial to understand at this stage, and could safely be skipped.)

In the definition of the `isTouching` and `removeTouching` methods, we have seen a parameter type with the name `java.lang.Class`. What does this mean?

Many types are defined by classes. Many of those classes are in the standard Java class library. You can see the documentation of the Java class library by choosing *Java Library Documentation* from Greenfoot's *Help* menu.

The Java class library contains thousands of classes. To make these a little easier to work with, they have been grouped into *packages* (logically related groups of classes). When a class name includes dots, such as `java.lang.Class`, only the last part is the name of the class itself, and the former parts are the name of the package. So here we are looking at the class named "Class" from the package "java.lang."

Try to find that class in the Java library documentation.

3.4 Creating new methods

In the previous few sections, we have added new behavior to the crab—turning at the edge of the world, occasional random turns, and eating worms. If we continue to do this in the way we have done so far, the act method will become longer and longer, and eventually really hard to understand. We can improve this by chopping it up into smaller pieces.

> **Concept**
>
> A **method definition** defines a new action for objects of this class. The action is not immediately executed, but the method can be called with a method call later to execute it.

We can create our own additional methods in the `Crab` class for our own purposes. For example, instead of just writing some code that looks for a worm and removes it into the `act` method, we can add a new method for this purpose. To do this, we first have to decide on a name for this method. Let us say we call it `lookForWorm`. We can then create a new method by adding the following code:

```
/**
 * Check whether we have stumbled upon a worm.
 * If we have, eat it. If not, do nothing.
 */
public void lookForWorm()
{
    if ( isTouching(Worm.class) )
    {
        removeTouching(Worm.class);
    }
}
```

Concept

Comments are written into the source code as explanations for human readers. They are ignored by the computer.

The first four lines are a *comment*. A comment is ignored by the computer—it is written for human readers. We use a comment to explain to other human readers what the purpose of this method is.

When we define this method, the code does not immediately get executed. In fact, by just defining this method, it does not get executed at all. We are just defining a new possible action ("looking for a worm") that can be carried out later. It will only be carried out when this method is called. We can add a call to this method inside the act method:

```
lookForWorm();
```

Note that the call has the parentheses for the (empty) parameter list. The complete source code after this restructuring is shown in Code 3.3.

Code 3.3

Splitting code into separate methods

```
public void act()
{
    if ( isAtEdge() )
    {
        turn(17);
    }

    if ( Greenfoot.getRandomNumber(100) < 10 )
    {
        turn(Greenfoot.getRandomNumber(90)-45);
    }

    move(5);
    lookForWorm();
}

/**
 * Check whether we have stumbled upon a worm.
 * If we have, eat it. If not, do nothing.
 */
public void lookForWorm()
{
    if ( isTouching(Worm.class) )
    {
        removeTouching(Worm.class);
    }
}
```

Note that this code change does not change the behavior of our crab at all. It just makes the code easier to read in the long run. As we add more code to the class, methods tend to become longer and longer. Longer methods are harder to understand. By separating our code into a number of shorter methods, we make the code easier to read.

> **Exercise 3.8** Create another new method named **randomTurn** (this method has no parameters and returns nothing). Select the code that does the random turning, and move it from the act method to the **randomTurn** method. Then call this new **random-Turn** method from your act method. Make sure to write a comment for this method.

Create yet another method named **turnAtEdge** (it also has no parameters and returns nothing). Move the code that checks whether we are at the edge of the world (and does the turn if we are into the **turnAtEdge** method). Call the **turnAtEdge** method from your act method. Your act method should now look like the version shown in Code 3.4.

Code 3.4

The new act method after creating methods for the sub-tasks

```
public void act()
{
    turnAtEdge();
    randomTurn();
    move(5);
    lookForWorm();
}
```

By convention, method names in Java always start with a lowercase letter. Method names cannot contain spaces (or many other punctuation characters). If the method name logically consists of multiple words, we use capitals in the middle of the method name to mark the start of each word.

3.5 Adding a Lobster

We are now at a stage where we have a crab that walks more or less randomly through our world, and eats worms if it happens to run into them.

To make it a little more interesting again, let us add another creature: a lobster (Figure 3.4).

Lobsters, in our scenario, like to chase crabs.

Figure 3.4
Adding an
enemy: a lobster

Exercise 3.9 Add a new class to your scenario. The class should be a subclass of **Actor**, called **Lobster** (with a capital "L"), and it should use the prepared image *lobster.png*.

Exercise 3.10 What do you expect lobsters to do when you place them into the world as they are? Compile your scenario and try it out.

We now want to program our new lobsters to eat crabs. This is quite easy to do, since the behavior is very similar to the behavior of crabs. The only difference is that lobsters look for crabs, while crabs look for worms.

Exercise 3.11 Copy the complete act method from the **Crab** class into the **Lobster** class. Also copy the complete **lookForWorm**, **turnAtEdge**, and **randomTurn** methods.

Exercise 3.12 Change the **Lobster** code so that it looks for crabs, rather than worms. You can do that by changing every occurrence of "Worm" in the source code to "Crab." For instance, where **Worm.class** is mentioned, change it to **Crab.class**. Also change the name **lookForWorm** to **lookForCrab**. Make sure to update your comments.

Exercise 3.13 Place a crab, three lobsters, and many worms into the world. Run the scenario. Does the crab manage to eat all worms before it is caught by a lobster?

You should now have a version of your scenario where both crabs and lobsters walk around randomly, looking for worms and crabs, respectively.

Now let us turn this program into a game.

3.6 Keyboard control

To get game-like behavior, we need to get a player involved. The player (you!) should be able to control the crab with the keyboard, while the lobsters continue to run randomly by themselves, as they already do.

The Greenfoot environment has a method that lets us check whether a key on the keyboard has been pressed. It is called isKeyDown, and, like the getRandomNumber method that we encountered in Section 3.1, it is a method in the Greenfoot class. The method signature is

```
static boolean isKeyDown(String key)
```

We can see that the method is static (it is a class method) and the return type is boolean. This means that the method returns either *true* or *false* and can be used as a condition in an if-statement.

We also see that the method expects a parameter of type *String*. A String is a piece of text (such as a word or a sentence), written in double quotes. The following are examples of Strings:

```
"This is a String"
"name"
"A"
```

In this case, the String expected is the name of the key that we want to test. Every key on the keyboard has a name. For those keys that produce visible characters, that character is their name, e.g., the A-key is called "A." Other keys have names too. For instance, the left cursor key is called "left." Thus, if we want to test whether the left cursor key has been pressed, we can write

```
if (Greenfoot.isKeyDown("left"))
{
    ... // do something
}
```

Note that we need to write "Greenfoot." in front of the call to isKeyDown, since this method is defined in the Greenfoot class.

If, for example, we want our crab to turn left by 4 degrees whenever the left cursor key is being pressed, we can write

```
if (Greenfoot.isKeyDown("left"))
{
    turn(-4);
}
```

The idea now is to remove the code from the crab that does the random turning and also the code that turns automatically at the world edge and replace them with the code that lets us control the crab's turn with our keyboard.

Exercise 3.14 Remove the random turning code from the crab.

Exercise 3.15 Remove the code from the crab that does the turn at the edge of the world.

Tip

Greenfoot automatically saves classes and scenarios when their windows are closed. To keep a copy of interim stages of scenarios, use **Save As**... from the Scenario menu.

Exercise 3.16 Add code into the crab's act method that makes the crab turn left whenever the left cursor key is pressed. Test.

Exercise 3.17 Add another—similar—bit of code to the crab's act method that makes the crab turn right whenever the right cursor key is pressed.

Exercise 3.18 If you have not done so in the first place, make sure that the code that checks the key-presses and does the turning is not written directly in the act method, but is instead in a separate method, maybe called `checkKeypress`. This method should be called from the act method.

Exercise 3.19 Currently, if you have simply copied the crab code to the lobster, both walk with the same speed. You can make them walk at different speeds by changing the parameter to the `move(5)` method call in either of them. Try making lobsters faster or slower. Try out how the game feels if you do that. Choose a speed for the crab and lobster that suits you.

Try solving the tasks by yourself first. If you get stuck, have a look on the next page. Code 3.5 shows the crab's complete `act` and `checkKeypress` methods after this change. The solution is also available in the book scenarios, as *little-crab-3*. This version includes all the changes we have discussed so far.

You are now ready to have a first try at playing your game! Place a crab, some worms, and a few lobsters into the world, and see whether you can get all the worms before the lobsters catch you. (Obviously, the more lobsters you place, the harder it gets....)

3.7 Ending the game

One simple improvement we can make is to end execution of the game when the crab is caught by a lobster. Greenfoot has a method to do this—we just need to find out what it is called.

Concept

The **API Documentation** lists all classes and methods available in Greenfoot. We often need to look up methods here.

To find out what the available methods in Greenfoot are, we can look at the documentation of the Greenfoot classes.

In Greenfoot, choose *Greenfoot Class Documentation* from the *Help* menu. This will show the documentation for all the Greenfoot classes in a Web browser (Figure 3.5).

This documentation is also called the *Greenfoot API* (Application Programmers' Interface). The API shows all available classes and for each class, all the available methods. You can see that Greenfoot offers seven classes: `Actor`, `Greenfoot`, `GreenfootImage`, `GreenfootSound`, `MouseInfo`, `UserInfo`, and `World`.

Code 3.5

The Crab's "act" method: controlling the crab with the keyboard

```java
/**
 * Act - do whatever the crab wants to do.
 */
public void act()
{
    checkKeypress();
    move(5);
    lookForWorm();
}
```

```java
/**
 * Check whether a control key on the keyboard has been pressed.
 * If it has, react accordingly.
 */
public void checkKeypress()
{
    if (Greenfoot.isKeyDown("left"))
    {
        turn(-4);
    }
    if (Greenfoot.isKeyDown("right"))
    {
        turn(4);
    }
}
```

The method we are looking for is in the **Greenfoot** class.

> **Exercise 3.20** Open the Greenfoot API in your browser. Select the **Greenfoot** class. In its documentation, find the section titled "Method Summary." In this section, try to find a method that stops the execution of the running scenario. What is this method called?
>
> **Exercise 3.21** Does this method expect any parameters? What is its return type?

We can see the documentation of the Greenfoot classes by selecting them in the list on the left. For each class, the main panel in the browser displays a general comment, details of its constructors, and a list of its methods. (Constructors will be discussed in a later chapter.)

If we browse through the list of available methods in the class **Greenfoot**, we can find a method named **stop**. This is the method that we can use to stop execution when the crab gets caught.

We can make use of this method by writing

```java
Greenfoot.stop();
```

into our source code.

Figure 3.5

The Greenfoot API in a browser window

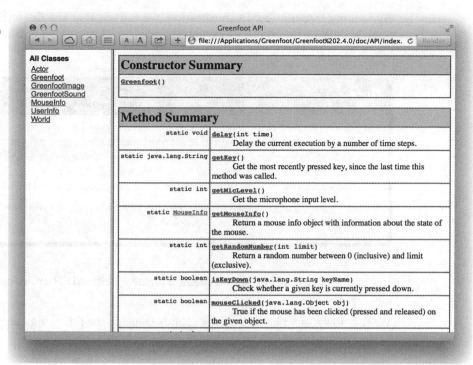

> **Exercise 3.22** Add code to your own scenario that stops the game when a lobster catches the crab. You will need to decide where this code needs to be added. Find the place in your code that is executed when a lobster catches a crab, and add this line of code there.

We will use this class documentation frequently in the future to look up details of methods we need to use. We will know some methods by heart after a while, but there are always methods we need to look up.

3.8 Adding sound

Another improvement to our game is the addition of sounds. Again, a method in the Greenfoot class helps us with this.

> **Exercise 3.23** Open the Greenfoot Class Documentation (from the Help menu) to find out about playing sounds. There is a **GreenfootSound** class for full sound control, and also a convenience method in the **Greenfoot** class to produce a sound quickly and easily. Find the details of the method in the **Greenfoot** class. What is its name? What parameters does it expect?

By looking through the documentation, we can see that the `Greenfoot` class has a method called `playSound`. It expects the name of a sound file (a String) as a parameter, and returns nothing.

Note

You may like to look at the structure of a Greenfoot scenario in your file system. If you look into the folder containing the book scenarios, you can find a folder for each Greenfoot scenario. For the crab example, there are several different versions (*little-crab*, *little-clab-2*, *little-crab-3*, etc.). Inside each scenario folder are several files for each scenario class, and several other support files. There are also two media folders: *images* holds the scenario images and *sounds* stores the sound files.

You can see the available sounds by looking into this folder, and you can make more sounds available by storing them here.

In our crab scenario, two sound files are already included. They are called *"slurp.wav"* and *"au.wav."*

We can now easily play one of the sounds by using the following method call:

```
Greenfoot.playSound("slurp.wav");
```

Try it out!

Exercise 3.24 Add playing of sounds to your scenario: when a crab eats a worm, play the "slurp.wav" sound. When a lobster eats the crab, play the "au.wav" sound. To do this, you have to find the place in your code where this should happen.

The *little-crab-4* version of this scenario shows the solution to this. It is a version of the project that includes all the functionality we have discussed so far: worms, lobsters, keyboard control and sound (Figure 3.6).

3.9 Making your own sounds

There are various ways to add your own sounds to a Greenfoot scenario. You can, for example, find sound effects in various sound libraries on the Internet or produce your own using some sound recording and effects software.

Using sounds sometimes gets a bit tricky because sounds on a computer can be stored in many different file formats, and Greenfoot can play some, but not others. Greenfoot can generally play sound files in MP3, AIFF, AU, and WAV formats (although certain WAV files cannot be played—it gets complicated).

Figure 3.6

The crab game with worms and lobsters

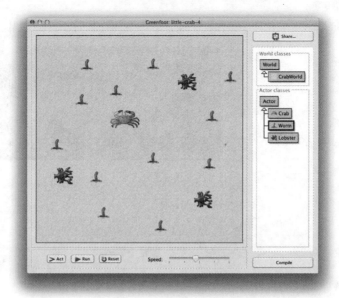

We will discuss sound more completely in Chapter 10; here, we will use the easiest method to get our own sounds into our scenario: recording them ourselves directly in Greenfoot.

Both of the sound effects we used in the previous section were recorded by simply speaking into the microphone. Greenfoot has a sound recorder built-in for you to do the same.

To get started, use the *Show Sound Recorder* function from the *Controls* menu. You will see the Greenfoot sound recorder control (Figure 3.7).

Using this sound recorder, you can now record your own sounds by pressing the *Record* button and speaking into the microphone.[1] Press *Stop Recording* when you are finished. You can use the *Play* button to check what your recording sounds like.

There is only one edit operation available: *Trim to selection*. The purpose is to cut off unwanted sections of the recording at the beginning and then end. Often you will have a bit of noise or silence at the beginning of the recording, and this will not sound good in your program: silence at the beginning will make your sound appear delayed.

To remove the unwanted parts, select the part of the sound you want to keep with your mouse (Figure 3.8) and then press *Trim to selection*.

Finally, choose a name for your sound, type it into the filename field, and click *Save*. The sound will be saved in WAV format and will automatically receive a ".wav" filename suffix. So if you, for example, call your sound file "bark," it will be saved as "bark.wav." Greenfoot will automatically save it to the right location (the "sounds" folder in your scenario folder).

---

[1] Obviously, this only works if your computer has a microphone. Most recent laptops have microphones built-in. For some desktop computers, you will have to connect an external microphone. If you do not have a microphone, just skip this section.

Figure 3.7
The Greenfoot sound recorder

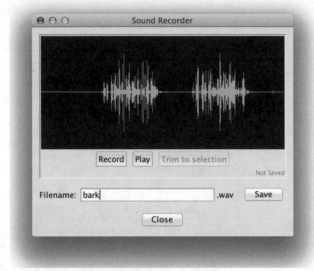

Figure 3.8
Selecting the good part of the sound for trimming

You can then use it in your code using the method we have seen before:

```
Greenfoot.playSound("bark.wav");
```

It's time to try for yourself.

Exercise 3.25 If you have a microphone on your computer, make your own sounds to use when the worms or the crab get eaten. Record them, then use them in your code.

Figure 3.9
Using code completion (CTRL+Space)

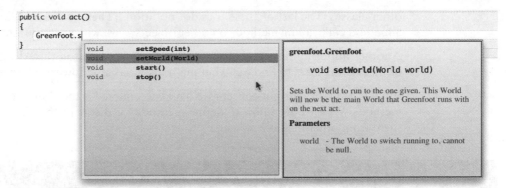

3.10 Code completion

A useful productivity tip is to use *code completion* to enter your method calls (Figure 3.9). You can use code completion whenever you are about to type the name of a method you want to call. It is activated by typing CTRL+Space.

For example, if you type

    Greenfoot.

and the cursor is behind the dot, and then you type CTRL+Space, a dialog will pop up listing all the methods you can call here (in this case: all the methods of the Greenfoot class). If you then start to type the beginning of a method name (for example, in Figure 3.9 we have typed the letter "s"), the list of methods reduces to those starting with what you have typed.

You can select methods from this list using your cursor keys or with your mouse, and insert them into your code by using the *Return* key.

Using code completion is useful to investigate which methods exist, to find a method that you know exists but cannot remember the exact name of, to look up parameters and documentation, or just to save yourself some typing and speed up entry of your code.

Summary of programming techniques

In this chapter we have seen more examples of using an if-statement, this time for turning at random times and reacting to key presses. We have also seen how to call methods from another class, namely, the getRandomNumber, isKeyDown, and playSound methods from the Greenfoot class. We did this by using dot notation, with the class name in front of the dot.

Altogether, we have now seen examples of calling methods from three different places: we can call methods that are defined in the current class itself (called *local methods*), methods that were defined in a superclass (*inherited methods*), and static methods from other classes. The last of these uses dot notation. (There is one additional version of a method call: calling methods on other objects —we will encounter that a little later.)

Another important aspect that we explored was how to read the API documentation of an existing class to find out what methods it has and how to call them.

Finally, a very important concept we have encountered is the ability to define our own methods. We have seen how to define methods for distinct subtasks, and how to call them from other methods.

Concept summary

- When a method we wish to call is not in our own class or inherited, we need to specify the class or object that has the method before the method name, followed by a dot. This is called **dot notation**.

- Methods that belong to classes (as opposed to objects) are marked with the keyword **static** in their signature. They are also called **class methods**.

- A **method definition** defines a new action for objects of this class. The action is not immediately executed, but the method can be called with a method call later to execute it.

- **Comments** are written into the source code as explanations for human readers. They are ignored by the computer.

- The **API Documentation** lists all classes and methods available in Greenfoot. We often need to look up methods here.

Drill and practice

The concepts that we want to reinforce here are if-statements (again), reading API documentation, calling a method from another class, and creating our own methods.

To do this, we will use another scenario: *stickman*. Find it in the book scenarios and open it.

Reading API documentation

Exercise 3.26 The `Greenfoot` class has a method to get the noise level from the computer's microphone. Find this method in the API documentation. How many parameters does it have?

Exercise 3.27 What is the return type of this method? What does this tell us?

Exercise 3.28 What are the possible values returned from this method?

Exercise 3.29 Is this method *static* or not? What does that tell us?

Exercise 3.30 How do we call this method? Write down a correct method call to this method.

Calling class methods/if-statements

Exercise 3.31 In your *stickman* scenario, make the stickman move to the right, so that when you run your scenario, he walks over to the right side of the screen.

Exercise 3.32 Using an if-statement and the microphone input method you found above, make the stickman move right only when you make some noise. Experiment with different values for the noise level. This will depend on your microphone and your environment. A good starting point is to make him move when the microphone level is greater than 3. Test.

Exercise 3.33 Make the stickman move left when you make some noise, but move continuously right if there is no noise. Test. Try to keep him near the center of the screen by shouting.

Defining methods

Exercise 3.34 Move the code that moves left when you make noise into its own method. Call this method `moveLeftIfNoise`. Test. Make sure it works as before.

Exercise 3.35 Add another method to your class called `gameOver`. This method should be called if the stickman reaches the edge of the screen. When called, the method plays a game-over sound and stops the scenario.

Exercise 3.36 Move the check for the game-over condition itself into a separate method called `checkGameOver`. The `act` method should call `checkGameOver`, which in turn calls `gameOver` if appropriate.

Exercise 3.37 Make the stickman float up when there is noise. The height he floats should be proportionate to the noise level. He comes down if there is no noise. Note: the proportionate height requirement is quite difficult—it requires you to look up some things we have not discussed yet. If you find it too hard, leave this out.

Exercise 3.38 Introduce another actor (maybe an animal) that starts at the left screen edge and moves sideways. If it reaches the right edge of the screen, it gets reset to the left side. On its path across the screen, it should touch the stickman if he is resting. You can then make the stickman jump over the animal by making some noise.

Exercise 3.39 Stop the scenario (with game-over sound) when the stickman touches the animal.

> topics: world initialization, setting images, animating images
>
> concepts: constructors, state, variables (instance variables and local variables), assignment, **new** (creating objects programmatically)

In this chapter, we will finish the crab game. "Finish" here means that this is where we stop discussing this project in this book. Of course, a game is never finished—you can always think of more improvements that you can add. We will suggest some ideas at the end of this chapter. First, however, we will discuss a number of improvements in detail.

4.1 Adding objects automatically

We are now getting close to having a playable little game. However, a few more things need to be done. The first problem that should be addressed is the fact that we always have to place the actors (the crab, lobsters, and worms) manually into the world. It would be better if that happened automatically.

There is one thing that happens automatically every time we successfully compile: the world itself is created. The world object, as we see it on screen (the sand-colored square area), is an instance of the CrabWorld class. World instances are treated in a special way in Greenfoot: while we have to create instances of our actors ourselves, the Greenfoot system always automatically creates one instance of our world class and displays that instance on screen.

Let us have a look at the CrabWorld's source code (Code 4.1). (If you do not have your own crab game at this stage, use *little-crab-4* for this chapter.)

Code 4.1
Source code of the
CrabWorld class

```
import greenfoot.*;  // (Actor, World, Greenfoot, GreenfootImage)

public class CrabWorld extends World
{
    /**
     * Create the crab world (the beach). Our world has a size
     * of 560x560 cells, where every cell is just 1 pixel.
     */
    public CrabWorld()
    {
        super(560, 560, 1);
    }
}
```

In this class, we see the usual import statement in the first line. (We will discuss this statement in detail later—for now it is enough to know that this line will always appear at the top of our Greenfoot classes.)

Then follows the class header, and a comment (the block of lines in a blueish color starting with asterisks—we have encountered them already in the last chapter). Comments usually start with a /** symbol and end with */.

Next comes the interesting part:

```
public CrabWorld()
{
    super(560, 560, 1);
}
```

Concept

A **constructor** of a class is a special kind of method that is executed automatically whenever a new instance is created.

This is called the *constructor* of this class. A constructor looks quite similar to a method, but there are some differences:

- A constructor has no return type specified between the keyword "public" and the name.

- The name of a constructor is always the same as the name of the class.

A constructor is a special kind of method that is always automatically executed whenever an instance of this class is created. It can then do what it wants to do to set up this new instance into a starting state.

In our case, the constructor sets the world to the size we want (560 by 560 cells) and a *resolution* (1 pixel per cell). We will discuss world resolution in more detail later in the book.

Since this constructor is executed every time a world is created, we can use it to automatically create our actors. If we insert code into the constructor to create an actor, that code will be executed as well. For example:

```java
public CrabWorld()
{
    super(560, 560, 1);
    Crab myCrab = new Crab();
    addObject(myCrab, 250, 200);
}
```

This code will automatically create a new crab, and place it at location x=250, y=200 into the world. The location 250,200 is 250 cells from the left edge of the world, and 200 cells from the top. The origin—the 0,0 point—of our coordinate system is at the top left of the world (Figure 4.1).

We are using four new things here: a variable, an assignment, the new statement to create the new crab, and the addObject method. Let us discuss these elements one by one.

Figure 4.1

The coordinate system of the world

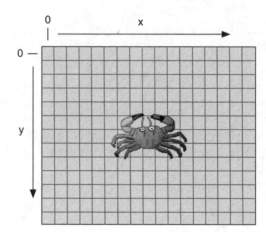

Creating new objects

4.2

If we want to add a crab into the world, the first thing we need is a crab. The crab in our case is an object of the Crab class. Previously, we have created crab objects interactively, by right-clicking the Crab class and selecting "new Crab()" from the pop-up menu.

Now, we want our constructor code to create the new crab object for us automatically.

The Java keyword new allows us to create new objects of any of the existing classes. For example, the expression

```java
new Crab()
```

creates a new instance of class Crab. The expression to create new objects always starts with the keyword new, followed by the name of the class we wish to create and a parameter list (which is empty in our example). The parameter list allows us to pass parameters to the new object's constructor. Since we did not specify a constructor for our Crab class, the default parameter list is empty. (You might have noticed that the instruction that we select from the class's pop-up menu to create objects is exactly this statement.)

In our constructor code above, you find the `new Crab()` instruction as the right half of the first line we inserted.

When we create a new object, we have to do something with it. In our case, we *assign it* to a *variable*.

4.3 Variables

In programming, we often need to store some information to remember and use it later. This is done by using *variables*.

A variable is a bit of storage space. It always has a name to refer to it. When we draw diagrams of our objects or code fragments, we usually draw variables as white boxes with their name to the left side.

Figure 4.2, for example, shows a variable called `age`. (We might want to store the age of the crab.)

age ☐

Variables also have a *type*. The type of a variable states what kind of data can be stored in it. For example, a variable of type `int` can store whole numbers, a variable of type `boolean` can store true/false values, and a variable of type `Crab` can store crab objects.

In our source code, when we need a variable, we can create one by writing a *variable declaration*. A variable declaration is very simple: we just write the type and the name of the variable we want, followed by a semicolon. For example, if we want an `age` variable as shown in Figure 4.2 to store whole numbers, we can write

```
int age;
```

This will create our `age` variable, ready to store `int` values.

4.4 Assignment

Once we have a variable, we are ready to store something in it. This is done using an *assignment statement*.

An assignment is a Java instruction written as an equal sign: =.

For example, to store the number 12 into our age variable, we can write

```
age = 12;
```

It is best to read assignment statements from right to left: *The value 12 is stored into the variable age.* After this assignment statement is executed, our variable will hold the value 12. In our diagrams, we show this by writing the value into the white box (Figure 4.3).

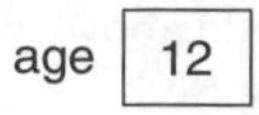

Figure 4.3

A variable storing an
integer value

age | 12 |

The general form of an assignment statement is

variable = *expression*;

That is, on the left hand side is always the name of a variable, and on the right hand side is an expression that is evaluated, and its value is stored into the variable.

Often in our programs, we want to declare a variable and store a value in it. So often we will find the variable declaration and assignment statements together:

```
int age;
age = 12;
```

Because this is so common, Java allows us to write these two statements together in one line:

```
int age = 12;
```

This single line creates the integer variable **age** and assigns the value 12 to it. It does exactly the same as the two-line version above.

Assignments overwrite any value previously stored in it. Thus, if we have our **age** variable now storing the value 12, and then we write

```
age = 42;
```

the **age** variable will now store the value 42. The 12 is overwritten, and we cannot get it back.

4.5 Object variables

We mentioned above that variables cannot only store numbers, they can also store objects.

Java distinguishes *primitive types* and *object types*. Primitive types are a limited set of often used data types, such as **int**, **boolean** and **char**. There are not many of them—Appendix D lists all primitive types in Java.

Every class in Java also defines a type, and these are called object types. So with our class **Crab**, for example, we get a type **Crab**, our **Lobster** class defines a type **Lobster**, and so on. We can declare variables of these types:

```
Crab myCrab;
```

Note that again, as before, we write the type at the front (**Crab**), followed by the name which we can make up (**myCrab**), and a semicolon.

> **Concept**
>
> Variables of **primitive types** store numbers, booleans and characters; variables of **object types** store objects.

Figure 4.4
An object variable
storing a reference
to an object

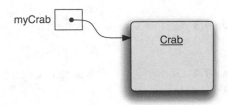

Once we have an object variable, we can store objects into it. We can now put this together with our instruction to create a crab object, which we saw in Section 4.2.

```
Crab myCrab;
myCrab = new Crab();
```

As before, we can also write this in a single line:

```
Crab myCrab = new Crab();
```

This single line of code does three things:

- It creates a variable called myCrab of type Crab.

- It creates a crab object (an object of type Crab).

- It assigns the crab object to the myCrab variable.

Concept

Objects are stored in variables by storing a **reference** to the object.

When we have an assignment statement, the right hand side of the assignment is always executed first (the crab object is created), and then the assignment to the variable on the left takes place.

In our diagrams, we draw object variables storing objects using an arrow (Figure 4.4). Here, the variable myCrab stores a reference to the crab object. The fact that object variables always store references to the objects (and not objects directly) will become important later, so we will be careful to always accurately draw it like this.

The type of the variable and the type of the value assigned to it must always match. You can assign an int value to an int variable, and you can assign a Crab object to a Crab variable. But you cannot assign a Crab object to an int variable (or any other non-matching combination).[1]

Exercise 4.1 Write a variable declaration for a variable of type **int** where the variable has the name "score."

Exercise 4.2 Declare a variable named "isHungry" of type **boolean**, and assign the value "true" to it.

---

[1] When we say "the types must match," this does not actually mean that they must be the same. There are situations where types match that are not the same. For example, we can assign a subclass to a superclass type, such as assigning a Crab to an Actor variable (because a crab *is an* actor). These are subtleties that we shall discuss later.

> **Exercise 4.3** Declare a variable named "year" and assign the value 2014 to it. Then assign the value 2015.
>
> **Exercise 4.4** Declare a variable of type **Crab**, named "littleCrab," and assign a new crab object to it.
>
> **Exercise 4.5** Declare a variable of type **Control**, named "inputButton," and create and assign an object of type **Button**.
>
> **Exercise 4.6** What is wrong with the following statement: `int myCrab = new Crab();`

4.6 Using variables

Once we have declared a variable and assigned a value, we can use it by just using the name of the variable.

For example, the following code declares and assigns two integer variables:

```
int n1 = 7;
int n2 = 13;
```

We can then use them on the right hand side of another assignment:

```
int sum = n1 + n2;
```

After this statement, sum contains the sum of n1 and n2. If we write

```
n3 = n1;
```

then the value of n1 (7, in this case) will be copied into n3 (assuming a variable n3 has been declared previously). n1 and n3 now both contain the value 7.

> **Exercise 4.7** Declare a variable called **children** (of type **int**). Then write an assignment statement that assigns to this variable the sum of two other variables named **daughters** and **sons**.
>
> **Exercise 4.8** Declare a variable named **area** of type **int**. Then write an assignment statement that assigns to **area** the product of two variables called **width** and **length**.
>
> **Exercise 4.9** Declare two variables x and y of type **int**. Assign the values 23 to x and 17 to y. Then write some code to swap those values (so that afterwards x contains 17, and y contains 23).

4.7 Adding objects to the world

We have now seen how we can create a new crab and store it in a variable. The last thing to do is to add this new crab into our world.

In the code fragment in the constructor code shown in Section 4.1, we have seen that we can use the following line:

```
addObject(myCrab, 250, 200);
```

The `addObject` method is a method of the `World` class, and it allows us to add an actor object to the world. We can look it up by looking at the class documentation for class `World`. There we see that it has the following signature:

```
void addObject(Actor object, int x, int y)
```

Reading the signature from start to finish, this tells us the following:

- The method does not return a result (void return type).

- The name of the method is *addObject*.

- The method has three parameters, named *object*, *x*, and *y*.

- The type of the first parameter is *Actor*, the type of the other two is *int*.

This method can be used to add a new actor into the world. Since the method belongs to the `World` class and `CrabWorld` is a `World` (it inherits from the `World` class), this method is available in our `CrabWorld` class, and we can just call it.

We have just created a new crab and stored it in our `myCrab` variable. Now we can use this crab (by using the variable it is stored in) as the first parameter to the `addObject` method call. The remaining two parameters specify the x and y coordinate of the position where we wish to add the object.

All the constructs together (variable declaration, object creation, assignment, and adding the object to the world) look like this:

```
Crab myCrab = new Crab();
addObject(myCrab, 250, 200);
```

We can use an object of type `Crab` for the `Actor` parameter, because a crab is an actor (class `Crab` is a subclass of class `Actor`).

Exercise 4.10 Add code to the `CrabWorld` constructor of your own project to create a crab automatically, as discussed above.

Exercise 4.11 Add code to automatically create three lobsters in the `CrabWorld`. You can choose arbitrary locations for them in the world.

Exercise 4.12 Add code to create two worms at arbitrary locations in the `CrabWorld`.

4.8 Save the World

We will now introduce an easier method to achieve the same thing.

First, remove the code again that you introduced in the last set of exercises, so that the objects are not created automatically. When you compile your scenario again, the world should be empty. Then do the following exercises.

> **Exercise 4.13** Compile your scenario. Then place the following actors into your world (interactively): one crab, three lobsters, and ten worms.
>
> **Exercise 4.14** Right-click on the world background. The world's context menu will pop up. From this menu, select **Save the World**.

When you place some objects into your world and then select the *Save the World* function (Figure 4.5), you will notice that your CrabWorld source code opens, and some new code has been inserted in this class. Study this code carefully.

Figure 4.5

The "Save the World" function

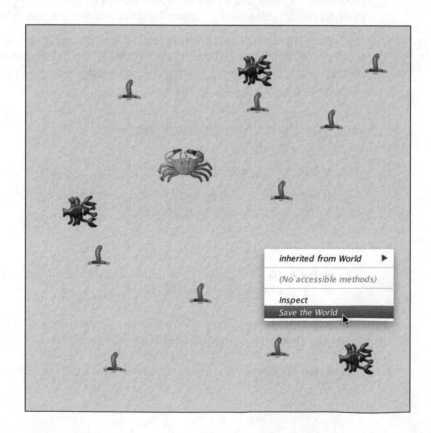

You will see that this code does the following:

- The constructor now includes a call to a new method named `prepare()`.

- A method definition for this method has been added.

- The `prepare()` method contains code that creates and adds all the actors that we have just created interactively.

So what is happening here?

When we create objects interactively, and then select *Save the World*, Greenfoot writes code into our world class to recreate the situation just as we set it up by hand. It does this by creating and calling a method called `prepare()`.

The effect is that now, every time we click *Compile* or *Reset*, the actors are immediately created again.

Our previous exercises to write the code manually to create and place the actors help us understand how this method works. In many cases, we do not need to write this code manually—and can use *Save the World* instead—but is important to understand it in detail. There are other occasions where we want a more sophisticated setup, where we will still write the initialization code by hand.

4.9 Animating images

Now that we have managed to start our game off with a good setup automatically, we can spend a bit of time improving some details.

We will next work on animating the image of the crab. To make the movement of the crab look a little better, we plan to change the crab so that it moves its legs while it is walking.

Animation is achieved with a simple trick: we have two different images of the crab (in our scenario, they are called *crab.png* and *crab2.png*), and we simply switch the crab's image between these two versions fairly quickly. The position of the crab's legs in these images is slightly different (Figure 4.6).

The effect of this (switching back and forth between these images) will be that the crab looks as if it is moving its legs.

In order to do this, we have to use some more variables and also discuss how to work with Greenfoot images.

Figure 4.6

Two slightly different images of the crab

a) crab with legs out   b) crab with legs in

4.10   Greenfoot images

Greenfoot provides a class called `GreenfootImage` that helps in using and manipulating images. We can obtain an image by constructing a new `GreenfootImage` object—using Java's `new` keyword—with the file name of the image file as a parameter to the constructor. For example, to get access to the *crab2.png* image, we can write

```
new GreenfootImage("crab2.png")
```

The file we name here must exist in the scenario's *images* folder.

All Greenfoot actors have images. By default, actors get their image from their class. We assign an image to the class when we create it, and every object created from that class will receive, upon creation, a copy of that same image. That does not mean, however, that all objects of the same class must always keep the same image. Every individual actor can decide to change its image at any time.

> **Exercise 4.15** Check the documentation of the **Actor** class. There are two methods that allow us to change an actor's image. What are they called, and what are their parameters? What do they return?

If you did the exercise above, you will have seen that one method to set an actor's image expects a parameter of type `GreenfootImage`. This is the method we shall use. We can create a `GreenfootImage` object from an image file as described above and assign it to a variable of type `GreenfootImage`. Then we use the actor's `setImage` method to use it for the actor. Here is a code snippet to do this:

```
GreenfootImage image2 = new GreenfootImage("crab2.png");
setImage(image2);
```

To set the image back to the original image, we write:

```
GreenfootImage image1 = new GreenfootImage("crab.png");
setImage(image1);
```

This creates the image objects from the named image files (*crab.png* and *crab2.png*) and assigns them to the `image1` and `image2` variables. Then we use these variables to set our new image as the actor's image. To create the animation effect, we just have to set it up somehow so that these two code fragments are executed in alternating sequence: first one, then the other, back and forth.

We could go ahead now and add code similar to this to our `act` method. However, before doing this, we shall discuss one improvement: we want to separate the creation of the image objects from the setting of the image.

The reason is efficiency. When our program runs with the image animation, we will change the image many times, several times per second. With the code as we have written it, we would also read the image from the image file and create the image objects many times. This is not necessary, and it is wasteful. It is enough to create the image objects once and then just set them back and forth many times. In other words, we want to separate the code fragments like this:

Do this only once at the beginning:

```
GreenfootImage image1 = new GreenfootImage("crab.png");
GreenfootImage image2 = new GreenfootImage("crab2.png");
```

Do this many times over and over:

```
setImage(image1);
```

or

```
setImage(image2);
```

Thus, we shall first create the images and store them, and later we shall use the stored images (without creating them again) over and over to alternate our displayed image.

To achieve this, we need a new construct that we have not used before: an instance variable.

4.11 Instance variables (fields)

Java provides different kinds of variables. The ones we have seen before are called *local variables*, and the ones we shall discuss now are *instance variables*. (Instance variables are also sometimes called *fields*.)

The first difference is the place where they are declared in our source code (Code 4.2): local variables are declared inside a method, while instance variables are declared inside the class, but before any methods.

Code 4.2
Instance variables and local variables in a class

```
public class Crab extends Actor                         ┌─ Instance variables
{
    private GreenfootImage image1;
    private GreenfootImage image2;
    private int age;

    /**
     * Make out crab act.
     */
    public void act()                          ┌─ Local variables
    {
        boolean isAlive;
        int n;

        // ... acting code omitted
    }
}
```

Concept

Instance variables (also called **fields**) are variables that belong to an object (rather than a method).

The next easily visible difference is that instance variables have the keyword `private` in front of them (see Code 4.2).

More important, however, is the difference in behavior: local variables and instance variables behave differently, especially regarding their *lifetime*.

Local variables belong to the method they are declared in, and disappear as soon as the method finishes executing. Every time we call the method, the variables are created again, and can be used while the method executes, but they do not survive between method calls. Values or objects stored in them are lost when the method ends.[2]

Instance variables, on the other hand, belong to the object they are declared in, and survive as long as the objects exist. They can be used over and over again, over multiple method calls and by multiple methods. Thus, if we want an object to store information for a longer time, an instance variable is what we need.

Instance variables are defined at the top of the class,[3] following the class header, using the keyword private followed by the type of the variable and the variable name:

```
private variable-type variable-name;
```

In our case, since we want to store objects of type `GreenfootImage`, the variable type is `GreenfootImage` and we use the names `image1` and `image2` as in our code snippets before (Code 4.3).

Code 4.3

The Crab class with two instance variables

```
import greenfoot.*;  // (World, Actor, GreenfootImage, and Greenfoot)
// comment omitted

public class Crab extends Actor
{
    private GreenfootImage image1;
    private GreenfootImage image2;

    // methods omitted

}
```

---

[2] To be exact: local variables belong to the *scope* they are declared in and exist only to the end of that scope. Often this is a method, but if the variable is declared, for example, inside an if-statement, it will disappear at the end of that if-statement.

[3] Java does not enforce instance variables being at the top of the class, but we will always do this as it is good practice and helps us find the variable declarations easily when we need to see them.

Exercise 4.16 Before adding this code, right-click a crab object in your world and select *Inspect* from the crab's pop-up menu. Make a note of all the variables that are shown in the crab object.

Exercise 4.17 Why do you think the crab has any variables at all, even though we have not declared any in our crab class?

Exercise 4.18 Add the variable declarations shown in Code 4.3 above to your version of the **Crab** class. Make sure that the class compiles.

Exercise 4.19 After adding the variables, inspect your crab object again. Take a note of the variables and their values (shown in the white boxes).

In our diagrams, we show objects as colored boxes with rounded corners, and instance variables as white boxes inside an object (Figure 4.7). Note that the declaration of these two GreenfootImage variables does not give us two GreenfootImage objects. It just gives us some empty space to store two objects.

Figure 4.7
A crab object with two empty instance variables

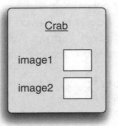

Next we have to create the two image objects and store them into the instance variables. The statement for the creation of the objects has already been shown above. It was achieved with the code snippet

```
new GreenfootImage("crab2.png")
```

Now we just need to create both image objects and assign them to our instance variables:

```
image1 = new GreenfootImage("crab.png");
image2 = new GreenfootImage("crab2.png");
```

Following these statements, we have three objects (one crab and two images), and the crab's variables contain references to the images. This is shown in Figure 4.8.

The last remaining question is where to put the code that creates the images and stores them into the variables. Since this should be done only once when the crab object is created, and not every time we act, we cannot put it into the act method. Instead, we put this code into a constructor.

Figure 4.8
A crab object with two variables, pointing to image objects

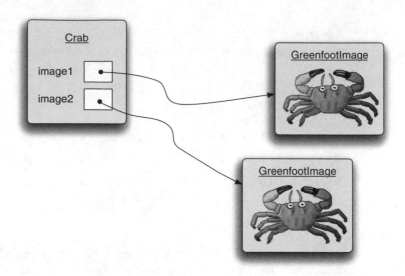

4.12 Using actor constructors

At the beginning of this chapter we have seen how to use the constructor of the world class to initialize the world. In a similar manner, we can use a constructor of an actor class to initialize the actor. The code in the constructor is executed once when the actor is created. Code 4.4 shows a constructor for the **Crab** class that initializes the two instance variables by creating images and assigning them to the variables.

Code 4.4
Initializing the variables in the constructor

```
import greenfoot.*;  // (Actor, World, Greenfoot, GreenfootImage)

// comment omitted

public class Crab extends Actor
{
    private GreenfootImage image1;
    private GreenfootImage image2;

    /**
     * Create a crab and initialize its two images.
     */
    public Crab()
    {
        image1 = new GreenfootImage("crab.png");
        image2 = new GreenfootImage("crab2.png");
        setImage(image1);
    }

    // methods omitted
}
```

The same rules described for the `World` constructor apply to the `Crab` constructor:

- The signature of a constructor does not include a return type.
- The name of the constructor is the same as the name of the class.
- The constructor is automatically executed when a crab object is created.

The last rule—that the constructor is automatically executed—ensures that the image objects are automatically created and assigned when we create a crab. Thus, after creating the crab, the situation will be as depicted in Figure 4.8.

Pitfall

Note carefully that there is no type before the variable name in the assignment in the constructor. The variable is defined before the constructor using the statement

```
private GreenfootImage image1;
```

and assigned in the constructor using the line

```
image1 = new GreenfootImage("crab.png");
```

If instead we write in the constructor

```
GreenfootImage image1 = new GreenfootImage("crab.png");
```

then something entirely different happens: we would declare an *additional* local variable called **image1** in the constructor (we then have two variables called **image1**: one *local*, one *instance*) and assign our image to the local one. It would then be lost as soon as the constructor ends, and our instance variable is still empty.

This is a very subtle error, easy to make and difficult to find. So make sure you have your variable declaration at the top, and only an assignment without the declaration in the constructor.

The last line of the constructor sets the first of the two created images as the crab's current image:

```
setImage(image1);
```

We can later use a similar method call to swap the images in the act method.

Exercise 4.20 Add this constructor to your **Crab** class. You will not yet see any change in the behavior of the crab, but the class should compile, and you should be able to create crabs.

Exercise 4.21 Inspect your crab object again. Take a note again of the variables and their values. Compare those to the notes you took previously.

Alternating the images

We have now reached a stage where the crab has two images available to do the animation. But we have not done the animation itself yet. This is now relatively simple.

To do the animation, we need to alternate between our two images. In other words, at every step, if we are currently showing `image1`, we now want to show `image2`, and *vice versa*. Here is some pseudo-code to express this:

```
if (our current image is image1) then
    use image2 now
else
    use image1 now
```

Pseudo-code, as used here, is a technique expressing a task in a structure that is partly like real Java code, and partly plain English. It often helps in working out how to write our real code. We can now show the same in real Java code (Code 4.5).

Code 4.5

Alternating between two images

```
if ( getImage() == image1 )
{
    setImage(image2);
}
else
{
    setImage(image1);
}
```

In this code segment, we notice several new elements:

- The method `getImage` can be used to receive the actor's current image.

- The operator == (two equal signs) can be used to compare one value with another. The result is either *true* or *false*.

- The if-statement has an extended form that we have not seen before. This form has an `else` keyword after the first body of the if-statement, followed by another block of statements. We investigate this new form of the if-statement in the next section.

Concept

We can test whether two things are **equal** by using a double equals symbol: ==.

Pitfall

It is a common mistake to get the assignment operator (=) and the operator to check equality (==) mixed up. If you want to check whether two values or variables are equal, you must write two equal symbols.

4.14 The if/else statement

Before moving on, let us investigate the if-statement again in some more detail. As we have just seen, an if-statement can be written in the form

```
if ( condition )
{
    statements;
}
else
{
    statements;
}
```

This if-statement contains two blocks (pairs of curly brackets surrounding a list of statements): the *if-clause* and the *else-clause* (in this order).

When this if-statement is executed, first the condition is evaluated. If the condition is true, the if-clause is executed, and then execution continues below the else-clause. If the condition is false, the if-clause is not executed; instead we execute the else-clause. Thus, one of the two statement blocks is always executed, but never both.

The else part with the second block is optional—leaving it off leads to the shorter version of the if-statement we have seen earlier.

We have now seen everything we need to finalize this task. It is time to get our hands on the keyboard again to try it out.

Exercise 4.22 Add the image switching code, as shown in Code 4.5, to the `act` method of your own **Crab** class. Try it out! (If you get an error, fix it. This should work.) Also try clicking the *Act* button instead of the *Run* button in Greenfoot—this allows us to observe the behavior more clearly.

Exercise 4.23 In Chapter 3, we discussed using separate methods for subtasks, rather than writing more code directly into the **act** method. Do this with the image switching code: Create a new method called `switchImage`, move your image switching code to it, and call this method from within your **act** method.

Exercise 4.24 Call the `switchImage` method interactively from the crab's pop-up menu. Does it work?

4.15 Counting worms

The final thing we want to achieve is to add functionality so that the crab counts how many worms it has eaten. If it has eaten eight worms, we win the game. We also want to play a short "winning sound" when this happens.

To make this happen, we will need a number of additions to our crab code. We need

- an instance variable to store the current count of worms eaten;
- an assignment that initializes this variable to zero at the beginning;
- code to increment our count each time we eat a worm; and
- code that checks whether we have eaten eight worms, and stops the game and plays the sound if we have.

Let us do the tasks in the order in which we have listed them here.

We can define a new instance variable by following the pattern introduced above. Below our two existing instance variable definitions, we add the line

```
private int wormsEaten;
```

Here the type `int` indicates that we want to store integers (whole numbers), and the name `wormsEaten` indicates what we intend to use it for.

Next we add the following line to the end of our constructor:

```
wormsEaten = 0;
```

This initializes the `wormsEaten` variable to zero when the crab is created. Strictly speaking, this is redundant, since instance variables of type `int` are initialized to zero automatically. However, sometimes we want the initial value to be something other than zero, so writing our own initialization statement is good practice.

The last bit is to count the worms and check whether we have reached eight. We need to do this every time we eat a worm, so we find our `lookForWorm` method, where we have our code that does the eating of the worms. Here, we add a line of code to increment the worm count:

```
wormsEaten = wormsEaten + 1;
```

As always in an assignment, the right hand side of the assignment symbol is evaluated first (`wormsEaten + 1`). Thus, we read the current value of `wormsEaten` and add 1 to it. Then we assign the result back to the `wormsEaten` variable. As a result, the variable will be incremented by 1.

Following this, we need an if-statement that checks whether we have eaten eight worms yet, and plays the sound and stops execution if we have. Code 4.6 shows the complete `lookForWorm` method with this code. The sound file used here (*fanfare.wav*) is included in the *sounds* folder in your scenario, so it can just be played.

Code 4.6

Counting worms
and checking
whether we win

```java
/**
 * Check whether we have stumbled upon a worm.
 * If we have, eat it. If not, do nothing. If we have
 * eaten eight worms, we win.
 */
public void lookForWorm()
{
    if ( isTouching(Worm.class) )
    {
        removeTouching(Worm.class);
        Greenfoot.playSound("slurp.wav");

        wormsEaten = wormsEaten + 1;
        if (wormsEaten == 8)
        {
            Greenfoot.playSound("fanfare.wav");
            Greenfoot.stop();
        }
    }
}
```

Exercise 4.25 Add the code discussed above into your own scenario. Test it, and make sure that it works.

Exercise 4.26 As a further test, open an object inspector for your crab object (by selecting *Inspect* from the crab's pop-up menu) before you start playing the game. Leave the inspector open and keep an eye on the **wormsEaten** variable while you play.

4.16 More ideas

The scenario *little-crab-5*, in the book scenarios folder, shows a version of the project that includes all the extensions discussed here.

We will leave this scenario behind now and move on to a different example, although there are many obvious things (and probably many more less obvious things) you can do with this project. Ideas include

- using different images for the background and the actors;
- using different kinds of actors;
- not moving forward automatically, but only when the up-arrow key is pressed;
- building a two-player game by introducing a second keyboard-controlled class that listens to different keys;
- making new worms pop up when one is eaten (or at random times); and
- many more that you can come up with yourselves.

Exercise 4.27 The crab image changes fairly quickly while the crab runs, which makes our crab look a little hyperactive. Maybe it would look nicer if the crab image changed only on every second or third act cycle. Try to implement this. To do this, you could add a counter that is incremented in the `act` method. Every time it reaches two (or three), the image changes, and the counter is reset to zero.

Summary of programming techniques

In this chapter, we have seen a number of important new programming concepts. We have seen how constructors can be used to initialize objects—constructors are always executed when a new object is created.

We have seen instance variables and local variables. Instance variables, also called fields, are used—together with assignment statements—to store information in objects, which can be accessed later. Local variables are used to store information for a short period of time—within a single method execution—and are discarded at the method end.

We have used the new statement to programmatically create new objects, and finally, we have seen the full version of the if-statement, which includes an *else* part that is executed when the condition is not true.

With all these techniques together we can now write quite a good amount of code already.

Concept summary

- A **constructor** of a class is a special kind of method that is executed automatically whenever a new instance is created.

- Java objects can be created programmatically (from within your code) by using the **new** keyword.

- **Variables** can be used to store information (objects or values) for later use.

- Variables can be created by writing a **variable declaration**.

- We can store values into variables by using an **assignment statement** (=).

- Variables of **primitive types** store numbers, booleans, and characters; variables of **object types** store objects.

- Objects are stored in variables by storing a **reference** to the object.

- Greenfoot actors maintain their visible image by holding an object of type **GreenfootImage**. These are stored in an instance variable inherited from class Actor.

- **Instance variables** (also called **fields**) are variables that belong to an object (rather than a method).

- **Lifetime of instance variables**: Instance variables persist as long as the object exists that holds them.

- **Lifetime of local variables**: Local variables persist only during a single method execution.

- We can test whether two things are **equal** by using a double equals symbol: **==**.

- The **if/else statement** executes a segment of code when a given condition is true, and a different segment of code when it is false.

Drill and practice

This time, we do some more exercises with calling methods, including a new inherited `Actor` method, and practice more use of variables.

More crab work

Exercise 4.28 Make the lobsters a bit more dangerous. The `Actor` class has a method called `turnTowards`. Use this method to make the lobsters turn toward the center of the screen occasionally. Experiment with the frequency of doing this, and also with different walking speeds for lobsters and the crab.

Exercise 4.29 Add a time counter to the crab. You can do this by adding an `int` variable that is incremented each time the crab acts. (You are, in effect, counting act cycles.) Should this be a local variable or an instance variable? Why?

Exercise 4.30 Play your game. Once you manage to win (eat eight worms), inspect the crab object and check how long you took. How many act cycles did it take?

Exercise 4.31 Move your time counter from the `Crab` class to the `CrabWorld` class. (It makes more sense for the world to manage time, than an individual crab.) The variable is easy to move. To move the statement that increments the time, you need to define an `act` method in the `CrabWorld` class. `World` subclasses can have `act` methods just like `Actor` subclasses. Just copy the signature of the crab's `act` method to create a new `act` method in `CrabWorld` and place your time counting statement here.

Exercise 4.32 Modify your game's time counter to be a game timer. That is: Initialize the time variable to some value (for example, 500), and count down (decrement the variable by one) at every act step. If the timer reaches zero, make the game end with a "time is up" sound. Experiment with different values for the game time.

Exercise 4.33 Investigate the `showText` method of the World class. How many parameters does it have? What are they? What does it return? What does it do?

Exercise 4.34 Display the game timer on screen using the `showText` method. You can do this in the `CrabWorld`'s `act` method. You need a statement similar to this:

```
showText("Time left: "+ time, 100, 40);
```

where **time** is the name of your timer variable. (Note: this statement uses the plus operator and a text string, which we will explain in Chapter 5.)

Bouncing ball practice

Exercise 4.35 Create a new scenario. In it, create a World and an Actor class called *Ball*. (Give it a ball-like image.) Program the ball so that it moves at constant speed, and bounces off the edges of the world.

Exercise 4.36 Program your ball so that it counts how often it has bounced off the edge. Run your scenario with the ball's object inspector open to test.

Exercise 4.37 Program your scenario so that three balls are automatically present at the start.

Exercise 4.38 Change your setup code, so that the three balls appear at random locations.

Exercise 4.39 Change the bouncing-off-the-edge code so that the balls bounce off the edge at somewhat random angles.

Sharing your scenarios

In this section, we will not introduce new programming techniques but rather go on a quick detour to discuss how you can share what you have created with others. The "others" may be your friend sitting next to you or another Greenfoot programmer on the other side of the world.

I1.1 Sharing your scenario

When you have finished writing a scenario—maybe a game or a simulation—you may want to enable others to use it. Those users should have the opportunity to start (and restart) the game, but they do not need access to the class diagram or the source code. They should not modify the game; instead they just use it.

For a scenario to work well when shared, it is important that it automatically creates all the actors you want to see on the screen at the start of the game. Users will not be able to create objects interactively.

In Greenfoot, this is done by *sharing* the scenario. You can share your scenario by clicking the *Share* button at the top right of the Greenfoot main window. This will show a dialog that lets you choose from four options: *Publish*, *Webpage*, *Application*, and *Project*.

I1.2 Publishing to the Greenfoot website

The most common way to share your scenario is to publish it to the Greenfoot website. The Greenfoot site is a public website (at the address *http://www.greenfoot.org /home*) that allows Greenfoot users to upload their Greenfoot scenarios. When you share your scenario on the Greenfoot site, it becomes public to the world—anyone with Internet access can see it and run it.

The share dialog (Figure I1.1) shows the site address at the top. Click here to open the website and see what is there. It is probably best if you have a look through the site first.

Figure I1.1
Publish to the
Greenfoot website

On the Greenfoot site, everyone can view and run scenarios, but if you want to rate them, leave comments, or upload your own scenarios, you need to create an account on the site. This is quick and easy.

After creating an account, you can easily upload your own scenario using the dialog shown in Figure I1.1. The dialog allows you to add an icon, a description, and tags that identify your scenario.

If you choose to publish the source code (using the *Publish source code* checkbox), your full source code will be copied to the Greenfoot site, where everybody else can then download it, read it, and make their own versions of your scenario.

You can change and improve your published scenarios later just by exporting again with the same title.

Publishing your scenarios to the Greenfoot site can be a good way to get feedback from other users: comments on what works and what doesn't, and suggestions what you could add to the program. The Greenfoot site is also a good place to get ideas for further functionality, or to learn how to do things. It includes a discussion section where you can ask and answer questions, and discuss programming techniques and ideas. Or you can look for scenarios with source code, download the source, and check how other programmers have implemented their classes.

I1.3 Export to a Web page

Concept

An **applet** is a version of a Java program that can run on a web page inside a web browser.

The second option is to export your scenario to your own Web page (Figure I1.2). You can choose a location and a name for your export, and Greenfoot will create a folder with your chosen name. In this folder, Greenfoot creates a Web page (in HTML format) and converts your scenario to an *applet* that will run in that Web page. An applet is a version of your Java program that can run embedded in a Web page in a Web browser.

You can execute your scenario by opening the generated Web page in a Web browser.

Initially, this Web page will be usable only on your own computer. If you want to include it in a Web page visible by others, you need to have access to a Web server somewhere to publish it.

The "Lock scenario" option disables the moving of actors in the world before starting the application, as well as removing the Act button and the execution speed slider. If you have a game, you typically want to lock the scenario, whereas for simulations or other more experimental scenarios you may want to leave it unlocked to allow users to experiment more.

Figure I1.2

Export to a Web page

Figure I1.3
Exporting a
scenario to an
application.

I1.4

Export to application

Concept

A **jar file** is a
single file with
the suffix *jar*
that contains all
Java classes that
belong to a Java
application.

The next export option is an export to an application. An application is a stand-alone program that users can execute locally on their computer.

To do this, choose *Application* in the export dialog. You can then choose a location and a name for the executable scenario that you are about to create (Figure I1.3).

Using this function will create an *executable jar file*. This is a file with a ".*jar*" suffix (short for *Java Archive*), which can be executed on many different operating systems (as long as Java has been installed on that machine). Just double-click the jar file to execute it.

I1.5

Export to Greenfoot archive

Concept

A **gfar file** is
a single file
that contains
a Greenfoot
scenario. It can
be opened with
Greenfoot.

The last export option is an export to a single-file Greenfoot archive (Figure I1.4). It creates a file with the suffix ".*gfar*" (*Greenfoot Archive*). *gfar* files contain the entire Greenfoot scenario, including all files from the scenario folder. When double-clicked, they expand to a standard Greenfoot scenario folder and start Greenfoot, opening the scenario.

gfar files make it easier to transfer Greenfoot scenarios between computers, for example, by attaching them to an email.

Figure I1.4
Export to Greenfoot archive

5

Scoring

topics: constrained movement, displaying text messages, keeping score, object interaction

concepts: Strings, String concatenation, abstraction (first look), casting, this (keyword)

One obvious element that is missing from our crab example is keeping score. We have done a part of it: the crab internally keeps track of the number of worms it has eaten, using an integer variable. We have seen that variables are an important part of keeping a score, but this is not a complete solution. Firstly, we might want other actions to contribute to gaining or losing points, and secondly, we have not yet displayed the score on the screen. To get some more variety, we shall discuss this with a different example. After reading this chapter, you can, if you like, go back to the crab game and add a scoring system there as well—you should have learnt how to do this by the end of this chapter.

For this discussion, we shall use a scenario called "WBC" (for "White Blood Cell," Figure 5.1). This is a little game where we control a white blood cell floating in the bloodstream of some creature, and we have the job to catch and remove bacteria. To make things a bit more interesting, there are viruses, too, and we imagine that our type of white blood cell can only neutralize bacteria but not viruses. The virus is too strong for us and damages our cell, so it must be avoided.

This chapter is divided into three parts: we first have a quick look at the starting scenario and analyze it (Sections 5.1 to 5.4), then add some more objects and functionality, using techniques we have already encountered in previous chapters (Sections 5.5 to 5.10). We shall go over these parts fairly quickly, since we have covered the concepts before. Lastly, we shall move on to investigate some new constructs to add the scoring.

Figure 5.1
The WBC ("White Blood Cell") scenario

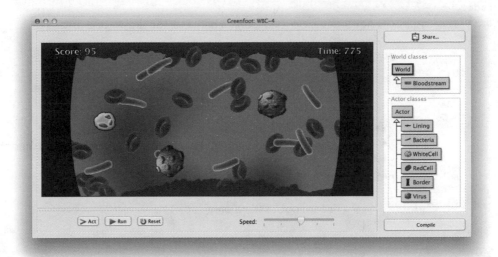

5.1 WBC: The starting point

Open the scenario *WBC-1*, which you find in the book projects, and try it out.

> **Exercise 5.1** Open the scenario *WBC-1* and run it. Describe what you observe.
>
> **Exercise 5.2** For each of the classes in the scenario, write a short (one- or two-sentence) description about what they represent.
>
> **Exercise 5.3** Open the source code for each of the four classes. Study the code and try to work out how it works. Note any section in the code that is unclear to you.

You should be able to work out most of what is going on. We will quickly go through the interesting elements of these classes.

The Lining class is trivial—it does not do anything. Objects of this class are just for decoration; they are placed along the upper and lower edge of the screen, and do not interact with any of the other objects.

The other classes are worth a closer look.

5.2 WhiteCell: constrained movement

The WhiteCell class defines a white blood cell—this is our game object which we control with our keyboard. The structure of its code is quite straightforward: its act method only calls one method to check for key input, which reacts to the "up" and "down" keys (Code 5.1).

Code 5.1

The WhiteCell methods

```
/**
 * Act: move up and down when cursor keys are pressed.
 */
public void act()
{
    checkKeyPress();
}
```

```
/**
 * Check whether a keyboard key has been pressed and react if it has.
 */
private void checkKeyPress()
{
    if (Greenfoot.isKeyDown("up"))
    {
        setLocation(getX(), getY()-4);
    }

    if (Greenfoot.isKeyDown("down"))
    {
        setLocation(getX(), getY()+4);
    }
}
```

The only interesting parts are two lines of the form

```
setLocation(getX(), getY()-4);
```

This is the line that actually moves the object. We use three methods from the `Actor` class that we have not seen before: `setLocation(x,y)`, `getX()`, and `getY()`.

> **Exercise 5.4** Look up these three methods in the documentation for class `Actor`. Write down their signature.

The `getX()`, and `getY()` methods return the current x- and y-coordinates, respectively, as an integer value.

The `setLocation` method expects two parameters, an x- and a y-coordinate, and places the actor at that location. Its signature is

```
void setLocation(int x, int y)
```

Concept

The **setLocation** method sets an actor's location to a position specified by x- and y-coordinates.

So, for example, calling this method with coordinates 120,200, like this:

```
setLocation(120, 200);
```

would teleport our blood cell to location 120,200.

We can now use the `getX()` and `getY()` methods in place of the expected coordinates:

```
setLocation(getX(), getY());
```

When a method call (`getX()`) is written as a parameter to another method call (`setLocation(..)`), the inner method call is evaluated first, and the result is used as the parameter for the outer method call.

Written like this, we would first retrieve our current x-coordinate, then retrieve the current y-coordinate, and then set our location to these coordinates. Thus, this statement would have no visible effect: we would position us where we already are.

However, with one small modification we can create movement:

```
setLocation(getX(), getY()-4);
```

Here, we retrieve our y-coordinate, then subtract 4, and set the result as our new y-coordinate. We leave the x-coordinate unchanged. This places us four cells higher than where we were before.

We have chosen this method of movement, instead of using the `move()` method as before, because this way movement is independent from turning. The `move()` method moves in the direction the object is facing, whereas we want to move always up or down without changing our rotation.

Concept

Access modifiers (private or public) determine who can call a method.

Concept

Private methods are only visible from within the class they are declared in. They are used to improve the structure of the code.

Note: private versus public

You may have noticed that we used the word **private** in the declaration of the `checkKeyPress` method:

```
private void checkKeyPress()
```

This is called a **private method**. Previously, we have declared all methods **public**.

The keywords `private` and `public` are called **access modifiers**, and they determine who can see and call a method. When a method is public, it can be called from other classes in our program. When a method is private, it can be called only from methods within the same class. It will not be visible from the outside.

For example, when you right-click the `WhiteCell` object in your current scenario, you will see the `act` method in its popup menu (it is public), but not the `checkKeyPress` method (it is private).

The purpose of public methods is to offer functionality to other parts of the system, so that our object can be called to do something. The purpose of private methods is to improve the structure of our code by breaking tasks down into smaller subtasks. They are not intended to be called from outside.

From now on, we will declare methods private if they are intended to be called only internally. We will declare them public if they are to be called from other classes.

Variables will always be private. (Java allows them to be made public, but this is considered very bad style.)

5.3 Bacteria: making yourself disappear

You have seen that the bacteria objects float from right to left, slowly rotating. The `Bacteria`'s act method makes this happen (Code 5.2).

The first line uses the same method to create movement as we have seen in the `WhiteCell` class: `setLocation(x,y)` together with `getX()` and `getY()`. This time we move to the left by subtracting from the x-coordinate. Again, we cannot use the `move()` method, because we want the direction of movement to be independent of the rotation.

Code 5.2

The Bacteria act method

```
/**
 * Float along the bloodstream, slowly rotating.
 */
public void act()
{
    setLocation(getX()-2, getY());
    turn(1);

    if (getX() == 0)
    {
        getWorld().removeObject(this);
    }
}
```

The second line is simple: we call the `turn` method to do the slow rotation.

After this follows an if-statement to remove the object from the world when it reaches the left edge of the screen. We can check that we have reached the left edge by checking whether the x-coordinate is zero and, if it is, remove ourselves from the world using the following line of code:

```
getWorld().removeObject(this);
```

Here, we use the `removeObject` method from the `World` class. Its signature is

```
void removeObject(Actor object)
```

We can call this method to remove an object from the world. We need to be aware of two aspects:

■ We must pass an object as a parameter. This is the object to be removed from the world.

■ This method is defined in the `World` class. It must be called on a `World` object.

The `this` keyword

To pass an object as a parameter, we use the Java keyword `this`. The "`this`" keyword refers to the current object that is executing at the moment. Thus, by saying that "`this`" should be removed from the world, the bacterium removes itself.

Chaining method calls

The `removeObject` method belongs to the world object, but we are writing code in the `Bacteria` class. So we cannot just call

```
removeObject(this);
```

This would try to invoke the method on the `Bacteria` object, but this object does not have such a method.

To invoke a method on another object, we must specify that object first, then use a dot, and then the method call:

```
my-world-object.removeObject(this);
```

Thus, we need to get access to the world object—the world we are currently in. Luckily, the `Actor` class has a method to do just that. It is called

```
getWorld()
```

and returns a reference to the current world object. We can now use this method call in place of the world object:

```
getWorld().removeObject(this);
```

Here we chain two method calls: `getWorld()` and `removeObject(..)`. First `getWorld()` is called, and it returns the world object to us. Then `removeObject(..)` is called on that world object that we just received. Thus, we are telling the world object to remove ourselves from the world.

5.4 Bloodstream: creating new objects

The last class to look at is our world subclass, called `Bloodstream`. It has the usual constructor, including a call to the `prepare()` method to place the initial objects (the white blood cell and lining).

The interesting part of this class is its `act` method (Code 5.3). When the scenario runs, this method will place new `Bacteria` objects into the world at random intervals. When a random number out of 100 is less than three—that is, on average three times in every 100 act cycles—a new bacterium will be created.

The x-coordinate to place this new object is always 779—the right edge of the screen (note that the world has a size of 780 by 360 cells, so 779 is the largest possible x-coordinate).

Code 5.3

The Bloodstream
act method

```
/**
 * Create new floating objects at irregular intervals.
 */
public void act()
{
    if (Greenfoot.getRandomNumber(100) < 3)
    {
        addObject(new Bacteria(), 779, Greenfoot.getRandomNumber(360));
    }
}
```

The y-coordinate is a random number out of 360—the height of the world. Thus, the y-position of the new bacterium is a random position at any possible height. We have seen all these constructs before; they are just used here for a new purpose.

5.5 Side-scroll movement

You should now be able to understand the code as it is present, and be ready to add some more objects and functionality to make this project more interesting. We will do this in a series of exercises that apply some of the constructs we already know.

First, we want to create the impression that our white blood cell is continuously moving right through the blood stream. However, we do not actually want to move the blood cell, as we want to keep it permanently on screen. Instead, we move the background—the lining objects—to the left to create the impression of movement. This is an often used technique in many side-scrolling video games.

To do this, we need to do three things:

- Move the Lining objects slowly to the left.
- Remove the Lining objects when they reach the left edge.
- Create new Lining objects on the right.

Exercise 5.5 Make the Lining objects move continuously left. They should move by one cell per act cycle. You can do this by copying the first line of the **Bacteria**'s **act** method, and changing the movement distance to 1.

Exercise 5.6 Make the Lining objects disappear when they reach the left edge. Again, an example of this is in the Bacteria class, and you can use this for guidance.

Exercise 5.7 Write a suitable comment for the **act** method.

Exercise 5.8 Make new `Lining` objects appear on the right of the screen. Do this in the `Bloodstream`'s `act` method. They should appear with a one percent probability (on average once every 100 act cycles).

The last exercise can be done by copying the if-statement in the `Bloodstream`'s `act` method two more times: once for `Lining` objects at the top of the screen, and once for objects at the bottom. Change the 3 in the if-statement to 1 to make them less frequent. Then change the class of the object to be created to `Lining`, and the y-coordinate from a random value to a fixed value: 0 for the top of the screen, and 359 for the bottom. For example,

```
addObject(new Lining(), 779, 359);
```

adds a `Lining` object at the bottom of the screen.

If you have trouble, you can find all the exercises we are discussing here implemented in the scenario *WBC-2*.

Figure 5.2

A virus

5.6 Adding viruses

Our task in this game will be to catch the floating bacteria. To make this a bit more challenging, let us add some danger: viruses. Viruses also float through the bloodstream, but our cell must avoid them.

Exercise 5.9 Add a new class for a virus to your scenario (as a subclass of **Actor**). Call it `Virus`. There is an image already prepared in the scenario for you to use (Figure 5.2).

Exercise 5.10 Extend the `Bloodstream`'s `act` method to add new virus objects at the right edge of the screen. Make the y-coordinate random. Make the probability of new objects 1 percent (one in a hundred act cycles). Test it. (Virus objects should occasionally appear at the right edge, but not yet move.)

Exercise 5.11 Make `Virus` objects move left and rotate (just like bacteria). However, viruses move four cells per act cycle (not two), and rotate anti-clockwise.

Exercise 5.12 Comment your `Virus` class. (That is: fill in the class comment at the top and the method comment above the `act` method.)

5.7 Collision: removing bacteria

Next let us check whether we are touching bacteria (and remove them if we do), or a virus (in which case we lose and the game ends). This is very similar to what we have done with the crab, worms, and lobsters.

Exercise 5.13 Create a new private method in class `WhiteCell`, called `checkCollision`. The method body can initially be empty. Call this method from your `act` method.

Exercise 5.14 In the checkCollision method, add code that removes bacteria if we are touching any. (Use the `isTouching()` and `removeTouching(..)` methods, just like in the crab scenario.)

Exercise 5.15 Play a sound when removing bacteria. The "slurp.wav" sound is included again in the scenario—you can use this one.

Exercise 5.16 Using the same sound effect again is a bit lazy. Make and use a new sound for removing bacteria.

Exercise 5.17 Add similar code to the `checkCollision` method again (another if-statement) to check whether we are touching a virus. If we are, play a sound (a sound called "game-over.wav" is included for this purpose) and stop Greenfoot.

A solution to all the exercises set so far is included in the scenario version *WBC-2*.

Note

If you look carefully, you might notice that you sometimes lose and the game stops when the white blood cell is near a virus, but not actually touching it yet. There is still a little distance between them.

This is caused by the way images are stored in computers, and is discussed in more detail in Chapter 9. Look at Figure 9.2 and the surrounding explanation if you are curious.

5.8 Variable speed

To create more interesting looking movement (and more interesting gameplay), we want to make the movement speed of the bacteria variable. Currently, the speed is 2 (bacteria move two cells per act cycle). We want to change this so that the movement speed is a random value between 1 and 3.

To do this, we will create a variable for the speed, initialize it to an appropriate random value, and use it in our movement statement.

> **Exercise 5.18** In your Bacteria class, add an instance variable of type `int`, named `speed`.
>
> **Exercise 5.19** In the Bacteria constructor, assign a random value to the speed variable, in the range 1 to 3.

You may wonder how to set a random range of 1 to 3, when we have previously learned that random numbers coming from Greenfoot's `getRandomNumber` method always start at 0. The answer is simple: Get a number from 0 to 2, and then add 1:

```
speed = Greenfoot.getRandomNumber(3) + 1;
```

Adding 1 is important, because we never want a speed of 0—the bacterium would never move away.

> **Exercise 5.20** Change the movement statement in your **act** method so that you subtract the variable **speed** from your x-coordinate, instead of subtracting 2. Test.

This is all that is needed. Each bacterium now gets its own speed assigned when it is created, between one and three, and will move at that speed. Watch carefully, and you should see some bacteria moving faster than others.

5.9 Red blood cells

Let us add some red blood cells to the mix. This is purely cosmetic: our other objects do not interact with red blood cells, and they do not influence the gameplay. But they look good!

> **Exercise 5.21** Add a new class called **RedCell**. You will find an image for it in your scenario.
>
> **Exercise 5.22** Make the red cells move just like bacteria, that is: They move right to left at variable speed, slowly rotating. There is one small difference: The speed range of red cells is only 1 to 2 (instead of 1 to 3). Our red cells are slow.

> **Exercise 5.23** Extend your `act` method in class `Bloodstream` to create red blood cells. This is very similar to creating bacteria or viruses, but red blood cells are more frequent: give them a 6 percent chance (6 out of every 100 act cycles) to appear.

This is looking better! It is getting a bit crowded in our bloodstream now, and that is good.

Before moving on to the next task, we can make one very minor improvement. Red blood cells, when they are created, all have the same rotation (they are all created with rotation 0). As a result, all blood cells created closely together rotate in unison. This looks a bit too much like synchronized swimming, and not random enough.

To fix this, we want red blood cells to start off with random rotation. We can do this by adding a statement in the red blood cell's constructor to set the rotation to a random number:

```
setRotation(Greenfoot.getRandomNumber(360));
```

> **Exercise 5.24** Initialize your red blood cells with a random rotation, using the statement shown above.

5.10 Adding borders

We will make one last cosmetic improvement before moving on to the more interesting new material: adding borders at the sides of the screen.

The main reason is to deal with an annoying effect: in Greenfoot, objects are positioned by specifying the coordinate of the center of the object's image. Therefore, when we place a new object on the right edge of the screen, half of its image suddenly appears at once, instead of moving in slowly from the side. The same problem exists at the other end when disappearing: Objects disappear when half their image is still visible on screen. This makes our objects look a bit jerky. It does not look nice.

To deal with this problem, we use a simple trick: we place black border objects on the left and right sides of our screen to cover the problematic space. This is intended to look as if we are looking at our blood stream through a microscope (see Figure 5.1). The objects will now appear behind the borders, out of view, and then slowly move into view.[1]

> **Exercise 5.25** Create a new `Actor` subclass called `Border`. There is a prepared image for it.

---

[1] There is another way we could deal with this problem: we could create an *unbounded world*, which would allow us to place actors outside of the world boundary, and then slowly move them in. This can be done by invoking another `World` superclass constructor, which you can find documented in the `World` class documentation. However, this gets more complicated, and we will not do this here.

We could now add a border object on the right and left side of the screen manually, and use the Save the World function to save them there. However, we want to place them at very precise locations, and that is hard to do by hand. So it is easier to write code to place the objects.

In the Bloodstream's prepare() method, we can add the following code:

```
Border border = new Border();
addObject(border, 0, 180);
Border border2 = new Border();
addObject(border2, 770, 180);
```

Exercise 5.26 Add the code shown above to the Bloodstream's prepare() method. Test it. What remaining problems do you observe?

We need to fix two minor problems: first, our white blood cell is now partly obscured, and second, our objects appear on top of the border, instead of below it. Let us fix both.

Exercise 5.27 In the Bloodstream's prepare() method, find the place where the initial x-coordinate for the white blood cell is defined. Change it to a larger value, so that the cell is a bit further to the right.

Exercise 5.28 In the constructor of Bloodstream, add the following statement:

setPaintOrder(Border.class);

This will make the border objects appear on top of the other objects. Test it.

The setPaintOrder method lets us specify which objects should be painted on top of other objects. The method has a variable length parameter list, and we are allowed to specify as many classes as we like. For example:

```
setPaintOrder(Class1.class, Class2.class, Class3.class);
```

In this example, objects of Class1 would be painted on top, objects of Class2 below it, Class3 objects below that, and all objects of classes not mentioned below these in an unspecified order.

By writing

```
setPaintOrder(Border.class);
```

we state that `Border` objects should be on top (and we do not care about the ordering of any other objects).

All exercises discussed so far are included in the scenario version *WBC-3*. If you had any trouble, you may like to compare your own scenario to that one.

> **Exercise 5.29** Add the ability for the white blood cell to move right and left as well as up and down.

5.11 Finally: adding a score

We will now move on to introduce a few rules for gaining a game score, and implement them. The first obvious idea is that we should get points for neutralizing bacteria. Let us say that we get 20 points for every bacterium we catch.

We can start by implementing this in the `WhiteCell` class. We will need an integer variable to hold our score, count the score every time we catch a bacterium, and display the score on screen.

> **Exercise 5.30** Add an instance variable of type `int` to your `WhiteCell` class. Name it `score`.
>
> **Exercise 5.31** Add a statement to increment the score by 20 when we catch a bacterium.

We have seen in the previous chapter how to add instance variables. We write

```
private int score;
```

at the top of the class, above the first method.

We can then add 20 points to our score by using the following statement immediately after removing the `Bacteria` object:

```
score = score + 20;
```

What is left to do is to display the score on screen. To do this, we use a method called `showText(..)` from the `World` class.

> **Exercise 5.32** Look up the `showText` method from the `World` class. How many parameters does it have? What are they?

Again, we have to call a method from the world class, as we already did earlier to remove an object from the world. We use the same technique as before: we call getWorld() to get access to the world object, and then chain our showText(..) method call to the end of it:

```
getWorld().showText(…);
```

What is left is to work out the parameters for the showText method. Its signature is

```
void showText(String text, int x, int y)
```

The last two parameters are simple: they are the x- and y-coordinates where we want the text to appear. The first parameter is the text we want to show, and it is of a type we have seen but not really discussed before: *String*.

> **Concept**
>
> The type **String** is used to represent text, such as words or sentences. Strings are written in double quotes.

Variables of type String can store text, such as characters, words or sentences. Strings are written in double quotes. For example:

```
String name = "Fred";
```
```
String message = "Game over";
```

We have seen a String before when we played a sound:

```
Greenfoot.playSound("slurp.wav");
```

> **Concept**
>
> Variables of type **String** can store String objects.

The playSound method expects a String parameter, and the value "slurp.wav" is a String we passed into it. We can do the same with the showText method. For example:

```
getWorld().showText("Hello", 80, 25);
```

will show the word "Hello" on our screen at the specified location.

> **Exercise 5.33** Insert the statement above so that it writes the word "Hello" to the screen when you catch a bacterium.
>
> **Exercise 5.34** Change the statement to write your name instead.
>
> **Exercise 5.35** Change the text again to show the word "Score:" (including the colon).

> **Concept**
>
> **String concatenation** merges two Strings into one. It is written with a plus symbol (+).

String concatenation

We have seen how we can display some text—all that is left is to find out how to display our score, which is held in an int variable. We will use *String concatenation*.

String concatenation is written using a plus symbol (+) and joins two Strings together into one:

```
"abc" + "def"
```

becomes

```
"abcdef"
```

and

```
"Wolfgang" + "Amadeus" + "Mozart"
```

becomes

```
"WolfgangAmadeusMozart"
```

(Note that String concatenation does not automatically insert spaces. If you want a space between the two parts, you need to write it.)

The same works with a String and an integer variable. If we "add" a String and an integer, the integer value is converted to a String and then concatenated:

> **Concept**
>
> **String concat-enation** can also be used with a String and an integer.

```
"Score: " + 20
```

becomes

```
"Score: 20"
```

We can also use a variable in place of the integer value:

```
"Score: " + score
```

that will convert the value stored in our `score` variable to a String, and then join it with the "`Score: `" String. And now we have everything we need to display our score on screen. All elements together are shown in Code 5.4.

Exercise 5.36 Show the score in your game.

Exercise 5.37 The game currently seems a bit too easy. Speed it up! You might like to try the following values: Bacteria have a random speed (cells per act cycle) between 1 and 5. The white cell moves sideways with speed 4, and up and down with speed 8. Viruses move at speed 8. Also, speed up the whole scenario using the speed slider at the bottom of the main window: set it just over 50 percent. Experiment with your own speeds to make it challenging, but not impossible.

5.12 Scoring in the World

So far, adding the scoring has been quite straightforward. However, there is a disadvantage to doing the scoring in the `WhiteCell` class: it makes it hard to add scores for other events.

Code 5.4

Scoring in the
WhiteCell class

```java
// import statement and comment omitted
public class WhiteCell extends Actor
{
    private int score;

    // other methods omitted

    /**
     * Check whether we are touching a bacterium or virus. Remove
     * bacteria. Game over if we hit a virus.
     */
    private void checkCollision()
    {
        if (isTouching(Bacteria.class))
        {
            Greenfoot.playSound("slurp.wav");
            removeTouching(Bacteria.class);
            score = score + 20;
            getWorld().showText("Score: " + score, 80, 25);
        }

        if (isTouching(Virus.class))
        {
            Greenfoot.playSound("game-over.wav");
            Greenfoot.stop();
        }
    }
}
```

Consider this: we want our full scoring rules to be:

- Neutralizing a bacterium scores 20 points. (That's done.)

- We lose 15 points for any bacterium that reaches the left screen edge.

- Being hit by a virus does not immediately end the game; instead, we lose 100 points.

- If our points fall below zero, we lose and the game ends.

These are more interesting scoring rules. However, we have a problem. The second event (a bacterium escaping) will be noticed in a Bacteria object. From here, we do not have access to our score variable, which is held in the WhiteCell object. We could try to get access to the WhiteCell object to tell it to update the score. However, it is easier to move the score variable to our World subclass (Bloodstream), since all other objects can easily get access to this object (using the getWorld() method).

Then, the Bloodstream object holds the current score, and the WhiteCell and Bacteria objects will call the Bloodstream object to tell it to update the score when necessary.

Let's get started.

> **Exercise 5.38** Move the score variable from `WhiteCell` to `Bloodstream`.
>
> **Exercise 5.39** Add a line to the `Bloodstream`'s constructor to initialize the score to zero. This is not strictly necessary, because the default value for instance variables is zero, but it is good practice.
>
> **Exercise 5.40** Add a public method called `addScore()` to the `Bloodstream` class. Move the code to increment the score and to show it on screen into this method. Note that you can now omit the `getWorld()` call at the beginning of the `showText(..)` call, because we are already in the world (see Code 5.5).
>
> **Exercise 5.41** Comment your new method.

Code 5.5

A first attempt at an addScore method

```
public void addScore()
{
    score = score + 20;
    showText("Score: " + score, 80, 25);
}
```

Lastly, we have to get the `WhiteCell` object to notify the world object when it wants a score recorded. A first—unfortunately incorrect—attempt, might be to try to write

```
getWorld().addScore();
```

This is a reasonable idea, but it will not work because of a tricky problem: the `getWorld()` method, as defined in Greenfoot's `World` class, returns an object of type `World`. And `World` does not have an `addScore()` method. However, *our* world object is actually a `Bloodstream` object, and *does* have this method.

We need to use a construct—called a *cast*—to tell the Greenfoot compiler that our world is of type `Bloodstream` and then store it in a `Bloodstream` variable. After doing this, we can call the `addScore()` method.

A cast is written by writing the type (`Bloodstream`) in parentheses in front of the method call:

```
Bloodstream bloodstream = (Bloodstream)getWorld();
bloodstream.addScore();
```

Casting is a tricky concept, and you will most likely not understand it completely at this stage. Don't worry—we will come back to this and discuss it more fully later (in Section 9.6), when we know a bit more about the details of typing and subtyping.

> **Exercise 5.42** Add the code to call the Bloodstream's `addScore()` method to your `WhiteCell` class. Test it. Your scenario should now run again, and catching bacteria should score points.

On the surface, we are back to where we were: catching bacteria scores points, and these are displayed when they change. Moving the code to keep score from the white blood cell to the world has—so far—no visible effect. But we now have one big advantage: we can now add other scoring events.

5.13   Abstraction: generalizing the scoring

Our next task is to implement the second scoring rule: we lose 15 points when a bacterium escapes to the left edge of the screen.

Calling the `Bloodstream`'s `addScore()` method is now easy: we can add the same code to the `Bacteria` class that we used in the `WhiteCell` class. However, this would then add a score (20 points), rather than subtract it.

We could make a new method in `Bloodstream`, called `losePoints()` or something similar, which subtracts 15 points from the score, and call that one. While this would work, we will use a more elegant solution: we will generalize our `addScore()` method so that it can be used to add or subtract any number of points.

We can do this by changing the `addScore` method to expect a parameter for the actual number of points to be added (see Code 5.6).

Code 5.6

The addScore method with a parameter

```
/**
 * Add a score
 */
public void addScore(int points)
{
    score = score + points;
    showText("Score: " + score, 80, 25);
}
```

Our improved `addScore` method now receives the number of points to be added to the score as a parameter. Where the new score is assigned, we now add the parameter `points` instead of just adding 20.

Having defined our new `addScore` method, we can now use it to add different scores:

```
bloodstream.addScore(20);
```

would add 20 points, while

```
bloodstream.addScore(100);
```

adds 100 points. We can also easily subtract points by using a negative number:

```
bloodstream.addScore(-15);
```

What we have just done here is an example of *abstraction*—an important concept in programming. Instead of writing a method that can do one specific thing—*adding 20 points*—we write a method that can do many similar things—*adding any number of points*—so that it can be used more generally in different situations.

Generalizing methods by adding parameters so that they are more flexible is generally a good idea.

Exercise 5.43 Change your **addScore** method to expect a parameter for the points, as discussed above.

Exercise 5.44 Change the code in the **WhiteCell** class accordingly: pass a parameter to **addScore**, so that neutralizing a bacterium scores 20 points again.

Exercise 5.45 Add code in your **Bacteria** class, so that you lose 15 points when a bacterium exits the screen.

When adding the scoring code to the **Bacteria** class, it is important not to call getWorld() again after removing the object itself from the world. If the object has been removed from the world, a call to getWorld() afterwards will not work, because we are not in a world anymore. (It would return the special value null, and trying to access the world would result in an error called a NullPointerException.) Code 5.7 is carefully written to ensure this. It also shows that we can now use the bloodstream variable to call the removeObject method, instead of calling getWorld() again. We do not need to get the world again, because we have already stored it in our local variable.

Another small glitch is that the score is not displayed on screen until we score the first points. It would really be nicer if it were displayed from the start. The following exercises make this change.

Code 5.7

Bacteria: losing points, then disappearing

```java
/**
 * Float along the bloodstream, slowly rotating.
 */
public void act()
{
    setLocation(getX()-speed, getY());
    turn(1);

    if (getX() == 0)
    {
        Bloodstream bloodstream = (Bloodstream)getWorld();
        bloodstream.addScore(-15);
        bloodstream.removeObject(this);
    }
}
```

Exercise 5.46 In `Bloodstream`, make a new private method called **showScore()**. It has no parameters and returns nothing. Move the **showText** statement that displays the score into this method. Where **showText** was called previously, call **showScore** instead now.

Exercise 5.47 In the constructor of `Bloodstream`, add a call to **showScore**. This will cause the score to be displayed at the start.

In addition to showing the score from the constructor, we have also made a separate method for it. It is always good practice to make a dedicated method for any task that needs to be done more than once, even if that task is short.

We are now ready to implement our last two scoring rules.

Exercise 5.48 Change your program so that touching a virus does not immediately end the game. Instead, the virus is removed and you lose 100 points. (Note: it is important to remove the virus. Otherwise we would keep touching it and lose 100 points repeatedly in every act cycle!)

Exercise 5.49 Make a new sound for touching a virus.

Exercise 5.50 Move the game-over functionality (playing the game-over sound and stopping Greenfoot) into the addScore method, so that the game is over if the score falls below zero. (You need an if-statement after changing and displaying the score.)

If you have problems, the scenario *WBC-4* shows the full implementation of this (as well as the additional changes discussed below). However, try to solve it yourself if you can—you should know everything you need by now.

5.14 Adding game time

The one last thing missing now is a way to win this game.

We will do this by adding a timer that counts down; if we make it to the end of the timer without losing, we win.

Adding the timer uses very similar constructs to those we have used when adding the score, so we should be able to do this now in the following sequence of exercises.

Exercise 5.51 In class `Bloodstream`, add an instance variable of type `int`, called `time`.

Exercise 5.52 In the constructor, initialize the time to 2000. (We will try to survive for 2000 act cycles.)

Exercise 5.53 Define a new private method called `showTime` that displays the time left (the `time` variable) near the top right of the screen. Call this method from the constructor to show the initial time.

Exercise 5.54 Define a new private method called `countTime` that decrements the time by 1 every time it is called and then shows the current time (by calling `showTime`). Call this method from your `act` method.

Exercise 5.55 In your `countTime` method, add an if-statement that stops execution when the timer reaches 0.

Exercise 5.56 Add a new private method called `showEndMessage`. When called, it displays a message telling us that we won, and how many points we have, near the middle of the screen. For example:

Time is up—you win!

Your final score: 1455 points

Call this method when the timer runs out and we win.

Summary of programming techniques

In this chapter we have gained more practice with important concepts that we really need to know: using variables and defining and calling methods.

We have also seen a first example of object interaction: our actor objects had to call our world object to ask it to do something (changing the score or removing an object). We encountered the String type and String concatenation.

Importantly, we have seen a first example of abstraction for generalization: we saw that adding a parameter to a method can make the method more generally useful, so that we can call the method from different contexts to carry out slightly different (but related) actions. This is better than writing separate methods for every case.

We will see more of abstraction throughout the coming chapters.

Concept summary

- The **setLocation** method sets an actor's location to a position specified by x- and y-coordinates.

- **Access modifiers** (private or public) determine who can call a method.

- **Private methods** are only visible from within the class they are declared in. They are used to improve the structure of the code.

- The keyword **this** can be used to refer to the current object.

- The **getWorld** method gives us access to the world from an actor object.

- The type **String** is used to represent text, such as words or sentences. Strings are written in double quotes.

- Variables of type **String** can store String objects.

- **String concatenation** merges two Strings into one. It is written with a plus symbol (+).

- **String concatenation** can also be used with a String and an integer.

- **Parameterizing** methods (adding parameters) can make them more flexible and more useful.

Drill and practice

In this chapter we will not have the usual drill-and-practice section; the last section—adding game time—already served this purpose and gave us the chance to practice our new constructs and techniques.

Instead, you can do some work to personalize your scenario.

Exercise 5.57 Experiment with the parameters of this game to make it more playable and more interesting. You can adjust

- the speed with which each of the actors moves;
- the numbers of points you gain and lose;
- the amount of time available;

- the sound effects;
- the frequency of new actors appearing;
- the execution speed of the scenario;

and anything else you can think of.

Exercise 5.58 Change the scenarios images to put the game into an entirely new setting. For example, you could make it a spaceship flying through space, collecting astronauts and avoiding asteroids, or a rabbit running over a field, catching carrots, and avoiding dogs.

Anything you like really. Make up something. Be creative.

If you are happy with your idea and images, it would be good to change the class names, too.

Different settings might give you different ideas for additional functionality.

6 Making music: an on-screen piano

topics:	sound
concepts:	abstraction, loops, arrays, OO structure

In this chapter we shall start on a new scenario: a piano that we can play with our computer keyboard. Figure 6.1 shows what it could look like once we're finished.

We start again with opening a scenario from the book scenarios: *piano-1*. This is a version of our project that has the resources in it that we will need (the images and the sound files), but not much else. We shall use this as the base scenario to start writing the code to build the piano.

Figure 6.1
The goal for this chapter: an on-screen piano

Exercise 6.1 Open the scenario *piano-1* and examine the code for the two existing classes, **Piano** and **Key**. Make sure you know what code is there and what it does.

> **Exercise 6.2** Create an object of class **Key** and place it into the world. Create several of them and place them next to each other.

6.1 Animating the key

When you examine the existing code you see that not much is there at present: The `Piano` class only specifies the size and resolution of the world, and the `Key` class contains only method stubs (empty methods) for the constructor and the `act` method (shown in Code 6.1).

Code 6.1

The initial "Key" class

```
import greenfoot.*;  // (World, Actor, GreenfootImage, and Greenfoot)

public class Key extends Actor
{
    /**
     * Create a new key.
     */
    public Key()
    {
    }

    /**
     * Do the action for this key.
     */
    public void act()
    {
    }
}
```

We can start experimenting by creating an object of class `Key` and placing it into the world. You see that its image is that of a simple white key, and it does nothing at all when we run the scenario.

Our first task will be to animate the piano key: when we press a key on the keyboard, we would like the piano key on screen to change so that it appears to be pressed down. The scenario as it is already contains two image files named *white-key.png* and *white-key-down.png*, which we can use to show these two states. (It also contains two more image files, *black-key.png* and *black-key-down.png*, which we will use later for the black keys.) The *white-key.png* image is the one that we currently see when we create a key.

We can create the effect of the key being pressed quite easily by switching between the two images when a specific key on the keyboard is pressed. Code 6.2 shows a first attempt at this.

Code 6.2

First version of
the act method:
changing images

```
/**
 * Do the action for this key.
 */
public void act()
{
    if ( Greenfoot.isKeyDown("g") ) {
        setImage("white-key-down.png");
    }
    else {
        setImage("white-key.png");
    }
}
```

In this code, we have chosen an arbitrary key on the computer keyboard (the "g" key) to react to. Which key we use at this stage does not really matter—eventually we want to attach different piano keys to several of our keyboard keys. When the key is pressed on the keyboard we show the "down" image; when it is not being pressed we show the "up" image.

> **Exercise 6.3** Implement this version of the `act` method in your own scenario. Test it—make sure it works.

While this version works, it has a problem: the image is set not only once when it changes, but continuously. Every time the `act` method executes, the image is set to either one of the two images, even though it might already show the correct image. For example, if the "g" key is not being pressed, the image will be set to *white-key.png*," even if this was already the displayed image.

This problem does not seem too serious at first. After all, setting the image when it is not needed is merely unnecessary, but not incorrect. There are several reasons why we want to fix this, though. One reason is that it is good practice to not waste processor resources by doing unnecessary work. Another reason is that we will add sound for the key soon, and then it does matter. When we press a key, it makes a big difference whether the key's sound is heard once, or over and over again.

So, let us improve our code by ensuring that the image is only set when it actually changes. To do this, we add a boolean field to our class to remember whether the key is currently down or not. We call this field `isDown`, and its declaration looks as follows:

```
private boolean isDown;
```

We will store `true` in this field while the piano key is down, and `false` while it isn't.

We can then check whether our keyboard key has just now been pressed: if our `isDown` field is `false`, but the "g" key on the keyboard is being pressed, it must have been pressed just a moment ago. Conversely, if our `isDown` field is `true` (we think the key is down), but the "g" key on the keyboard is not down, then it must have been released just now. In these two situations, we can then change the image. Code 6.3 shows the complete act method implementing this idea.

Code 6.3

Only set the image when it needs to change

```
public void act()
{
    if ( !isDown && Greenfoot.isKeyDown("g") ) {
        setImage("white-key-down.png");
        isDown = true;
    }
    if ( isDown && !Greenfoot.isKeyDown("g") ) {
        setImage("white-key.png");
        isDown = false;
    }
}
```

In both cases, we make sure to set the isDown field to the new state if we detect a change.

This code makes use of two new symbols: the exclamation mark (!) and the double ampersand (&&).

Both are logical operators. The exclamation mark means *NOT*, while the double ampersand means *AND*.

Concept

Logic operators, such as **&&** (AND) and **!** (NOT) can be used to combine multiple boolean expressions into one boolean expression.

Thus, the following lines from the act method

```
if ( !isDown && Greenfoot.isKeyDown("g") ) {
    setImage ("white-key-down.png");
    isDown = true;
}
```

can be read a little more informally (attention: not Java code!) as

```
if ( (not isDown) and Greenfoot.isKeyDown("g") ) …
```

The same code, even more informally, can be read as

```
if ( the-piano-key-is-not-down and the-keyboard-key-is-down ) {
    change the image to show the "down" image;
    remember that the piano key is down now;
}
```

Have a look at Code 6.3 again, and make sure you understand the code shown there.

A full list of all available logic operators is given in Appendix D.

Exercise 6.4 Implement the new version of the **act** method in your own scenario. It will not appear to do anything different from before, but it is a necessary preparation for what we shall do next. Don't forget that you also have to add the **boolean isDown** field at the beginning of your class.

6.2 Producing the sound

The next thing we shall do is to ensure that pressing the key makes a sound. To do this, we add a new method to the `Key` class, called `play`. We can add this method in the editor, below the `act` method. For a start, we can write the comment, signature, and an empty body for the new method:

```
/**
 * Play the note of this key.
 */
public void play()
{
}
```

While this code does not do anything (the method body is empty) it should compile.

The implementation for this method is quite simple: we just want to play a single sound file. The *piano-1* scenario, which you used to start this project, has a collection of sound files included (in the *sounds* subfolder), each of which contains the sound of a single piano key. The names of the sound files are *2a.wav*, *2b.wav*, *2c.wav*, *2c#.wav*, *2d.wav*, *2d#.wav*, *2e.wav*, and so on. Of these, let us just pick a more or less random note—say *3a.wav*, a middle *a*—to play for our test key.

To actually play this note, we can use the `playSound` method from the `Greenfoot` class again:

```
Greenfoot.playSound("3a.wav");
```

This is the only code needed in the `play` method. The complete method implementation is shown in Code 6.4.

Code 6.4

Playing the note for the key

```
/**
 * Play the note of this key.
 */
public void play()
{
    Greenfoot.playSound("3a.wav");
}
```

Exercise 6.5 Implement the `play` method in your own version of the scenario. Make sure that the code compiles.

Exercise 6.6 Test your method. You can do this by creating an object of class **Key**, right-clicking the object, and invoking the `play` method from the object's pop-up menu.

We are almost there now. We can produce the key's sound by interactively invoking the play method, and we can run the scenario and press a keyboard key ("g") to create the appearance of the piano key being pressed.

All we need to do now is to play the sound when the keyboard key is pressed.

To play the sound programmatically (from your code), we can just call our own play method, like this:

```
play();
```

> **Exercise 6.7** Add code to your **Key** class so that the key's note is played when the associated keyboard key is pressed. To do this, you need to figure out where the call to the **play** method should be added. Test it.
>
> **Exercise 6.8** What happens when you create two keys, run the scenario, and press the "g" key? Do you have any ideas what we need to do to make them react to different keyboard keys?

All the changes described thus far are available in the book scenarios as *piano-2*. If you had problems that you could not solve, or if you just want to compare your solution to ours, have a look at this version.

6.3 Abstraction: creating multiple keys

We have reached a stage where we can create a piano key that reacts to one key on our computer keyboard and plays a single piano note. The problem now is obvious: when we create multiple keys, they all react to the same keyboard key, and all produce the same note. We need to change that.

The current limitation comes from the fact that we *hard-coded* the keyboard key name ("g") and the sound file name ("3a.wav") into our class. That means: we used these names directly, without a chance to change them short of changing the source code and recompiling.

When writing computer programs, writing code that can solve one very specific task— such as finding the square root of 1,764 or playing a middle-*a* piano key sound—is not very useful. Generally, we would like to write code that can solve a whole *class* of problems (such as finding the square root of any number, or playing a whole range of piano key sounds). If we do this, our program becomes much more useful. We have seen an example of this in the previous chapter, when we parameterized our addScore method so that instead of adding 20 points every time it was able to add any number of points. We need to do something similar now.

The principle we shall use is called *abstraction*. Abstraction occurs in computing in many different forms and contexts—this is one of them.

> **Concept**
>
> **Abstraction** occurs in many different forms in programming. One of them is the technique to write code that can solve a whole class of problems, rather than a single specific problem.

We will use abstraction to turn our Key class from a class that can create objects that play a middle-*a* when the "g" key is pressed on the keyboard into one that can create objects that can play a range of notes when different keyboard keys are pressed.

The way to achieve this is to use a variable for the name of the keyboard key we react to, and another variable for the name of the sound file we then want to play.

Code 6.5 shows the start of a solution to this. Here, we use two additional fields—key and sound—to store the name of the key and the sound file we want to use. We also add two parameters to the constructor, so that these bits of information can be passed in when the key object is being created, and we make sure that we store these parameter values into the fields in the constructor body.

Code 6.5

Generalizing for multiple keys: making the key and note variable

```
public class Key extends Actor
{
    private boolean isDown;
    private String key;
    private String sound;

    /**
     * Create a new key linked to a given keyboard key, and
     * with a given sound.
     */
    public Key(String keyName, String soundFile)
    {
        key = keyName;
        sound = soundFile;
    }

    // methods omitted
}
```

We have now made an abstraction of our Key class. Now, when we create a new Key object, we can specify which keyboard key it should react to, and which sound file it should play. Of course, we haven't written the code yet that actually uses these variables—that remains to be done.

We will leave this as an exercise for you.

Exercise 6.9 Implement the changes discussed above. That is: add fields for the key and the sound file, and add a constructor with two parameters that initializes those fields.

Exercise 6.10 Modify your code so that your key object reacts to the key and plays the sound file specified on construction. Test it! (Construct multiple keys with different sounds.)

We have now reached a point where we can create a set of keys to play a range of notes. (Currently, we have only white keys, but we can already build half a piano with this.) This version of the project is in the book scenarios as *piano-3*.

Constructing all the keys, however, is a bit tedious. Currently, we have to create every piano key by hand, typing in all the parameters. What's worse: every time we make a change to the source code, we have to start all over again. It is time to write some code to create the keys for us.

6.4 Building the piano

We would now like to write some code in the `Piano` class that creates and places the piano keys for us. Adding a single key (or a few keys) is quite straight forward: by adding the following line to the `Piano`'s constructor, a key is created and placed into the world each time we re-initialize the scenario:

```
addObject(new Key("g", "3a.wav"), 300, 180);
```

Remember that the expression

```
new Key("g", "3a.wav")
```

creates a new key object (with a specified key and sound file), while the statement

```
addObject( some-object , 300, 180);
```

inserts the given object into the world at the specified *x*- and *y*-coordinates. The exact coordinates 300 and 180 are picked somewhat arbitrarily at this stage.

> **Exercise 6.11** Add code to your piano class so that it automatically creates a piano key and places in into the world.
>
> **Exercise 6.12** Change the y-coordinate at which the key is placed, so that the piano key appears exactly at the top of the piano (that is: the top of the piano key should line up with the top of the piano itself). Hint: the key image is 280 pixels high and 63 pixels wide.
>
> **Exercise 6.13** Write code to create a second piano key that plays a middle-*g* (sound file name "3g.wav") when the "f" key is pressed on the keyboard. Place this key exactly to the left of the first key (without any gap or overlap).

Earlier in this book, we have discussed the value of using separate methods for separate tasks. Creating all the keys is a logically distinct task, so let us place the code for it into a separate method. It will do exactly the same thing, but the code is clearer to read.

> **Exercise 6.14** In the `Piano` class, create a new method named `makeKeys()`. Move your code that creates your keys into this method. Call this method from the `Piano`'s constructor. Make sure to write a comment for your new method.

We could now go ahead and insert a whole list of `addObject` statements to create all the keys we need for our keyboard. That is, however, not the best way of achieving what we want to do.

6.5 Using loops: the while loop

Programming languages offer you a specific construct to do a similar task repeatedly: a *loop*.

A loop is a programming language construct that allows us to express commands such as "*Do this statement 20 times*" or "*Call these two methods 3 million times*" easily and concisely (without writing 3 million lines of code). Java has several different kinds of loop. The one we shall investigate now is called a *while loop*.

A while loop has the following form:

```
while ( condition )
{
    statement;
    statement;
    ...
}
```

The Java keyword *while* is followed by a condition in parentheses and a block (a pair of curly brackets) containing one or more statements. These statements will be executed over and over, as long is the condition is *true*.

A very common pattern is a loop that executes some statements a given number of times. To do this, we use a *loop variable* as a counter. It is common practice to name a loop variable *i*, so we shall do this as well. Here is an example that executes the body of the while loop 100 times:

```
int i = 0;
while (i < 100)
{
    statement;
    statement;
    ...
    i = i + 1;
}
```

Concept

A **loop** is a statement in programming languages that can execute a section of code multiple times.

Concept

A **loop variable** is a local variable that is used for counting the number of iterations in a loop. For a while loop, it should be declared immediately before the loop.

There are several things worth noting in this code. First, it uses a construct that we have seen before: a local variable. Our variable is called *i* and we initialize it to zero. Then we repeatedly execute the body of the while loop, counting up *i* every time we do so. We continue this as long as *i* is less than 100. When we reach 100, we stop the loop. Execution will then continue with the code following the loop body.

There are two further details worth pointing out:

- We use the statement i = i + 1; at the end of the loop body to increment our loop variable by one every time we have executed the loop. This is important. It is a common error to forget to increment the loop counter. The variable would then never change, the condition would always remain true, and the loop would continue looping forever. This is called an *infinite loop*, and is the cause of many errors in programs.

- Our condition says that we execute the loop while *i* is less than (<) 100, not less than or equal (<=). So the loop will not be executed when *i* is equal to 100. At first glance, one might think that this means that the loop executes only 99 times, not 100 times. But this is not so. Because we started counting at zero, not at one, we do execute 100 times (counting from 0 to 99). It is very common to start counting from zero in computer programs—we will see some advantages of doing so soon.

Now that we know about a while loop, we can use this construct to create all our piano keys.

Our piano will have 12 white keys. We can now create 12 keys by placing our statement to create a key inside the body of a loop that executes 12 times:

```
int i = 0;
while (i < 12)
{
    addObject (new Key ("g", "3a.wav"), 300, 140);
    i = i + 1;
}
```

Exercise 6.15 Replace the code in your own **makeKeys** method with the loop shown here. Try it out. What do you observe?

Trying out this code, it first looks as if only one key was created. This is deceptive, however. We do indeed get 12 keys, but since they have all been placed at exactly the same coordinates, they are all lying right on top of each other, and we cannot see them very well. Try moving the keys in the piano world with your mouse pointer and you will see that they are all there.

Exercise 6.16 How can you change your code so that the keys do not all appear at exactly the same place? Can you change your code so that they get placed exactly next to each other?

The reason the keys all appeared on top of each other is that we inserted them all at the fixed location 300,140 into the world. We now want to insert every key at a different location. This is now actually quite easy to do: we can make use of our loop variable i to achieve this.

Exercise 6.17 How many times does our loop body execute? What are the values of i during each of the executions?

We can now replace the fixed x-coordinate 300 with an expression that includes the variable i:

```
addObject(new Key("g", "3a.wav"), i*63, 140);
```

(The asterisk "*" is the operator for multiplication. Appendix D lists other operators that you can use with integer numbers.)

We have chosen i*63, because we know that the image of each key is 63 pixels wide. The values for i, as the loop executes, are 0, 1, 2, 3, and so on. So the keys will be placed at x-coordinates 0, 63, 126, 189, and so on.

When we try this, we notice that the left-most key is not placed very well. Since object placement in Greenfoot refers to the center point of an object, the center of the first key is placed at x-coordinate zero, which places the key half out of the screen. To fix this, we just add a fixed offset to each key coordinate. The offset is chosen so that the keys as a whole appear in the middle of our piano:

```
addObject(new Key("g", "3a.wav"), i*63 + 54, 140);
```

The y-coordinate can remain constant, since we want all keys at the same height.

Exercise 6.18 Challenge exercise (Do this exercise only if you are fairly confident about your programming. If you are just beginning, you may like to skip this exercise.)

Using fixed numbers in your code, such as the 140 or 63 in the statement above, is usually not the best solution, since it makes your code vulnerable to breaking when things change. For example, if we replace the key images with nicer images that have a different size, our code would not place them correctly.

We can avoid using those numbers directly by calling the `getWidth()` and `getH-eight()` methods of the key's image. To do this, first assign the key object to a local variable of type `Key` when you create it, and then use `key.getImage().getWidth()` in place of the 63. Do a similar thing with the height.

Replacing the 54 requires you to also use the `getWidth()` method of the piano's image.

After doing this, our code will always place the keys nicely, even if their size changes.

Our code now places our white keys nicely—that's a good step forward. The most obvious problem now is that all piano keys react to the same keyboard key and play the same note. Fixing this requires a new programming construct: an *array*.

6.6 Using arrays

Currently, our 12 keys are created, and placed at appropriate locations on the screen, but they all react to the "g" key, and they all play the same note. This is despite the fact that we have prepared our keys to accept different keyboard keys and sound files in the constructor. However, since all our keys are created by the same line of source code (executed in a loop), they are all created with "g" and "3a.wav" as parameters.

The solution is similar to the change we made in regards to the *x*-coordinate: we should use variables for the keyboard key and the sound file name, and assign different values to them each time the loop executes.

This is more problematic than in the case with the *x*-coordinate, though. The correct keys and sound file names cannot be computed as easily. So where do we get the values from?

The answer is: we will store them in an array.

An array is an object that can hold many variables, and thus can store many values. We can show this in a diagram. Assume we have a variable named "name" of type `String`. To this variable, we assign the String "Fred":

```
String name;

name = "Fred";
```

Figure 6.2 illustrates this example.

> **Concept**
>
> An **array** is an object that holds multiple variables. These can be accessed using an **index**.

Figure 6.2
A simple String variable

String name   "Fred"

This case is very simple. The variable is a container that can hold a value. The value is stored in the variable.

In case of an array, we get a separate object—the array object—that holds many variables. We can then store a reference to that array object in our own variable (Figure 6.3).

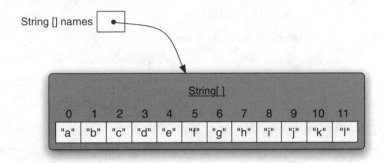

The Java code to create this situation is as follows:

```
String[] names;
names = { "a","b","c","d","e","f","g","h","i","j","k","l" };
```

In the variable declaration, the pair of square brackets ([ ]) indicates that the type of the variable is an array. The word before the brackets indicates the *element type* of the array, that is the type that each entry in the array should have. Thus, `String[]` denotes an array of Strings, while `int[]` denotes an array of integers.

The expression

```
{ "a","b","c","d","e","f","g","h","i","j","k","l" }
```

creates the array object and fills it with the Strings "a" to "l." This array object is then assigned to our variable `names`. We can see from the diagram that, when an array object is assigned to a variable, the variable then contains a pointer to that object.

Once we have our array variable in place, we can access individual elements in the array by using an *index*—a position number in the array object. In Figure 6.3, the index of each individual String is shown above each array element. Note that counting again starts at zero, so the String "a" is at position 0, "b" is at position 1, and so on.

In Java, we access array elements by attaching the index in square brackets to the array name. For example:

```
names[3]
```

accesses the element in the `names` array at index 3—the String "d."

For our piano project, we can now prepare two arrays: one with the names of the keyboard keys (in order) for our piano keys, and one with the names of the sound files for those piano keys. We can declare fields in the `Piano` class for those arrays and store the filled arrays. Code 6.6 illustrates this.

Code 6.6

Creating arrays for keys and notes

```
public class Piano extends World
{
    private String[] whiteKeys =
        { "a", "s", "d", "f", "g", "h", "j", "k", "l", ";", "'", "\\" };
    private String[] whiteNotes =
        { "3c", "3d", "3e", "3f", "3g", "3a", "3b", "4c", "4d", "4e",
          "4f", "4g" };

    // constructor and methods omitted

}
```

Note that the values in the `whiteKeys` array are the keys on the middle row of my computer keyboard. Keyboards are slightly different on different systems and in different countries, so you may have to change these to match your own keyboard. The other slightly odd thing here is the String "\\." The backslash character (\) is called an *escape character* and has a special meaning in Java Strings. To create a String that contains the backslash as a normal character, you have to type it twice. So typing the String "\\" in your Java source code actually creates the String "\."

Now we have arrays available listing the keys and sound file names that we want to use for our piano keys. We can now adapt our loop in the `makeKeys` method to make use of the array elements to create appropriate keys. Code 6.7 shows the resulting source code.

Code 6.7

Creating piano keys with keyboard keys and notes from arrays

```
/**
 * Create the piano keys and place them in the world.
 */
private void makeKeys()
{
    int i = 0;
    while (i < whiteKeys.length)
    {
        Key key = new Key(whiteKeys[i], whiteNotes[i] + ".wav");
        addObject(key, i*63 + 54, 140);
        i = i + 1;
    }
}
```

A number of things are worth noting:

■ We have moved the creation of the new key out of the `addObject` method call into a separate line, and assigned the key object initially to a local variable called `key`. This was just done for clarity: the line got very long and busy, and it was quite hard to read. Splitting it into two steps makes it easier to read.

- The parameters for the Key constructor access whiteKeys[i] and whiteNotes[i]. That is, we use our loop variable *i* as the array index to access all the different key strings and note file names in turn.

- We use a plus symbol (+) with whiteNotes[i] and a String (".wav"). The variable whiteNotes[i] is also a String, so this is string concatenation again, as we encountered in the previous chapter. We append the String ".wav" to the whiteNotes[i] value. This is because the name stored in the array is of the form "3c," while the file name on disk is "3c.wav." We could have stored the full file name in the array, but since the suffix is the same for all notes files, this seemed unnecessary. Just adding it here saves us some typing.

- We have also replaced the 12 in the condition of the while loop with whiteKeys.length. The ".length" attribute of an array will return the number of elements in this array. In our case, we do have 12 elements, so leaving the 12 in place would have worked. However, using the length attribute is safer. Should we one day decide to use more or fewer keys, our loop will still do the right thing, without the need to change the condition.

With these changes, our piano should now be playable with the middle row of keys on our keyboard, and it should produce different notes for different keys.

Exercise 6.19 Make the changes discussed above in your own scenario. Make sure that all keys work. If your keyboard layout is different, adapt the whiteKeys array to match your keyboard.

Exercise 6.20 The sounds folder of the piano scenario contains more notes than the ones we are using here. Change the piano so that the keys are one octave lower than they are now. That is, use the sound "2c" instead of "3c" for the first key, and move up from there.

Exercise 6.21 If you like, you can make your keys produce entirely different sounds. You can record you own sounds using Greenfoot's built-in sound recorder or other sound recording software, or you can find sound files on the Internet. Move the sound files into the sounds folder, and make your keys play them.

The version we have now is in the book scenarios as *piano-4*.

The missing part now is quite obvious: we have to add the black keys.

There is nothing really new in this. We essentially have to do very similar things again as we did for the white keys. We will leave this as an exercise for you to do. However, doing it all in one chunk is quite a substantial job. In general, when approaching a larger task, it is a good idea to break it down into several smaller steps. Thus, we will break this task down into a sequence of exercises that approaches the solution one step at a time.

Exercise 6.22 Currently, our **Key** class can only produce white keys. This is because we have hard-coded the file names of the key images ("white-key.png" and "white-key-down.png"). Use abstraction to modify the **Key** class so that it can show either white or black keys. This is similar to what we did with the key name and sound file name: introduce two fields and two parameters for the two image file names, and then use the variables instead of the hard-coded file names. Test by creating some black and white keys.

Exercise 6.23 Modify your **Piano** class so that it adds two black keys at an arbitrary location.

Exercise 6.24 Add two more arrays to the **Piano** class for the keyboard keys and notes of the black keys.

Exercise 6.25 Add another loop in the **makeKeys** method in the **Piano** class that creates and places the black keys. This is made quite tricky by the fact that black keys are not as evenly spaced as white keys—they have gaps (see Figure 6.1). Can you come up with a solution to this? Tip: create a special entry in your array where the gaps are, and use that to recognize the gaps. (Read the note below these exercises first before you start. This is a hard task! You may want to look at the solution in *piano-complete* if you cannot figure it out.)

Note: The String class

We have now used the *String* class several times and discussed some of its characteristics in the previous chapter. It is time to find out a bit more about it. Find this class in the **Java library documentation** and have a look at its methods. There are many, and some of them are often very useful.

You will see methods to create substrings, to find out the length of a string, to convert the case, and much more.

Especially interesting for Exercise 6.25 above may be the **equals** method that allows you to compare the string with another string. It will return **true** if the two strings are the same.

This is as far as we go with this project. The piano is more or less complete now. We can play simple tunes, and we can even play chords (multiple keys at the same time).

Feel free to extend this if you like. How about adding a second set of sounds, and then adding a switch on screen that allows you to switch from the piano sounds to your alternate sounds?

Summary of programming techniques

In this chapter, we have seen two very fundamental and important concepts for more sophisticated programming: loops and arrays. Loops allow us to write code that executes a sequence of statements many times over. The loop construct we have discussed is called a *while loop*. Java has other loops as well, which we will encounter shortly. We will use loops in many of our programs, so it is essential to understand them.

Within the loop, we often use the loop counter to perform calculations or to generate different values in every loop iteration.

The other major new concept we used was an array. An array can provide many variables (all of the same type) in one single object. Often, loops are used to process an array if we need to do something to each of its elements. Elements are accessed using square brackets.

Another very fundamental technique we encountered was abstraction. In this case, it appeared through the use of constructor parameters to create code that could handle a whole class of problems instead of a single specific problem.

We have also encountered a few new operators: we have seen the AND and NOT (&& and !) operators for boolean expressions, and we have again encountered string concatenation using the plus operator (+) on String operands. The String class is documented in the Java API documentation and has many useful methods.

Concept summary

- **Logic operators**, such as **&&** (AND) and **!** (NOT) can be used to combine multiple boolean expressions into one boolean expression.

- **Abstraction** occurs in many different forms in programming. One of them is the technique to write code that can solve a whole class of problems, rather than a single specific problem.

- A **loop** is a statement in programming languages that can execute a section of code multiple times.

- A **loop variable** is a local variable that is used for counting the number of iterations in a loop. For a while loop, it should be declared immediately before the loop.

- An **array** is an object that holds multiple variables. These can be accessed using an **index**.

- Individual **elements** in an array are accessed using square brackets (**[ ]**) and an **index** to specify the array element.

- The type **String** is defined by a normal class. It has many useful methods, which we can look up in the **Java library documentation**.

Drill and practice

This time, we will practice the most fundamental construct we have just learned: using the while loop. We will do this with a different scenario called *bubbles* (Figure 6.4). Open that scenario, and then do the following exercises.

Figure 6.4

Floating bubbles

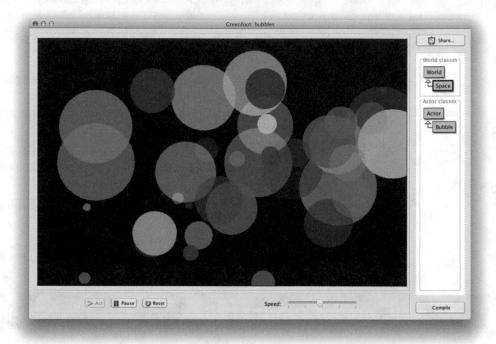

Exercise 6.26 Open the *bubble* scenario. You will see that the world is empty. Place some **Bubble** objects into the world, using the *default constructor*. (The default constructor is the one without parameters.) Remember: you can also do this by shift-clicking into the world. What do you observe?

Exercise 6.27 What is the initial size of a new bubble? What is its initial color? What is its initial direction of movement?

Exercise 6.28 In the world subclass, **Space**, create a new private method called **setup()**. Call this method from the constructor. In this method, create a new bubble, using the default constructor, and place it in the center of the world. Compile, then click **Reset** a few times to test.

Exercise 6.29 Change your **setup()** method so that it creates 21 bubbles. Use a while loop. All bubbles are placed in the center of the world. Run your scenario to test.

Exercise 6.30 Place the 21 bubbles at random locations in the world.

Exercise 6.31 Place the bubbles on a diagonal, with *x* and *y* distances of 30. The first bubble at 0,0, the next one at 30,30, the next at 60,60, and so on. The last one will be at 600,600 (for 21 bubbles). Use your loop counter variable to achieve this.

Exercise 6.32 Place the bubbles on a slightly different diagonal line, so that they go from the top left corner of the world to the bottom right corner. The last bubble should be at 900,600.

Exercise 6.33 Add a second while loop to your `setup()` method that places some more bubbles. This loop places 10 bubbles, in a horizontal line, starting at *x*=300, *y*=100, with *x* increasing by 40 every time and *y* being constant. (That is, the bubbles are at *300,100*, then *340,100*, then *380,100*, and so on.) The size of the bubble should also increase, starting with 10 for the first bubble, then 20, then 30, etc. Use the second `Bubble` constructor for this (the one with one parameter).

Exercise 6.34 Remove the existing loops from your `setup()` method. Write a new while loop that does the following: it creates 18 bubbles. The bubbles are all placed in the center of the world, and have sizes starting from 190, decreasing by 10. The last bubble has size 10. Make sure to create the largest first, and the smallest last, so that you have bubbles of sizes 190, 180, 170, etc., all lying on top of each other.

Use the third constructor of Bubble—the one with two parameters. It also lets you specify the initial direction. Set the direction as follows: the first bubble has direction 0, the next 20, the next 40, etc. That is, the direction between each two bubbles increases by 20 degrees.

Test.

CHAPTER

7

Object interaction: an introduction

topics:	communication with other objects, using classes from the Java library, using lists of objects
concepts:	null, Java class library, collection, list, for-each loop

This chapter introduces two very important concepts in preparation of the following chapter: communicating with other objects, and dealing with lists of objects. In Chapter 8, we will develop a fairly complex example—involving planets in space—that makes use of many new constructs, some of which require a bit of explanation and practice. To approach things step by step and not do too much at once, we will first introduce these two concepts with a smaller example here.

The scenario we discuss in this chapter is a practice ground for these constructs constructs; it is called *autumn* (Figure 7.1).

Figure 7.1

The "autumn" scenario

> **Exercise 7.1** Open the *autumn-1* scenario and investigate it. Run it and note what it does. Read the source code of the three scenario classes and note every bit of code that you do not fully understand.

7.1 Interacting objects

Objects can interact with ("talk to") other objects by calling methods on those other objects.

We have seen several examples of this in the previous chapters, but it is time to gather everything we have seen so far and discuss it systematically to make sure we have covered everything important. Object interaction is so central to object-oriented programming that we cannot afford to miss anything here.

7.2 Object references

For one object to talk to another, it must always have a reference to that other object. This reference is usually stored in a variable. If, for example, our `Block` object from the *autumn* scenario wants to talk to the `MyWorld` object, it must first have a reference to the `MyWorld` object. Figure 7.2 shows this situation: The object of type `Block` holds a reference to a `MyWorld` object in a variable called `world`.

Figure 7.2

A Block object holding a reference to a MyWorld object

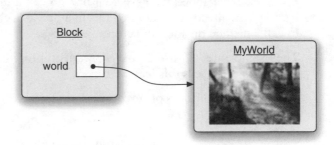

Once the block has a reference to the `MyWorld` object in a variable, it can call methods on it. For example:

```
world.addObject(new Leaf(), 100, 100);
```

Calling a method on another object serves to "talk to" that object. Often, this is to give instructions to that other object (in this case saying to the world object: "Please add a new leaf at location 100,100.")

7.3 Interacting with the world

Since we always need an object reference to talk to an object, one obvious question is: Where do we get this object reference from? Well, there are several possibilities.

In the example above, our block is talking to the world object. We can get a reference to the world object by using the `getWorld()` method that every actor possesses.

The `getWorld()` method gives us a reference to the currently instantiated world, which is always of the subclass of the `World` class. We can declare a variable of type `World` and store our world object into it. Doing this before calling our method gives us:

```
World world = getWorld();

world.addObject(new Leaf(), 100, 100);
```

> **Exercise 7.2** Add code to your **Block** class so that the block adds new leaves to the world whenever it hits the edge of the world. First, add the leaves at location 100,100, as in the example above.
>
> **Exercise 7.3** Modify your code so that the new leaf is added at the current location of the block. You can use the block's **getX()** and **getY()** methods to achieve this.

7.4 Interacting with actors

In the example above, we have seen how to call a method on the world object. (We had, in fact, already encountered this in a previous chapter.) Next we investigate how to call a method on another actor object.

The example we will use is that we want to program our block so that whenever it touches a leaf, it tells this leaf to turn.

Since `Leaf` is a subclass of `Actor`, and `Actor` has a `turn` method, we can call

```
leaf.turn(9);
```

This assumes that we have a variable called `leaf` which holds a reference to a `Leaf` object. The number 9 is an arbitrary value to turn the leaf a bit.

We can see that calling a method on an actor object looks just the same as with the world object. The difference is in obtaining the reference to the leaf in the first place—where do we get the reference from?

One way to get references to other actors in the world is via Greenfoot's *collision detection methods*. These are methods that check whether our actor intersects with another actor, and gives us a reference to that other actor if it does. Once we have a reference to the leaf we are touching, the rest is easy.

We will use a method called `getOneIntersectingObject`. This method returns to us a reference to the intersecting actor. (There are various other collision detection methods; they are further discussed in Chapter 9, and a full list is given in Appendix C.)

We call our method like this:

```
Leaf leaf = (Leaf) getOneIntersectingObject(Leaf.class);
```

> **Exercise 7.4** Look up the method `getOneIntersectingObject` in Greenfoot's class documentation. Which class does it belong to? What type does it return?

Here is what this line of code does in detail:

- We call the `getOneIntersectingObject` method. The parameter lets us specify what kinds of object we are interested in. We must specify a class. By using `Leaf.class` as the parameter, we are saying we want to check whether we are intersecting any `Leaf` objects.

- On the left hand side, we are declaring a new local variable called `leaf` (of type `Leaf`) to be ready to store a leaf object.

- If `getOneIntersectingObject` finds an intersecting leaf, it will return a reference to that leaf object to us, and we assign it to our `leaf` variable.

- We need to use a cast: `(Leaf)`. This is because the `getOneIntersectingObject` method is declared to return an `Actor`, not a `Leaf`. We need to tell our compiler that we are actually expecting an object of type `Leaf` here.

7.5 The `null` value

We have seen what happens if our method finds an intersecting leaf: It returns the reference and we are storing it in a variable. What if we are not intersecting any leaf?

If we call `getOneIntersectingObject`, but we are not intersecting any object of the requested type at the moment, the method will return the special value `null`.

The `null` value can be assigned to any object variable. If it is stored in a variable, it means that this variable is not currently holding any reference; it is essentially empty.

The `getOneIntersectingObject` method returns either `null` or an object reference, depending on whether we are intersecting an object. We can check this after the call to find out whether we were actually touching anything:

```
Leaf leaf = (Leaf) getOneIntersectingObject(Leaf.class);
if (leaf != null)
{
    // if we get here, we are touching a leaf
}
```

Concept

The value **null** is a special value that can be assigned to any object variable. If a variable contains **null**, it does not currently reference any object.

Here, we look at the `leaf` variable: If it is not `null`, then we know we touched a leaf, and the reference is stored in our variable. Thus, we can complete this task by entering our request for the leaf to turn in the body of the if-statement:

```
leaf.turn(9);
```

Exercise 7.5 In your class `Block`, create a new private method called `checkLeaf()`. The method does not return a value. In this method, enter the code as discussed above, to check whether we are intersecting a leaf, and ask it to turn if we do.

Exercise 7.6 Make sure you are actually checking for leaves: From your **act** method, call your `checkLeaf()` method. Test.

Exercise 7.7 Remove your code that adds leaves when the block hits the world edge. Instead, add some code to the `setUp()` method in the `MyWorld` class to add 18 leaves. Use a while loop. Add the leaves at random locations. Test.

7.6 Interacting with groups of actors

We have now seen one way to get a reference to another actor, and then to communicate with that actor by calling one of its methods.

The next interesting case is communication with several actors at once: sometimes we want to do something to every actor of a given class, or every actor within a given range around us.

The example we use here is somewhat artificial, but serves well to practice this: If the user clicks the mouse, we want to change the image of all leaves.

Exercise 7.8 The Leaf class has a method called `changeImage()` to set a different image. Try it out: With your scenario paused, call the `changeImage()` method interactively on some leaves (by right-clicking and choosing it from the leaf's menu).

The `Block` class already has a method to check for mouse clicks (Code 7.1). We can enter our code here. All we need to do is to work out how to call the `changeImage()` method on all leaves in the world.

Code 7.1

A method to check for mouse clicks

```java
/**
 * Check whether the mouse button was clicked. If it was, change all leaves.
 */
private void checkMouseClick()
{
    if (Greenfoot.mouseClicked(null))
    {
        // do this when the mouse is clicked. currently: nothing.
    }
}
```

The World class in Greenfoot has methods that give us access to objects within it.

Exercise 7.9 Look up Greenfoot's World class in the Greenfoot class documentation. Find all methods that give us access to objects within the world. Write them down.

The most interesting of those methods for us is this one:

```java
java.util.List getObjects(java.lang.Class cls)
```

This method gives us a list of all objects in the world of a particular class. It uses two types that look unusual: java.lang.Class for its parameter, and java.util.List as the return type. To understand this properly, we have to discuss two things: Java class libraries and the List type.

7.7 Using Java library classes

Concept

The **Java class library** is a large collection of ready-made classes, provided with the Java system. We can use these classes by writing an **import** statement.

The classes Class and List are two of the many classes from the *Java Standard Class Library*[1]. The Java system comes with a large collection of useful classes which we can just use. Over time, we will get to know many of them.

We can see documentation for all the classes in the class library by selecting *Java Library Documentation* from Greenfoot's *Help* menu. This will open the documentation for the Java libraries in a web browser (Figure 7.3).

The bottom left pane in this window shows a list of all classes in the Java library. (There are many of them!) We can look at the documentation for any particular class by finding it in this list and selecting it. When selected, the main part of the window will display the documentation for this class.

Exercise 7.10 Find the class Color in the class list. Select it. Look at the documentation of this class. How many constructors does it have?

---

[1] List is actually an *Interface*, not a class—we will discuss this later.

Figure 7.3

The Java library
documentation

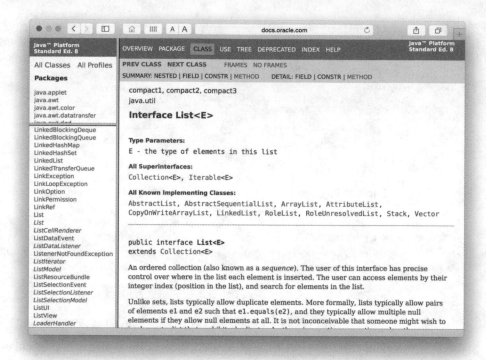

You can see that there are literally thousands of classes in the Java library. To get some sort of order into this long list, classes are grouped into *packages*. A package is a group of logically related classes. At the top of the documentation of any class, we can see what package the class is in. The class `Color`, for instance, is in a package called *java.awt*.

When we want to use any of the classes from the Java library in our own scenario, we need to *import* the class, using an import statement. The import statement is written at the very top of the class's source code and names the package and the class we want to use, with a dot in-between. For example, the `List` type is in the package *java.util*. To use it in our own code, we write

```
import java.util.List;
```

> **Exercise 7.11** Write the import statement for `List` into your own `Block` class, just below the import statement for `greenfoot.*` that is already there.

Using an asterisk (*) imports all classes from a given package. For example, `import greenfoot.*` imports all classes from the `greenfoot` package.

Importing a class makes it usable within our own scenario, just as if it were one of our own classes. After importing it, we can declare variables of this type, call methods, and do anything else we can do with any other class. Thus, in our own code, we could now declare a variable of type `List`:

```
List myList;
```

The package *java.lang* is special: it contains the most commonly used classes, and we do not need to import it explicitly; it is always automatically imported. Thus, we do not need to write an import statement for `java.lang.Class`.

The Java library is quite intimidating at first, because it has so many classes. Don't worry—we shall use only a small number of them, and we shall introduce them one by one when we need them.

Now that we know how to import the `List` type, let us have a closer look at how to use it.

7.8 The List type

Dealing with collections of objects is important both in Greenfoot programming and in programming in general. Several of the Greenfoot methods return collections of objects as their result, usually in the form of a list. The type of the returned object then is the `List` type from the `java.util` package.

Side Note: Interfaces

The `List` type is a little different from other object types we have seen: It is not a class, but an *interface*. Interfaces are a Java construct that provides an abstraction over different possible implementing classes. The details are not important to us right now—it is sufficient to know that we can deal with the `List` type in similar ways as with other types: We can look it up in the Java Library Documentation, and we can call the existing methods on the object. We cannot, however, create objects directly of type `List`. We will come back to this later.

Exercise 7.12 Look up `java.util.List` in the Java library documentation. What are the methods called to add an object to the list, remove an object from the list, and to find out how many objects are currently in the list?

Exercise 7.13 What is the full name of this type, as given at the top of the documentation?

When we looked at the `getObjects` method in the previous section, we noticed that it returns an object of type `java.util.List`. Thus, in order to store this object, we need to declare a variable of this type. We will do this in our `checkMouseClick` method.

The List type, however, is different from other types we have seen before. The documentation shows at the top

```
Interface List<E>
```

Apart from the word *interface* in place of *class*, we notice another new notation: the <E> after the type name.

Formally, this is called a *generic type*. This means that the type List needs an additional type specified as a parameter. This second type specifies the type of the elements held within the list.

For example, if we are dealing with a list of strings, we would specify the type as

```
List<String>
```

If, instead, we are dealing with a list of actors, we can write

```
List<Actor>
```

In each case, the element type within the angle brackets (<>) is the type of some other known kind of object.

7.9 A list of leaves

In our case, we shall call the `getObjects` method on our world to receive a list of leaves, so our variable declaration will read:

```
List<Leaf> leaves
```

We can then assign the list which we retrieve from the `getObjects` method to this variable. Together with getting the world object itself, this is what it looks like:

```
World world = getWorld();

List<Leaf> leaves = world.getObjects(Leaf.class);
```

After executing these lines, our variable `leaves` holds a list of all leaves that currently exist in the world. The last thing left to do is to call the `changeImage()` method for every leaf in our list. We will use a new kind of loop to achieve this: the *for-each loop*.

7.10 The for-each loop

We will now go through our list of leaves one by one, changing the image of each in turn.

Java has a specialized loop for stepping through every element of a collection, and we can use this loop here. It is called a *for-each* loop, and it is written using the following pattern:

```
for (ElementType variable : collection)
{
    statements;
}
```

In this pattern, *ElementType* stands for the type of each element in the collection, *variable* is a variable that is being declared here, so we can give it any name we like, *collection* is the name of the collection we wish to process, and *statements* is a sequence of statements we wish to carry out. This will become clearer with an example.

Using our list named `leaves`, we can write

```
for (Leaf leaf : leaves)
{
    leaf.changeImage();
}
```

(Remember that Java is case sensitive: `Leaf` with an uppercase "L" is different from `leaf` with a lowercase "l". The uppercase name refers to the class, the lowercase name refers to a variable holding an object. The plural version—`leaves`—is another variable that holds the whole list.)

We can read the *for-each* loop a little more easily if we read the keyword *for* as "for each," the colon as "in," and the opening curly bracket as "do." This then becomes:

for each leaf *in* leaves *do*: ...

This reading also gives us a hint as to what this loop does: It will execute the statements within the curly brackets once for each element in the list '`leaves`'. If, for example, there are ten elements in that list, the statements will be executed ten times. Every time, before the statements are executed, the variable `leaf` (declared in the loop header) will be assigned one of the list elements. Thus, the sequence of action will be

leaf = first element from 'leaves';
execute loop statements;
leaf = second element from 'leaves';
execute loop statements;
leaf = third element from 'leaves';
execute loop statements;
 ...

The variable `leaf` is available to be used in the loop statements to access the current element from the list. We could then, for example, call a method on that object, as in the example shown above, or pass the object on to another method for further processing.

We are now ready to put it all together and add the for-each loop to our code. Code 7.2 shows the complete method that implements the example we have just discussed.

Code 7.2

Changing the
images of all leaves
in the world

```
/**
 * Check whether the mouse button was clicked. If it was, change all leaves.
 */
private void checkMouseClick()
{
    if (Greenfoot.mouseClicked(null))
    {
        World world = getWorld();
        List<Leaf> leaves = world.getObjects(Leaf.class);

        for (Leaf leaf : leaves)
        {
            leaf.changeImage();
        }
    }
}
```

> **Exercise 7.14** Implement the functionality to change all leaves with a mouse click in your own scenario. Test.

If you are unsure about your solutions and want to compare them with ours: the *autumn-2* scenario includes all the functionality discussed in this chapter.

Summary of programming techniques

We have seen some important constructs in this chapter, and these constructs may at first not be easy to fully understand. You will need some time (and much more practice) to get used to them.

The first part was relatively easy: We have seen how to get access to the world object and call a method on it. Then we have discussed how to get access to another actor and call one of its methods. We gained access to that actor using one of Greenfoot's collision detection methods.

Finally—and this is the hard bit—we have seen how to receive a list of multiple objects, and we used a for-each loop to call a method on each of the objects in the list.

Working with lists and processing their elements is a very important concept, not only in Greenfoot, but in programming in general. This was just a brief look at a first example. We shall do more of this in the following chapters, and you will hopefully become more familiar with these techniques as you practice them repeatedly.

Concept summary

- The value **null** is a special value that can be assigned to any object variable. If a variable contains **null**, it does not currently reference any object.

- The **Java class library** is a large collection of ready-made classes, provided with the Java system. We can use these classes by writing an **import** statement.

- A **collection** is a kind of object that can hold many other objects.

- A **List** is an example of a collection. Some methods from the Greenfoot API return List objects.

- A **generic type** is a type that receives a second type name as a parameter.

- The **for-each loop** is another kind of loop. It is well suited to process all elements of a collection.

Drill and practice

The most important concepts to practice here are working with lists and the for-each loop. Here are some exercises to give you some practice with this. We will continue to use the *autumn* scenario.

Exercise 7.15 In your autumn scenario, introduce a new class called **Apple**. Give it an apple image. Write code in the **MyWorld** class to place 12 apples at random locations.

Exercise 7.16 Write code in your **Block** class to turn all apples by 90 degrees whenever the block hits the edge of the world.

Exercise 7.17 Create yet another class: **Pear**. Use a suitable image. Write code to place 8 pears into the world.

Exercise 7.18 Write code in the **Block** class so that every time the block hits the edge, all pears are moved 20 cells to the right (in addition to turning the apples).

Exercise 7.19 Modify your pear-moving code so that pears are only moved right if they are not already at the right edge. If they are at the right edge, they are moved to the left edge instead.

Exercise 7.20 Modify your method that handles the mouse click so that only the images of leaves in the left half of the world are changed (instead of changing all images).

This should be sufficient preparation for the next chapter: We will now move on and look at the next scenario, and get some more practice with lists as a part of that example.

8 Interacting objects: Newton's Lab

topics: more about objects interacting, using helper classes

concepts: overloading, more practice with lists, for-each loop

In this chapter, we will investigate more sophisticated interactions between objects in a world. As a start, we will look at one of the most universal interactions between objects anywhere: gravity.

In this scenario, we are dealing with celestial bodies (such as stars and planets). We shall simulate the motion of these bodies through space, using Newton's law of universal gravitation. (We now know that Newton's formulas are not quite accurate, and that Einstein's theory of general relativity describes the motions of planets more precisely, but Newton is still good enough for our simple simulation.)

If you are a little worried about dealing with physics and formulas, don't worry. We do not need to go very deeply into it, and the formula we will use is really quite simple. At the end, we will turn this scenario into an artistic experiment with sound and visual effects. If you are more technically interested, you can work more on the physics. If your interest is more artistic, you can concentrate on this aspect instead.

8.1 The starting point: Newton's Lab

We shall start this project by investigating a partly implemented version of this scenario. Open the *Newtons-Lab-1* scenario from the book scenario folder. You will see that a world subclass already exists (called Space). We also have classes SmoothMover, Body, and Vector (Figure 8.1).

Figure 8.1
The Newton's Lab
scenario

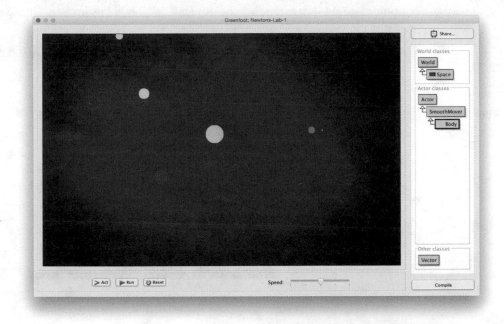

Figure 8.2
Isaac Newton and
Albert Einstein[1]

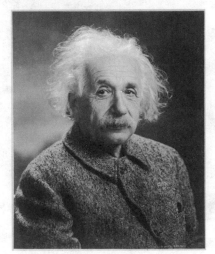

Exercise 8.1 Open the Newtons-Lab-1 scenario. Try it out (place some bodies into space). What do you observe?

When you try to run this scenario, you will notice that you can place objects (of type **Body**) into space, but these bodies do not move, and they do not act in any interesting way yet.

---

[1] Newton: from Georgios Kollidas/Shutterstock. Einstein: Courtesy of Library of Congress Prints and Photographs Division.

Before we get into extending the implementation, let us investigate the scenario a little more closely.

By right-clicking on the world background, we can see and invoke the public methods of the Space class (Figure 8.3).

Figure 8.3
The World
methods in
Newton's Lab

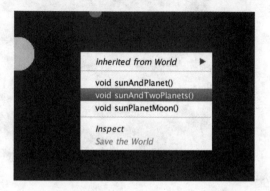

Exercise 8.2 Invoke the different public methods of the Space object. What do they do?

Exercise 8.3 When you have a star or planet in your world, right-click it to see what public methods it has. What are they?

Exercise 8.4 Invoke the `sunPlanetMoon` method from the public methods of Space. Find out and write down the mass of the sun, the planet, and the moon.

Exercise 8.5 Have a look at the source code of the Space class and see how the public methods here are implemented.

8.2 Helper classes: SmoothMover and Vector

In this scenario, we are using two general purpose helper classes: SmoothMover and Vector. These are classes that add functionality to a given scenario, and can be used in different scenarios for similar purposes. (These two classes are in fact used in a number of different existing projects.)

The SmoothMover class provides smoother movement for actors by storing the actor's coordinates as decimal numbers (of type `double`), rather than integers. Fields of type `double` can store numbers with decimal fractions (such as 2.4567), and thus are more precise than integers.

For displaying the actor on screen, the coordinates will still be rounded to integers, since the location for painting on screen must always be a whole pixel. Internally, however, the location is held as a decimal number.

A SmoothMover can, for example, have the x-coordinate 12.3. If we now move this actor along the x-coordinate in increments of 0.6, its successive location will be

12.3, 12.9, 13.5, 14.1, 14.7, 15.3, 15.9, 16.5, 17.1, ...

and so on. We will see the actor on screen at rounded x-coordinates. It will be painted at x-coordinate

12, 13, 14, 14, 15, 15, 16, 17, 17, ...

and so on. Altogether, even though it is still rounded to integers for display, the effect is smoother looking movement than could be achieved by use of int fields.

The second bit of functionality that the SmoothMover adds is a *velocity vector*—a vector that indicates a current direction and speed of movement. We can think of a vector as an (invisible) arrow with a given direction and length (Figure 8.4).

Figure 8.4
A SmoothMover object with a movement vector

The SmoothMover class has methods to change its movement by modifying its velocity vector, and a move method that moves the actor according to its current vector.

Side note: Abstract classes

If you right-click the **SmoothMover** class, you will notice that you cannot create objects of this class. No constructor is shown.

When we examine the source code of that class, we can see the keyword **abstract** in the class header. We can declare classes as abstract to prevent creation of instances of these classes. Abstract classes serve only as superclasses for other classes, not for creating objects directly.

Exercise 8.6 Place an object of class **Body** into the world. By examining the object's pop-up menu, find out what methods this object inherits from class **SmoothMover**. Write them down.

Exercise 8.7 Which of the method names appears twice? How do the two versions differ?

Terminology: Overloading

It is perfectly legal in Java to have two methods that have the same name, as long as their parameter lists are different. This is called **overloading**. (The name of the method is **overloaded**—it refers to more than one method.)

When we call an overloaded method, the runtime system figures out which of the two methods we mean by examining the parameters we supply.

We also say that the two methods have different *signatures*.

The second helper class, `Vector`, implements the vector itself, and is used by the `SmoothMover` class. Note that `Vector` is not listed in the `Actor` group of classes. It is not an actor—it will never appear in the world on its own. Objects of this class are only ever created and used by other actor objects.

Vectors can be represented in two different ways: either as a pair of distances in their x- and y-coordinates (dx, dy), or as a pair of values specifying the direction and its length (direction, length). The direction is usually specified as the angle from the horizontal.

Figure 8.5 shows the same vector with both possible specifications. We see that either the (dx, dy) pair, or the (direction, length) pair can describe the same vector.

Figure 8.5

Two possible ways to specify a vector

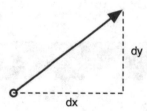
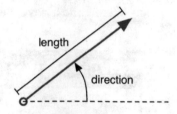

The first representation, using the x and y offsets, is called a *Cartesian* representation. The second, using the direction and length, is a *polar* representation. You will see these two names used in the source code of the `Vector` class.

For our purposes, sometimes the Cartesian representation and sometimes the polar representation is easier to use. Therefore our vector class is written in a way that it can deal with both. It will do the necessary conversions internally automatically.

Exercise 8.8 Familiarize yourself with the methods of the `SmoothMover` and `Vector` classes by opening the editor and studying their definition in *Documentation* view. (Remember: you can switch to *Documentation* view using the menu in the top right corner of the editor.) You can also read the source code, if you like, but this is not strictly necessary at this stage.

Exercise 8.9 Place a **Body** object into the world. Which of the methods inherited from **SmoothMover** can you call interactively (through the object's menu)? Which can you not call at this stage?

8.3   The existing Body class

Exercise 8.10 Open the source code of the **Body** class and examine it.

Looking at the source code of the Body class, two aspects are worth discussing a bit further. The first is the fact that the class has two constructors (Code 8.1). This is another example of overloading: it is absolutely fine to have two constructors in a class if they have different parameter lists.

In our case, one constructor has no parameters at all, and the other has four parameters.

Code 8.1
Constructors of
class *Body*

```
public class Body extends SmoothMover
{
    // some code omitted
    private double mass;

    /**
     * Construct a Body with default size, mass, velocity and color.
     */
    public Body()
    {
        this (20, 300, new Vector(0, 1.0), defaultColor);
    }

    /**
     * Construct a Body with a specified size, mass, velocity and color.
     */
    public Body(int size, double mass, Vector velocity, Color color)
    {
        this.mass = mass;
        addToVelocity(velocity);
        GreenfootImage image = new GreenfootImage (size, size);
        image.setColor (color);
        image.fillOval (0, 0, size-1, size-1);
        setImage (image);
    }

    // more code omitted
}
```

The default constructor makes it easy for us to create bodies interactively without having to specify all the details. The second constructor allows creation of a body with custom size, mass, velocity, and color. This constructor is used, for example, in the Space class to create the sun, planet, and moon.

The second constructor initializes the state of the actor using all its parameter values that have been passed in. The first constructor looks more mysterious. It has only one line of code:

```
this (20, 300, new Vector(90, 1.0), defaultColor);
```

Concept

The keyword **this** is used to call one constructor from another, or to refer to the current object.

The line looks almost like a method call, except that it uses the keyword this instead of a method name. Using this call, the constructor executes the *other* constructor (the one with the four parameters), and provides default parameters for all the four values. Using the this keyword in this way (like a method name) is only possible within constructors to call another constructor as part of the initialization.

There is a second use of the this keyword:

```
this.mass = mass;
```

Here we have another example of overloading: the same name is used for two variables (a parameter and an instance field). When we assign these values, we need to specify which of these two variables named mass we mean on each side of the assignment.

When we write mass without any qualification, then the closest definition of a variable with that name is used—in this case, the parameter. When we write this.mass, we specify that we mean the mass field of the current object. Thus, this line of code assigns the parameter named mass to the field named mass.

Exercise 8.11 Remove the "this." segment before the **mass** in the line of code shown above, so that it reads

```
mass = mass;
```

Does this code compile? Does it execute? What do you think this code does? What is its effect? (Create an object and use its *Inspect* function to examine the **mass** field. When you are finished experimenting, restore the code to how it was before.)

The second aspect worth exploring a little further are the two lines near the top of the class, shown in Code 8.2.

Code 8.2

Declaration of
constants

```
public class Body extends SmoothMover
{
    private static final double GRAVITY = 5.8;
    private static final Color defaultColor = new Color(255, 216, 0);

    // rest of code omitted

}
```

These two declarations look similar to field declarations, except that they have the two keywords `static final` inserted after the keyword `private`.

Concept

A **constant** is
a named value
that can be used
in ways similar
to a variable,
but can never
change.

This is what we call a *constant*. A constant has similarities to a field, in that we can use the name in our code to refer to its value, but the value can never change (it is *constant*). It is the `final` keyword that makes these declarations constants.

The effect of the `static` keyword is that this constant is shared between all actors of this class, and we do not need separate copies of it in every object. We encountered the `static` keyword before (in Chapter 3), in the context of class methods. Just as static methods belong to the class itself (but can be called from objects of that class), static fields belong to the class and can be accessed from its instances.

In this case, the constants declared are a value for gravity[2] (to be used later), and a default color for the bodies. This is an object of type `Color`, which we will discuss in more detail below.

It is good practice to declare fields constant that should not change in a program. Making the field constant will prevent accidental change of the value in the code.

8.4 First extension: creating movement

Okay, enough looking at what is there. It is time to write some code and make something happen.

The first obvious experiment is to make the bodies move. We have mentioned that the SmoothMover class provides a `move()` method, and since a Body is a SmoothMover, it, too, has access to this method.

Exercise 8.12 Add a call to the `move()` method into the `act` method of Body. (Make sure to call the `move()` method without a parameter, and not the one with an int parameter inherited from **Actor**.) Test it. What is the default direction of movement? What is the default speed?

---

[2] Our value of gravity has no direct relationship to any particular unit in nature. It is an arbitrary value made up for this scenario. Once we start implementing gravitation for our bodies, you can experiment with different amounts of gravity by changing this value.

Exercise 8.13 Create multiple **Body** objects. How do they behave?

Exercise 8.14 Call the public **Space** methods (**sunAndPlanet()**, etc.) and run the scenario. How do these objects move? Where is their initial movement direction and speed defined?

Exercise 8.15 Change the default direction of a body to be towards the left. That is, when a body is created using the default constructor, and its **move()** method is executed, it should move left.

As we see when we perform these experiments, just telling the bodies to move is enough to make them move. They will, however, move in a straight line. This is because movement (speed and direction) is dictated by their velocity vector, and currently nothing changes this vector. Thus, movement is constant.

8.5 The Color class

While reading the code above, in both the Body and Space classes, we have come across the Color class. The second constructor of the Body class expects a parameter of type Color, and the code in the Space class creates Color objects with expressions such as

```
new Color(248, 160, 86)
```

We have come across this class briefly in the previous chapter, as we read through the Java library documentation.

Exercise 8.16 Open the documentation of class **Color** again.

The three parameters of the Color constructor are the red, green, and blue components of this particular color. Every color on a computer screen can be described as a composite of these three base colors. (We will discuss color a little more in Chapter 10. There, in Section 10.9, you can also find a table of RGB color values. You can use any good graphics program to experiment with these yourself.)

Exercise 8.17 Look at the documentation of class **Color**. How many constructors does it have?

Exercise 8.18 Find the description of the constructor we have used (the one with three integers as parameters). What is the legal range for these integer numbers?

As we know, if we want to use any class from the Java library (other than those from the *java.lang* package), we have to import it. For the Color class, the import statement is:

```
import java.awt.Color;
```

Exercise 8.19 Where in the **Body** class do you find the import statement for class Color?

Exercise 8.20 What error would you get if you attempted to use class **Color**, but forgot the import statement? (Try it out!)

The Color class is useful in Greenfoot when we want to draw on images. In this case, for every celestial body we draw a colored circle onto the actor's image. We will see this class used again in later chapters.

What we want to do next is to add gravity to this scenario. That is, when we have more than one body in our space, the gravitational pull between these bodies should change each body's movement.

8.6 Adding gravitational force

Let us start by looking at the current act method in our Body class (Code 8.3). (If you have not done Exercise 8.12, then the call to the move method will not be there—you can add it now.)

Code 8.3

The current *act* method

```
/**
 * Act. That is: apply  the gravitation forces from
 * all other bodies around, and then move.
 */
public void act()
{
    move();
}
```

While the code currently contains only the move call, the comment actually describes correctly what we have to do: before we move, we should apply the forces caused by the gravitational pull of all other objects in space.

We can give an outline of the task in pseudo-code:

```
apply forces from other bodies:
    get all other bodies in space;
    for each of those bodies:
    {
        apply gravity from that body to our own;
    }
```

We can see that this again is a situation where we want to use a list of objects and a for-each loop, as we practiced in the previous chapter.

Since this is not a trivial thing to do, we start by making a separate method for this task (Code 8.4). At first, creating a separate (initially empty) method might seem not to accomplish much, but it greatly helps in breaking down our problem into smaller sub-problems, and it helps structuring our thoughts.

Code 8.4

Preparing to apply forces of gravity

```
/**
 * Act. That is: apply  the gravitation forces from
 * all other bodies around, and then move.
 */
public void act()
{
    applyForces();
    move();
}
```

```
/**
 * Apply the forces of gravity from all other celestial bodies in
 * this universe.
 */
private void applyForces()
{
    // work to do here
}
```

Exercise 8.21 If you feel confident in the use of the world's **getObjects** method, the **List** class, and the for-each loop, try to implement this now in your own **Body** class. (If you are less sure—read on. We will now do this step by step.)

Our pseudo-code of the task above gives us the outline of our `applyForces()` method. We can see that the first thing we need to do is to get access to all other bodies in space. We do this using the same `getObjects` method as in the previous chapter.

Exercise 8.22 Write, on paper, the call to get access to all objects of type **Body** in space. The objects will be returned as a list. Declare a variable for this list and assign the list of bodies you receive.

Exercise 8.23 Write, on paper at first, a for-each loop that iterates through the list of bodies.

The code we need to write here is very similar to the code we wrote for changing the images of all leaves in the previous chapter. Look at that code again if you are unsure.

Exercise 8.24 Once you are satisfied that your loop is correct on paper, write it into the `applyForces()` method in your **Body** class. Remember to add the import statement for `java.util.List`. Compile to check that the syntax is correct.

Once we have worked out how to write our loop, we have to decide what to write inside the loop's body. Our pseudo-code tells us that we want to apply the force of gravity from the other body to our own. Again, as before, when we encounter a somewhat difficult task where we do not immediately know how to solve it, we just insert a method call to a new method with an appropriate name, and worry about implementing this method afterwards.

Exercise 8.25 Make a method stub (empty method) for a private method named `applyGravity(Body body)`. Call this method from within the loop in your `applyForces()` method, passing the current list element as a parameter.

If you managed to do the exercises so far, you are almost finished. The full implementation of the `applyForces()` method is shown in Code 8.5. If you study this code, you will notice that there is one more construct added: the loop now contains an if-statement:

```
if (body != this)
{

    ...

}
```

The reason for this is that the `bodies` list contains all bodies in space, including the current object (the one we want to apply gravity to). We do not need to apply gravity of an object to itself, so we can add an if-statement that calls `applyGravity` only if the element from the list is not the current object itself. Note how the `this` keyword is used here to refer to the current object.

> **Exercise 8.26** Compare your own code with our code shown below. If necessary, complete your own `applyForces` method.

Code 8.5

Applying gravity from all other bodies in space

```
private void applyForces()
{
    List<Body> bodies = getWorld().getObjects(Body.class);

    for (Body body : bodies)
    {
        if (body != this)
        {
            applyGravity(body);
        }
    }
}

/**
 * Apply the gravity force of a given body to this one.
 */
private void applyGravity(Body other)
{
    // work to do here
}
```

8.7 Applying gravity

In Code 8.9, we have solved the task of accessing each object in space, but we have deferred the task of actually applying the gravitational force. The method `applyGravity` still needs to be written.

This is now a little easier than before, though, since this method now only needs to deal with two objects at a time: the current object, and one other object specified in its parameter. We now want to apply the gravitational force from the other object to this one. This is where Newton's Law comes into play.

Newton's formula for gravitation looks like this:

$$\text{force} = \frac{\text{mass1} \times \text{mass2}}{\text{distance}^2} \, G$$

In other words, to calculate the force we need to apply to the current object, we need to multiply the mass of this object with the mass of the other object, and then divide by the square of the distance between the two objects. Finally, the value gets multiplied by the constant G—the *gravitational constant*. (You may remember that we have already defined a constant for this value in our class, named *GRAVITY*.)

If you are very confident or adventurous, you may like to try to implement the `applyGravity` method yourself. You need to create a vector in the direction from the current body to the other body, with a length specified by this formula. For the rest of us, we now look at the finished implementation of that method (Code 8.6).

Code 8.6

Calculating and applying gravity from another body

```
/**
 * Apply the force of gravity of a given body to this one.
 * (Force is applied for one time unit; dt==1.)
 */
private void applyGravity(Body other)
{
    double dx = other.getExactX() - this.getExactX();
    double dy = other.getExactY() - this.getExactY();
    Vector dv = new Vector (dx, dy); //sets direction; length to be done
    double distance = Math.sqrt (dx*dx + dy*dy);
    double force = GRAVITY * this.mass * other.mass / (distance * distance);
    double acceleration = force / this.mass;
    dv.setLength (acceleration);
    addToVelocity (dv);
}
```

This method is not quite as complicated as it looks. First we calculate the distances between our object and the other object in the x- and y-coordinates (*dx* and *dy*). Then we create a new vector using these values. This vector now has the right direction, but not the correct length.

Next we calculate the distance between the two objects using the *Pythagoras theorem* ($a^2 + b^2 = c^2$ in right-angled triangles, see Figure 8.6).

Figure 8.6

The distance in relation to dx and dy

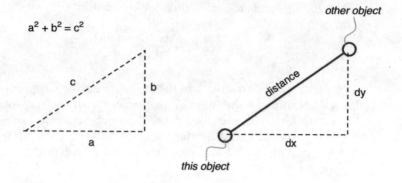

This tells us that the distance is the square root of dx squared plus dy squared. In our code (Code 8.6), we use a method called `sqrt` from the `Math` class to calculate the square root. (`Math` is a class in *java.lang*, and thus automatically imported.)

Exercise 8.27 Look up the class **Math** in the Java documentation. How many parameters does the `sqrt` method have? What types are they? What type does this method return?

Exercise 8.28 In the **Math** class, find the method that can be used to find the maximum of two integers. What is it called?

The next line in our code calculates the force of the gravitational pull by using Newton's formula of gravitation given above.

The final thing to do is to calculate the acceleration, since the actual velocity change to our object is not only determined by the force of gravity, but also the mass of our object: The heavier the object, the slower it will accelerate. Acceleration is computed using the following formula:

$$\text{acceleration} = \frac{\text{force}}{\text{mass}}$$

Once we have calculated the acceleration, we can set our new vector to the correct length and add this vector to the velocity of our body. Doing this is easy, using the `addToVelocity` method that is provided by the `SmoothMover` class.

Exercise 8.29 Map the variables in Code 8.6 to Newton's formula, the Pythagoras theorem, and the acceleration formula given above. Which variable corresponds to which part of which formula?

With this, our task is completed. (An implementation of the code described so far is also available in the book scenarios as *Newtons-Lab-2*.)

This task clearly involved more background knowledge in maths and physics than the others we have seen. It may seem complicated at first, and you may feel that you could not have written this on your own. Don't worry—that is normal. At this stage, the aim is for you to study and understand this code. If you understand it and can explain it, you are doing well. We do not expect you to be able to write code using unknown concepts on your own the first time they come up. Studying it here will help you write similar code later when you encounter related problems.

If maths and physics are not your favorite areas—don't worry, we shall return to less mathematical projects shortly. Remember: programming can do anything you like. You can make it very mathematical, but you can also make it very creative and artistic.

8.8 Trying it out

Now that we have completed our implementation of gravitational forces, it is time to try it out. We can start by using the three ready-made scenarios defined in the Space class.

Exercise 8.30 With your completed gravity code, try out the three initialization methods from the Space object again (`sunAndPlanet()`, `sunAndTwoPlanets()`, and `sunPlanetMoon()`). What do you observe?

Exercise 8.31 Experiment with changes in gravity (the `GRAVITY` constant at the top of the **Body** class).

Exercise 8.32 Experiment with changes to the mass and/or initial movement of the bodies (defined in the **Space** class).

Exercise 8.33 Create some new set-ups of stars and planets and see how they interact. Can you come up with a system that is stable?

Pitfall

Be careful when using the constructor of class **Vector**. The constructor is overloaded: one version expects an **int** and a **double** as parameters, the other expects two **doubles**. Thus

```
new Vector(32, 12.0)
```

will call one constructor, while

```
new Vector(32.0, 12.0)
```

will call the other constructor, resulting in an entirely different vector.

You will quickly see that it is very hard to configure the parameters so that the system remains stable for a long time. The combination of mass and gravity will often result in objects crashing into each other or escaping from orbit. (Since we have not implemented "crashing into each other," our objects can essentially fly through each other. However, when they get very close, their forces become very large and they often catapult each other onto strange trajectories.)

Some of these effects are similar to nature, although our simulation is somewhat inaccurate due to some simplifications we have made. The fact, for example, that all objects act in sequence, rather than simultaneously, will have an effect on their behavior and is not a realistic representation. It introduces small errors that add up and have an effect over time. To make the simulation more accurate, we would have to calculate all forces first (without moving) and then execute all moves according to the previous calculations. Also, our simulation does not model the forces accurately when two bodies get very close to each other, adding more unrealistic effects.

We can also ask the stability question about our own solar system. While the orbits of the planets in our solar system are quite stable, precise details about their movement are hard to predict accurately for a long time into the future. We are quite certain that none of the planets will crash into the Sun in the next few billion years, but small variations in orbit may happen. Simulations such as ours (just much more accurate and detailed, but similar in principle) have been used to try to predict the future orbits. We have seen, however, that this is very hard to simulate accurately. Simulations can show that minute differences in the initial conditions can make huge differences after a few billion years.[3]

Seeing how difficult it is to come up with parameters that create a system that is stable even for a limited time, we might be surprised that our solar system is as stable as it is. But there is an explanation: when the solar system formed, material from a gas cloud surrounding the Sun formed into lumps that slowly grew by colliding with other lumps of matter and combining to form ever-growing objects. Initially, there were countless of these lumps in orbit. Over time, some fell into the Sun, some escaped into deep space. This process ends when the only chunks left are well separated from one another and on generally stable orbits.

It would be possible to create a simulation that models this effect. If we correctly modeled the growth of planets out of billions of small, random lumps of matter, we would observe the same effect: some large planets form that are left in fairly stable orbits. For this, however, we would need a much more detailed and complicated simulation and a lot of time; simulating this effect would take a very, very long time, even on very fast computers.

---

[3] If you are interested to read more, Wikipedia is a good starting point: http://en.wikipedia.org /wiki/Stability_of_the_solar_system

8.9 Gravity and music

Before we leave our *Newton's Lab* scenario behind, we have one more thing to play with: adding music. Well, noise, in any case.[4]

The idea is as follows: we add a number of *Obstacles* into our world. When obstacles are touched by our planets, they make a sound. Then we create a few planets or stars, let them fly around, and see what happens.

We will not discuss this implementation in detail. Instead, we leave you to study it yourself, and just point out some of the more interesting features. You can find an implementation of this idea in the book scenarios as *Newtons-Lab-3*.

> **Exercise 8.34** Open the scenario named *Newtons-Lab-3* and run it. Have a look at the source code. Try to understand how it works.

Here is a summary of the most interesting changes we have made from the previous version to create this:

- We have added a new class `Obstacle`. You can easily see objects of this class on screen. Obstacles have two images: the orange rectangle you see most of the time, and a lighter version of the rectangle to show when they are touched. This is used to create the "lighting up" effect. Obstacles are also associated with a sound file, just as the piano keys were in our piano scenario. In fact, we are reusing the sound files from the piano scenario here, so they do sound the same.

- We have modified the `Body` class so that bodies bounce off the edges off the screen. This gives a better effect for this kind of scenario. We have also increased gravity a bit to get faster movement and modified the code so that bodies automatically slow down once they get too fast. Otherwise they might speed each other up more and more, indefinitely.

- Finally, we have added code in the `Space` class to create a fixed row of obstacles and to create five random planets (random size, mass, and color).

The implementation of these three changes includes a few interesting snippets of code that are worth pointing out.

- In the `Obstacle` class, we use the method `getOneIntersectingObject` again to check whether the obstacle is being hit by a planet. The code pattern is the following:

```
Object body = getOneIntersectingObject(Body.class);
if (body != null)
{
    ...
}
```

---

[4] The idea to add sound to a gravity project was inspired by *Kepler's Orrery* (see http://www.art .net/~simran/GenerativeMusic/kepler.html or search for "Kepler's Orrery" on YouTube).

We have seen the first use of this method in the previous chapter.

■ In the Space class, we have added a method called `createObstacles`. It creates the obstacles with their associated sound file names, quite similar to the initialization code in the piano example.

■ We have added another method in the Space class, called `randomBodies`. It uses a while loop to create a number of Body objects. The bodies are initialized with random values. The while loop counts down from a given number to zero, to create the right number of objects. It is worth studying as another example of a loop.

Hopefully this scenario gives you a few ideas of additional things you can try with this project. Once you start combining creativity and programming, there is no limit to what you can come up with.

Summary of programming techniques

In this chapter, we have touched on a number of new concepts. We have seen a new scenario—Newton's Lab—that simulates stars and planets in space. Simulations in general are a very interesting topic, and we will come back to them in Chapter 11.

We have seen two useful helper classes, SmoothMover and Vector, both of which help us to create more sophisticated movement.

Overloading of methods is another concept we have encountered, where the same method name may be used for more than one method. We also discovered various uses of the keyword this, which can be used to refer to the current object, access fields with names that are overloaded, and to call one constructor from another.

But most importantly—although not new—we have seen another use of a list of objects together with a for-each loop. This is the most important—and probably the most difficult—concept covered here, so we have to study it carefully.

Concept summary

- **Overloading** is the use of the same method name for two different methods or constructors.
- The keyword **this** is used to call one constructor from another, or to refer to the current object.
- A **constant** is a named value that can be used in ways similar to a variable, but can never change.

Drill and practice

The last version of the Newton's Lab scenario gives us a lot of opportunity to practice all sorts of different constructs. Here are some ideas.

Exercise 8.35 Change the number of bodies that are created by default in this scenario.

Exercise 8.36 Play with the movement parameters to see whether you can create nicer movement for the planets. The parameters are: the value for GRAVITY; the acceleration value used when bouncing off an edge (currently 0.9); the speed threshold (currently 7) and acceleration (0.9) used in the `applyForces` method to slow down fast objects; and the initial mass used for the planets (in the **Space** class).

Exercise 8.37 Create a different arrangement of obstacles in your scenario.

Exercise 8.38 Use different sounds (different sound files) for your obstacles.

Exercise 8.39 Use different images for your obstacles.

Exercise 8.40 Make planets change color every time they bounce off the edge of the universe.

Exercise 8.41 Make planets change color every time they hit an obstacle.

Exercise 8.42 Make a different kind of obstacle that gets switched on and off by being hit. When on, it continuously blinks and produces a sound at fixed intervals.

Exercise 8.43 Add some keyboard control. For example, pressing the right arrow key could add a small force to the right to all **Body** objects.

Exercise 8.44 Allow adding more planets. A mouse click into the universe while it is running should create a new planet at that location.

There are countless other possible ways to make this scenario more interesting and nicer to look at. Invent some of your own and implement them.

9 Collision detection: Asteroids

topics:	more about movement, keyboard control, and collision detection
concepts:	collections (again), for loop, for-each loop (again), array (again)

In this chapter, we shall have another look at loops (introducing a new kind of loop) and have a deeper look at collision detection. We are working with collections again (you have been warned that they would become important!) and bring together several topics we have touched on in earlier chapters. We shall revisit a scenario that we have encountered before, very early in this book: Asteroids (Figure 9.1).

The version of Asteroids that we use here is slightly different from the one we looked at earlier. It has some added features (such as a proton wave and a score counter), but

Figure 9.1

The new Asteroids scenario (with proton wave)

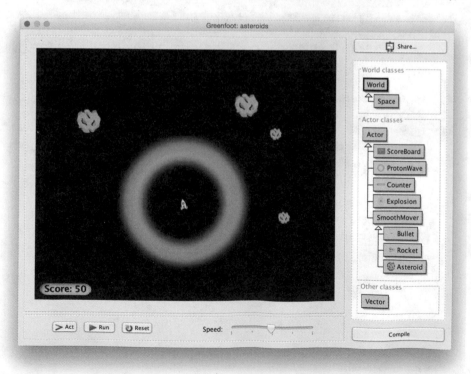

it is not fully implemented. Important parts of the functionality are still missing, and it will be our job in this chapter to implement them.

We will use this example to revisit movement and collision detection. In terms of Java programming concepts, we will use this to gain more practice with loops and collections.

9.1   Investigation: What is there?

We should start this project by examining the existing code base. We have a partially implemented solution, named *asteroids-1*, in the *chapter09* folder of the book scenarios. (Make sure to use the *chapter09* version, not the copy from *chapter01*.)

> **Exercise 9.1** Open the *asteroids-1* scenario form the *chapter09* folder of the book projects. Experiment with it to find out what it does, and what it does not do.
>
> **Exercise 9.2** Write down a list of things that should be added to this project.
>
> **Exercise 9.3** Which keyboard key is used to fire a bullet?
>
> **Exercise 9.4** Place an explosion into a running scenario (by interactively creating an object of class `Explosion`). Does it work? What does it do?
>
> **Exercise 9.5** Place a proton wave into a scenario. Does this work? What does it do?

When experimenting with the current scenario, you will have noticed that some fundamental functionality is missing:

- The rocket does not move. It cannot be turned nor can it be moved forward.
- Nothing happens when an asteroid collides with the rocket. It flies straight through it instead of damaging the rocket.
- As a result of this, you cannot lose. The game never ends and a final score is never displayed.
- The `ScoreBoard`, `Explosion`, and `ProtonWave` classes, which we can see in the class diagram, do not seem to feature in the scenario.

One thing that we can do, however, is fire bullets at asteroids. (If you have not yet found out how, try it out.) Asteroids break up when hit by a bullet or, if they are already fairly small, disappear.

The goal of this game would obviously be to clear the screen of asteroids without our rocket ship being hit itself. To make it a little more interesting, we also want to add another weapon—the proton wave. And we want to keep a score while we're playing. To achieve all this, we have a good amount of work to do.

- We have to implement movement for the rocket. Currently it can fire bullets, but nothing else. We need to be able to move forward and turn.
- We must ensure that the rocket explodes when we hit an asteroid.

- When the rocket explodes we want to put up a scoreboard that displays our final score.

- We want to be able to release a proton wave. The proton wave should start small around the rocket ship and then gradually spread out, destroying asteroids when it hits them.

But before we get into these functions, we start with one more minor cosmetic thing: painting stars into our universe.

9.2 Painting stars

In all our previous scenarios, we used a fixed image as the background for the world. The image was stored in an image file in our file system.

In this scenario, we'd like to introduce a different technique to make background images: painting them on the fly.

The Asteroid scenario does not use an image file for the background. A world that does not have a background image assigned will, by default, get an automatically created background image that is filled with plain white.

> **Exercise 9.6** Investigate the constructor of the **Space** class in your scenario. Find the lines of code that create the black background.

Looking at the *asteroids-1* scenario, we can see that the background is plain black. When we investigate the constructor of the **Space** class, we can find these three lines of code:

```
GreenfootImage background = getBackground();
background.setColor(Color.BLACK);
background.fill();
```

> **Exercise 9.7** Remove these three lines from your class. You can do this by just commenting them out. What do you observe? (Once done, put them back in.)

The first line retrieves the current background image from the world. This is the automatically generated (white) image. We then have a reference to the world background stored in the **background** variable.

The background object that we have stored here is of class **GreenfootImage**—we have seen this class before.

> **Exercise 9.8** Look up the documentation for the class **GreenfootImage**. What is the name of the method used to draw a rectangle? What is the difference between **drawOval** and **fillOval**?

Tip

If you want to remove some code temporarily, it is easier to "comment it out" rather than delete it. The Greenfoot editor has a function to do this. Just select the lines in question, and invoke "Comment" (F8) or "Uncomment" (F7) from the Edit menu.

The second line in the code fragment above sets the paint color to black. Doing this has no immediate effect (it does not change the color of the image). Instead, it determines the color that is used by all following drawing operations. The parameter is a constant from the `Color` class, which we encountered in the previous chapter.

Exercise 9.9 Look up the documentation of class `Color` again. (Do you remember which package it is in?) For how many colors does this class define constant fields?

The third line of the code fragment now fills our image with the chosen color. Note that we do not need to set this image again as the background of the world. When we got the image (using `getBackground()`), we got a reference to the background image, and the same image still remains the world background. It is not removed from the world just because we now have a reference to it.

When we paint onto this image, we are painting directly onto the background of the world.

Our task now is to draw some stars onto the background image.

Exercise 9.10 In class **Space**, create a new method named **createStars**. This method should have one parameter of type **int**, named **number**, to specify the number of stars it should create. It has no return value. The method body should—for now—be empty.

Exercise 9.11 Write a comment for the new method. (The comment should describe what the method does and explain what the parameter is used for.)

Exercise 9.12 Insert a call to this new method into your **Space** constructor. Three hundred stars may be a good amount to start with (although you can later experiment with different numbers and choose something that you think looks good).

Exercise 9.13 Compile the class **Space**. At this stage you should not see any effect (since our new method is empty), but the class should compile without problems.

Concept

The **for loop** is one of Java's loop constructs. It is especially useful for iterating a fixed number of times.

In the `createStars` method, we will now write code to paint some stars onto the background image. The exact amount of stars is specified in the method's parameter.

We will use yet another loop to achieve this: the *for loop*.

Previously, we have seen the *while loop* and the *for-each loop*. The *for loop* uses the same keyword as the *for-each loop* (`for`) but has a different structure. It is:

```
for (initialization; loop-condition; increment)
{
    loop-body;
}
```

An example of this loop can be seen in the `addAsteroids` method in the Space class.

Exercise 9.14 Examine the `addAsteroids` method in class **Space**. What does it do?

Exercise 9.15 Look at the *for loop* in that method. From the loop header, write down the *initialization* part, the *loop-condition*, and the *increment*. (See the definition of the for loop above.)

The initialization part of a for loop is executed exactly once before the loop starts. Then the loop condition is checked: If it is true, the loop body is executed. Finally, after the loop body has been completely executed, the increment section from the loop header is executed. After this, the loop starts over: the condition is evaluated again and, if true, the loop runs again. This continues until the loop condition returns false. The initialization is never executed again.

A for loop could quite easily be replaced by a while loop. A while loop equivalent of the for loop structure shown above is this:

```
initialization;
while (loop-condition)
{
    loop-body;
    increment;
}
```

The while loop structure shown here and the for loop structure shown above do exactly the same thing. The main difference is that, in the for loop, the initialization and the increment have been moved into the loop header. This places all elements that define the loop behavior in one place, and can make loops easier to read.

The for loop is especially practical if we know at the beginning of the loop already how often we want to execute the loop.

The for loop example found in the `addAsteroids` method reads

```
for (int i = 0; i < count; i++)
{
    int x = Greenfoot.getRandomNumber(getWidth()/2);
    int y = Greenfoot.getRandomNumber(getHeight()/2);
    addObject(new Asteroid(), x, y);
}
```

This shows a typical example of a for loop:

- The initialization part declares and initializes a loop variable. This variable is often called `i`, and often initialized to 0.

- The loop condition checks whether our loop variable is still less than a given limit (here: `count`). If it is, the loop will continue.

- The increment section simply increments the loop variable.

Different variations of the for loop are possible, but this example shows a very typical format.

Exercise 9.16 In your **Space** class, rewrite the for loop in **addAsteroids** as a while loop. Make sure that it does the same as before.

Exercise 9.17 Rewrite this method again with a for loop, as it was before.

Exercise 9.18 Implement the body of the **createStars** method that you created earlier. This method should include the following:

- Retrieve the world's background image.
- Use a for loop similar to the one in **addAsteroids**. The limit for the loop is given in the method parameter.
- In the body of the loop, generate random x- and y- coordinates. Set the color to white and then paint a filled oval onto the background image with a width and height of two pixels.

Test! Do you see stars in your world? If all went well, you should.

Exercise 9.19 Create stars of random brightness. You can do this by creating a random number between 0 and 255 (the legal range for RGB values for colors) and creating a new Color object using the same random value for all three color components (red, green, and blue). Using the same value for all color components ensures that the resulting color is a shade of neutral gray. Use this new random color for painting the star. Make sure to generate a new color for every new star.

These exercises are quite challenging, but you should know everything you need to solve them. If you have trouble, you can look at our version of the implementation which is provided in the *asteroids-2* version of this scenario. Alternatively, you can ignore this section for now, continue with the following tasks first, and come back to this later.

9.3 Turning

In the previous section we spent a lot of effort just on looks. We used a for loop to create the stars in the background. That was hard work for little effect. However, knowing the for loop will come in very handy later.

Now we want to achieve some real functionality: we want to make the rocket move. The first step is to make it turn when the right or left arrow key is pressed on the keyboard.

Exercise 9.20 Examine the **Rocket** class. Find the code that handles keyboard input. What is the name of the method that holds this code?

Exercise 9.21 Add a statement that makes the rocket rotate left while the "left" key is pressed. In every act cycle, the rocket should rotate 5 degrees to the left.

Exercise 9.22 Add a statement that makes the rocket rotate right while the "right" key is pressed. Test it!

If you managed to successfully complete the exercises, your rocket should be able to turn now when you press the arrow keys. Since it fires in the direction it is facing, it can also fire in all directions.

The next challenge is to make it move forward.

9.4 Flying forward

Our Rocket class is a subclass of the SmoothMover class, which we have already seen in the previous chapter. This means that it holds a velocity vector that determines its movement, and that it has a move() method that makes it move according to this vector.

Our first step is to make use of this move() method.

Exercise 9.23 In the Rocket's act method, add a call to the move() method (inherited from SmoothMover). Test. What do you observe?

Adding the call to move() to our act method is an important first step, but does not achieve much by itself. It causes the rocket to move according to its movement vector, but since we have not initiated any movement, this vector currently has length 0, so no movement takes place.

To change this, let us first introduce a small amount of automatic drift, so that the rocket starts off with some initial movement. This makes it more interesting to play, because it stops players from being able to just remain stationary for a long time.

Exercise 9.24 Add a small amount of initial movement to the rocket. To do this, create a new vector with some arbitrary direction and a small length (I used 0.7 for my own version) and then use the SmoothMover's addToVelocity method with this vector as a parameter to add this force to the rocket. You can do this in the Rocket's constructor. (Make sure to use an int as your first parameter in the Vector's constructor, in order to use the correct constructor.)

Test. If all went well, the rocket should drift all by itself when the scenario starts. Don't make this initial drift too fast. Experiment until you have a nice, slow initial movement.

Next, we want to add movement controls for the player. The plan is that pressing the "up" arrow key ignites the rocket's booster and moves us forward.

For the existing keyboard input, we have used code of the following pattern:

```
if (Greenfoot.isKeyDown("left"))
{
    turn(-5);
}
```

For the movement forward, we need a slightly different pattern. The reason is that, for the rotation shown here, we need to act only if the key is being pressed.

The movement forward is different: when we press the "up" key to move, we want to change the rocket's image to show the rocket engine firing. When we release the key, the image should return to the normal image. We want to act when the key is pressed, and also when it is released. Thus, we need a code pattern along these lines:

```
when "up" key is pressed:
    change image to show engine fire;
    add movement;

when "up" key is released:
    change back to normal image;
```

Showing the images is quite easy. The scenario already contains two different rocket images for this: *rocket.png* and *rocketWithThrust.png*. Both images are loaded into fields toward the top of the Rocket class.

Since we need to react in both cases, when the "up" key is pressed and when it is not pressed, we will define and call a separate method to handle this functionality.

In checkKeys, we can insert the following method call:

```
ignite(Greenfoot.isKeyDown("up"));
```

This line of code will first call the isKeyDown method from the Greenfoot class, which returns a boolean. This boolean value is then passed as a parameter to the ignite method (which we now have to write).

To write the ignite method, we have to arrange the following:

■ The method receives a boolean parameter (say, boosterOn) that indicates whether the booster should be on or off. This parameter is set by the result of the isKeyDown("up") call (if the key is down, boosterOn will be true, otherwise false).

■ If the booster is on, it sets the image to *rocketWithThrust.png* and uses addToVelocity to add a new vector. This vector should get its direction from the current rotation of the rocket (getRotation()) and have a small, constant length (say, 0.3).

■ If the booster is not on, set the image to *rocket.png*.

> **Exercise 9.25** Add the call to the ignite method to your **checkKeys** method, exactly as shown above.

Exercise 9.26 Define a method stub (a method with an empty body) for the `ignite` method. This method should have one boolean parameter, and a void return type. Make sure to write a comment. Test! The code should compile (but not do anything yet).

Exercise 9.27 Implement the body of the `ignite` method, as outlined in the bullet points above.

For the implementation of our `ignite` method, it is okay if the image gets set every time the method is called, even when it is not necessary (e.g., if the booster is off, and it was also off last time, we would not need to set the image again since it has not changed). Setting the image even when it is not strictly necessary has very little overhead and so avoiding it is not crucial.

Once you have completed these exercises, you have reached a stage where you can fly your rocket through space and fire at asteroids. You see the effect of using a movement vector, rather than just calling the actor's `move` method when the key is down: movement continues when you do nothing, and you have to press your keys to *change* the movement. We have implemented *momentum*.

A version of the project that implements the exercises presented so far in this chapter is provided as *asteroids-2* in the book scenarios.

9.5 Colliding with asteroids

The most obvious fault with our asteroids game at this stage is that we can fly right through the asteroids. That leaves not much of a challenge to play this game, since we cannot lose. We shall fix that now.

The idea is that our rocket ship should explode when we crash into an asteroid. If you did the exercises earlier in this chapter, then you have already seen that we have a fully functional `Explosion` class available in our project. Simply placing an explosion into the world will show an adequate explosion effect.

Thus, a rough description of the task to solve is this:

```
if (we have collided with an asteroid)
{
    place an explosion into the world;
    remove the rocket from the world;
    show final score (game over);
}
```

Before we look into solving these subtasks, we prepare our source code to implement this task, as we did with other functionality. We follow the same strategy as before: since this is a separate subtask, we shall put it into a separate method, in order to keep our code well structured and easily readable. You should usually start the implementation of new functionality like this. The next exercise achieves this.

Exercise 9.28 Create a new method stub (a method with an empty body) in class `Rocket` for checking for collisions with asteroids. Call it `checkCollision`. This method can be private and needs no return value and no parameters.

Exercise 9.29 In the rocket's `act` method, add a call to the `checkCollision` method. Ensure that your class compiles and runs again.

Concept

Greenfoot provides several methods for **collision detection**. They are in the Actor class.

The first subtask is to check whether we have collided with an asteroid. Greenfoot's `Actor` class contains a number of different methods to check for collisions, each with different functionality. We have seen one of them—`getOneIntersectingObject`—in the previous chapters. Let us now look at the rest of them as well.

Exercise 9.30 Look at the documentation of the **Actor** class and write down all methods related to collision detection.

Exercise 9.31 You will notice that there are also methods to tell you about other objects nearby (even if you are not colliding). Write those methods down as well.

Appendix C presents a summary of the different collision detection methods and their functionality. This might be a good time to have a quick look through it. At some stage, you should become familiar with all the collision detection methods.

Concept

The **bounding box** of an image is the enclosing rectangle of that image.

For our purpose, `getOneIntersectingObject` or `getIntersectingObjects` seem like a good fit. Two objects intersect if any of the pixels in their images intersect. This is pretty much what we need.

In Chapter 5 we have seen one surprising effect: If you look really carefully, you can see that sometimes a collision is detected when the objects do not actually seem to touch each other. This is caused by transparent pixels in the actor images.

Images in Greenfoot are always rectangles. When we see non-rectangular images, such as the rocket, it is because some pixels in the image are *transparent* (invisible; they contain no color). For the purpose of our program, however, they are still part of the image.

Figure 9.2 shows the rocket and asteroid images with their *bounding boxes*. The bounding box is the edge of the actual image. (The image of the rocket is a little bigger than what seems necessary to make it the same size as the second rocket image, *rocketWithThrust*, which shows the flame in the currently empty area.)

Figure 9.2

Two actor images and their bounding boxes

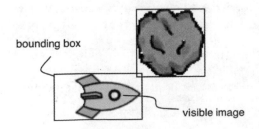

In Figure 9.2, the images intersect, even though their visible parts do not touch. The collision detection methods will report this as an intersection. They work with the bounding boxes and pay no attention to the non-transparent parts of the image.

As a result, our rocket will make "contact" with an asteroid even though, on screen, there seems to be still a little distance between them.

For our asteroids game, we choose to ignore this. First, the distance is small, so often players will not notice. Second, it is easy enough to come up with a story line to explain this effect ("flying too close to an asteroid destroys your ship because of the gravitational pull").

Sometimes it would be nice to check whether the actual visible (non-transparent) parts of an image intersect. This is possible, but much more difficult. We will not discuss this here.

Now that we have decided to go with intersection, we can look at the Actor methods again. There are two methods for checking object intersection. Their signatures are:

```
List getIntersectingObjects(Class cls)
Actor getOneIntersectingObject(Class cls)
```

Both methods accept a parameter of type Class (which means that we can check for intersections with a specific class of object if we want to). The difference is that one method will return a list of all objects that we currently intersect with, while the other returns only a single object. In case we intersect more than one other object, the second method randomly chooses one of them and returns it.

For our purpose, the second method is good enough. As in the WBC scenario in Chapter 5, it actually makes no difference to the game whether we crash into one asteroid or into two of them simultaneously. The rocket will explode just the same. The only question for us is: Did we intersect with any asteroid at all?

Thus, we shall use the second method. Since it returns an Actor, rather than a List, it is slightly simpler to work with. The code pattern for our first task—checking whether we have collided with an asteroid—then is the same we have seen before:

```
Asteroid a = (Asteroid) getOneIntersectingObject(Asteroid.class);
if (a != null)
{
    ...
}
```

Exercise 9.32 Add a check for intersecting with an asteroid, similar to the one shown here, to your own **checkCollision()** method.

Exercise 9.33 Add code to the body of the if-statement that adds an explosion to the world at the current position of the rocket, and removes the rocket from the world. (To do this, you need to use the **getWorld()** method to access the world's methods for adding and removing objects.)

For the last exercise above, we can use our own `getX()` and `getY()` methods to retrieve our current position. We can use this as the coordinates for placing the explosion.

An attempt at solving this might look like this:

```
World world = getWorld();
world.removeObject(this); // remove rocket from world
world.addObject(new Explosion(), getX(), getY());
```

This code looks reasonable at first glance, but will not work.

Exercise 9.34 Try out the code as shown above. Does it compile? Does it run? At what point does something go wrong, and what is the error message?

The reason this does not work is that we are calling the `getX()` and `getY()` methods *after* removing the rocket from the world. When an actor is removed from the world, it does not have any coordinates anymore—it has coordinates only while being in the world. Thus, the `getX()` and `getY()` method calls fail in this example.

This can easily be fixed by switching the last two lines of code: Insert the explosion first, and then remove the rocket from the world.

Exercise 9.35 This is a very advanced exercise, and you may want to skip it initially, and come back to it later.

The explosion used here is a fairly simple looking explosion. It is good enough for the moment, but if you want to create really good looking games, it can be improved. A more sophisticated way to show explosions is introduced in a series of Greenfoot tutorial videos named "Creating Explosions," available on the Greenfoot YouTube channel:

```
https://www.youtube.com/user/18km
```

Create a similar explosion for your rocket.

9.6 Game Over

Our game is now fairly playable. You may have noticed that the score counting does not work (we will look into that later) and that nothing happens when you lose. Next we shall add a big "Game Over" sign at the end, when the rocket crashes.

This is quite easy to do: There is already a `ScoreBoard` class in the project that we can use.

Exercise 9.36 Create an object of class `ScoreBoard` and place it into the world.

Exercise 9.37 Examine the source code of the `ScoreBoard` class. How many constructors does it have? What is the difference between them?

Exercise 9.38 Modify the `ScoreBoard` class: change the text shown on it, change the color of the text, change the background and frame colors, change the font size so that your new text fits well, and change the width of the scoreboard to suit your text.

As you have seen, the scoreboard includes a "Game Over" text and the final score (although the score is currently not correctly counted, but we shall worry about that later).

The `Space` class already has a method, named `gameOver`, that is intended to create and show a scoreboard.

Exercise 9.39 Find and examine the `gameOver` method in the `Space` class. What does its current implementation do?

Exercise 9.40 Implement the `gameOver` method. It should create a new `ScoreBoard` object, using the constructor that expects an `int` parameter for the score. For now, use 999 as the score—we will fix this later to use a real score. Write code to place the scoreboard into the world, exactly centered in the middle.

Exercise 9.41 Once implemented, test your `gameOver` method. Remember: You can call methods of the world class by right-clicking on the world background (see Figure 8.3).

Exercise 9.42 How can you ensure that the scoreboard gets placed in the middle of the world without hard-coding the location (That is, without using the numbers *300* and *250* directly as coordinates)? Hint: Make use of the width and height of the world. Implement this in your scenario.

So, it seems most of the work has been well prepared for us. Now we only need to call the `gameOver` method when we want the game to finish.

The place in our code where we want the game to be over is in our rocket's `checkCollision` method: If we detect a collision, the rocket should explode (we have done that), and the game is over.

Exercise 9.43 Add a call to the `gameOver` method in your `checkCollision` method. Compile it. What do you observe? If you see an error, what is the error message?

If you added the `gameOver` call without a cast, you will have noticed the problem. We have seen in earlier chapters that we have to use a cast if we want to call our own methods from the world subclass (such as the `gameOver` method here). The explanation we have given when we first encountered this, in Chapter 5, was a bit superficial, and we have glossed over some of the details. It is time to revisit this, and discuss it more fully.

Let us start by looking at the code so far, assuming we just added a call to the `gameOver` method to our `checkCollision` method, without a cast (Code 9.1). This code will not compile.

Code 9.1

A first (incorrect) attempt at calling the gameOver method

```
/**
 * Check whether we are colliding with an asteroid.
 */
private void checkCollision()
{
    Asteroid a = (Asteroid) getOneIntersectingObject(Asteroid.class);
    if (a != null)
    {
        World world = getWorld();
        world.addObject(new Explosion(), getX(), getY());
        world.removeObject(this);
        world.gameOver();                   // error: this will not work
    }
}
```

When trying to compile this code, we get an error message that reads

```
cannot find symbol - method gameOver()
```

This message is trying to tell us that the compiler cannot find a method with this name. We know, however, that such a method exists in our `Space` class. We also know that the `getWorld()` call used here gives us a reference to our `Space` object. So what is the problem?

The problem lies in the fact that the compiler is not quite as clever as we would like. The `getWorld()` method is defined in class `Actor`, and its signature is this:

```
World getWorld()
```

We can see that it states that it will return an object of type `World`. The actual world object that it returns in our case is of type `Space`.

This is not a contradiction: our world object can be of type `World` and of type `Space` at the same time because `Space` is a subclass of `World` (`Space` *is a* `World`; we also say that the type `Space` is a *subtype* of type `World`).

The error comes from the difference between the two: `gameOver` is defined in class `Space`, while `getWorld` gives us a result of type `World`. The compiler looks only at the declared return type of the method we are calling (`getWorld`). Because of this, the compiler searches for the `gameOver` method only there and it does not find it. That's why we get the error message.

To solve this problem, we need to tell the compiler explicitly that the world we are receiving is actually of type `Space`. We can do this by using the *cast* construct we have seen earlier.

```
Space space = (Space) getWorld();
```

Concept

Objects can be of **more than one type**: the type of their own class and the type of its superclass.

Casting is the technique of telling the compiler a more precise type for our object than it can work out for itself. In our case, the compiler can work out that the object returned from `getWorld` is of type `World`, and we are now telling that it is actually of class `Space`. We do this by writing the class name (`Space`) in parentheses before the method call. Once we have done this, we can then assign the result to a variable of type `Space` (instead of a `World` variable) and then call methods defined in `Space`:

```
space.gameOver();
```

It is worth noting that casting does not change the type of the object. Our world actually is of type `Space` all along. The problem is just that the compiler does not know this. With the cast, we are just giving additional information to the compiler.

Let's get back to our `checkCollision` method. Once we have cast our world to `Space` and stored it in a variable of type `Space`, we can call all methods on it: those defined in `Space` and the inherited ones defined in `World`. Thus, our existing calls to `addObject` and `removeObject` should still work, and the `gameOver` call should work as well. Code 9.2 shows the fixed method.

Code 9.2

A correct solution to calling the gameOver method

```
/**
 * Check whether we are colliding with an asteroid.
 */
private void checkCollision()
{
    Asteroid a = (Asteroid) getOneIntersectingObject(Asteroid.class);
    if (a != null)
    {
        Space space = (Space) getWorld();
        space.addObject(new Explosion(), getX(), getY());
        space.removeObject(this);
        space.gameOver();
    }
}
```

Exercise 9.44 Implement the call to the `gameOver` method, using the cast of the `World` object to `Space`, as discussed here. Test. This should now work, and the scoreboard should come up when the rocket explodes.

Exercise 9.45 What happens when you use a cast incorrectly? Try casting the world object to, say, `Asteroid` instead of `Space`. Does this work? What do you observe?

This work so far has achieved the display of our "Game Over" sign (still with an incorrect score). We shall leave the scoring as an exercise at the end of this chapter. If you really want to fix this now, you may like to jump ahead to the end-of-chapter exercises and look into this first. Here, we will look at proton waves next.

9.7 Adding fire power: the proton wave

Our game is getting pretty good. The final thing we shall discuss in detail in this chapter is the addition of a second weapon: the proton wave. This should give the game a little more variety. The idea is this: Our proton wave, once released, radiates outward from our rocket ship, damaging or destroying every asteroid in its path. Since it works in all directions simultaneously, it is a much more powerful weapon than our bullets. For the game, we should probably restrict how often or how frequently you can use it, so that the game does not become too easy to play.

> **Exercise 9.46** Run your scenario. Place a proton wave into the scenario—what do you observe?

The exercise shows us that we have a proton wave actor, which shows the wave at full size. However, this wave does not move, does not disappear, and does not cause any damage to asteroids.

Our first task will be to make the wave grow. We will start it very small, and then grow it until it reaches the full size that we have just seen.

> **Exercise 9.47** Examine the source code of class **ProtonWave**. What are the methods that already exist?
>
> **Exercise 9.48** What is the purpose of each method? Review the comments of each method and expand them to add a more detailed explanation.
>
> **Exercise 9.49** Try to explain what the `initializeImages` method does and how it works. Explain in writing, using diagrams if you like.

9.8 Growing the wave

We have seen that the `ProtonWave` class has a method—`initializeImages`—that creates 30 images of different sizes and stores them in an array (Code 9.3). This array, named "`images`," holds the smallest image at index 0, and the largest one at index 29 (see Figure 9.3). The images are created by loading a base image ("wave.png") and then, in a loop, creating copies of this image and scaling them to different sizes.

Code 9.3

Initializing the images for the proton wave

```
/**
 * Create the images for expanding the wave.
 */
public static void initializeImages()
{
    if (images == null)
    {
        GreenfootImage baseImage = new GreenfootImage("wave.png");
        images = new GreenfootImage[NUMBER_IMAGES];
        int i = 0;
        while (i < NUMBER_IMAGES)
        {
            int size = (i+1) * ( baseImage.getWidth() / NUMBER_IMAGES );
            images[i] = new GreenfootImage(baseImage);
            images[i].scale(size, size);
            i++;
        }
    }
}
```

Figure 9.3

An array of images
(some left out for space
reasons)

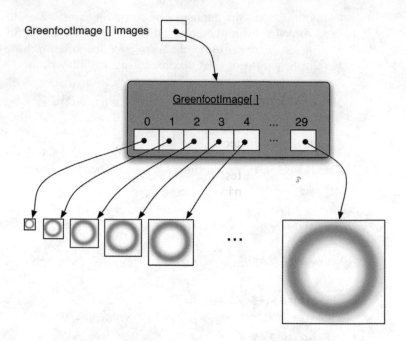

This method uses the `scale` method from the `GreenfootImage` class to do the scaling. It also uses a *while* loop for the iteration. However, this is an example where a *for* loop, which we encountered at the beginning of this chapter, would be more appropriate.

> **Exercise 9.50** Rewrite the `initializeImages` method to use a for loop instead of a while loop.

In practice, it is not very important which loop to use in this case. (We changed it here mainly to gain additional practice in writing for loops.) This is, however, a case where a for loop is a good choice, because we have a known number of iterations (the number of images) and we can make good use of the loop counter in calculating the image sizes. The advantage over the while loop is that the for loop brings all elements of the loop (initialization, condition, and increment) together in the header, so that we run less danger of forgetting one of its parts.

The `images` field and the `initializeImages` method are static (they use the `static` keyword in their definition). As we have briefly mentioned in Chapter 3, this means that the `images` field is stored in the `ProtonWave` *class*, not in the individual instances. As a result, all objects that we will create of this class can share this set of images, and we do not need to create a separate set of images for each object. This is much more efficient than using a separate image set each time.

Copying and scaling these images takes a fairly long time (up to two-tenths of a second on a current average computer). This may not seem very much, but it is long enough to introduce a visible, annoying delay when we do it in the middle of playing a game. To solve this, the code of this method is enclosed in an if-statement:

```
if (images == null)
{
    ...
}
```

This if-statement ensures that the main part of this method (the body of the if-statement) is executed only once. The first time, `images` will be `null`, and the method executes fully. This will initialize the `images` field to something other than `null`. From then on, the test of the if-statement is all that will be executed, and the body will be skipped. The `initializeImages` method is actually called every time a proton wave is created (from the constructor), but substantial work is only being done the first time.[1]

Now that we have a fair idea of the code and the fields that already exist, we can finally get to work and make something happen.

What we want to do is the following:

- We want to start the wave off with the smallest image.

- At every act step, we want to grow the wave (show the next larger image).

- After we have shown the largest image, the wave should disappear (be removed from the world).

The following exercises will achieve this.

Exercise 9.51 In the constructor of class **ProtonWave**, set the image to the smallest image. (You can use `images[0]` as the parameter to the `setImage` method.)

Exercise 9.52 Create an instance field named `currentImage` of type `int`, and initialize it to 0. We will use this field to count through the images. The current value is the index of the currently displayed image.

Exercise 9.53 Create a method stub for a new private method called `grow`. This method has no parameter and does not return a value.

Exercise 9.54 Call the `grow` method from your `act` method (even though it does not do anything at this stage).

---

[1] The method is actually called for the first time from the Space constructor, so it executes even before the first proton wave is created. This avoids a delay for the first proton wave as well. The call is included in the proton wave constructor only as a safety feature: if this class is ever used in another project, and this method is not called in advance, all will still work.

We're almost there. The only thing left is to implement the `grow` method. The idea, roughly, is this:

```
show the image at index currentImage;
increment currentImage;
```

We will also have to add an if-statement that first checks whether `currentImage` has reached the last image. In that case, we can remove the proton wave from the world and we are finished.

Exercise 9.55 Implement the `grow` method along the lines discussed above.

Exercise 9.56 Test your proton wave. If you interactively create a proton wave, and place it into the world while the scenario is running, you should see the wave expansion effect.

Exercise 9.57 Add some sound. A sound file named "proton.wav" is included with the scenario—you can just play it. You can place the statement to play the sound into the constructor of the proton wave.

Now that we have a functioning proton wave, we should equip our rocket to release it.

Exercise 9.58 In class **Rocket**, create a method stub named **startProtonWave** without parameters. Does it need to return anything?

Exercise 9.59 Implement this method: It should place a new proton wave object into the world, at the current coordinates of the rocket.

Exercise 9.60 Call this new method from the **checkKeys** method when the "z" key is pressed. Test.

Exercise 9.61 You will quickly notice that the proton wave can be released much too often now. For firing the bullets, a delay has been built into the **Rocket** class (using the **gunReloadTime** constant and the **reloadDelayCount** field). Study this code and implement something similar for the proton wave. Try out different delay values until you find one that seems sensible. Proton waves should not be available very often.

9.9 Interacting with objects in range

We now have a proton wave that we can release at the push of a button. The remaining problem is that this proton wave does not actually do anything to the asteroids.

We now want to add code that causes damage to the asteroids when they get hit by the proton wave.

Exercise 9.62 Prepare for this new functionality: In class **ProtonWave**, add a method stub for a method called **checkCollision**. The method has no parameters and does not return a value. Call this method from your **act** method.

Exercise 9.63 The purpose of this new method is to check whether the wave touches an asteroid, and cause damage to it if it does. Write the method comment.

This time we do not want to use the `getIntersectingObjects` method, since the invisible image areas at the corners of the proton wave image (included in the bounding box, but not part of the blueish circle) are fairly large, and asteroids would be destroyed long before the wave seems to reach them.

Instead, we will use another collision detection method, called `getObjectsInRange`.

The `getObjectsInRange` method returns a list of all objects within a given radius of the calling object (see Figure 9.4). Its signature is

```
List getObjectsInRange(int radius, Class cls)
```

When called, we can specify the class of objects we are interested in (as before), and we also specify a radius (in cells). The method will then return a list of all objects of the requested class that are found within this radius around the calling object.

To determine which objects are within the range, the center points of objects are used. For example, an asteroid would be within range 20 of a rocket if the distance of its center point to the center point of the rocket is less than 20 cell widths. The size of the image is not relevant for this method.

Using this method, we can implement our `checkCollision` method.

Figure 9.4

The range around an actor with a given radius

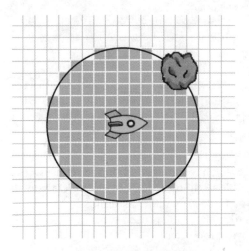

Our proton wave will have images of increasing size. At each act cycle, we can use the size of the current image to determine the range of our collision check. We can find out our current image size using the following method calls:

```
getImage().getWidth()
```

We can then use half of this size as our range (since the range is specified as a radius, not a diameter).

Exercise 9.64 In `checkCollision`, declare a local variable named `range` and assign half the current image width to it.

Exercise 9.65 Add a call to `getObjectsInRange` that returns all asteroids within the calculated range. Assign the result to a variable of type `List<Asteroid>`. Remember that you also have to add an import statement for the `List` type.

These exercises give us a list of all asteroids in the range of the proton wave. We now want to do some damage to each asteroid in range.

The `Asteroid` class has a method called `hit` that we can use to do this. This method is already being used to do damage to the asteroid when it is hit by a bullet, and we can use it again here.

We can use a for-each loop to iterate through all asteroids in the list we received from the `getObjectsInRange` call. (If you are unsure about writing for-each loops, look back to Section 7.10.)

Exercise 9.66 Find the `hit` method in the `Asteroid` class. What are its parameters? What does it return?

Exercise 9.67 The `ProtonWave` class has a constant defined toward the top called `DAMAGE`; it specifies how much damage it should cause. Find the declaration of this constant. What is its value?

Exercise 9.68 In method `checkCollision`, write a for-each loop that iterates over the asteroid list retrieved from the `getObjectsInRange` call. In the loop body, call `hit` on each asteroid using the `DAMAGE` constant for the amount of damage caused.

Once you have completed these exercises, test. If all went well, you should now have a playable version of this game that lets you shoot at asteroids and also release proton waves to destroy many asteroids instantly. You will notice that you should make the reload time for the proton wave quite long, since the game gets too easy if you can use the wave too often.

This version of the game, including all the changes made in the last few sections, is available in the book projects as *asteroids-3*. You can use this version to compare it to your own scenario, or to look up solutions if you get stuck in one of the exercises.

9.10 Further development

We are at the end of the detailed discussion of development of this scenario in this chapter. There are, however, a large number of further improvements possible to this game. Some are quite obvious, others you may like to invent yourself.

Below are some suggestions for further work, in the form of exercises. Many of them are independent of each other—they do not need to be done in this particular order. Pick those first that interest you most, and come up with some extensions of your own.

The Counter class and other helper classes

The **Counter** class included in this scenario is one of a small collection of useful helper classes provided with Greenfoot. You can import any of these classes by using the *Import Class…* function from the *Edit* menu in Greenfoot's main window. Try it to see what other classes are there.

We could have chosen to display the score by just writing it onto the world background, as we did in Chapter 5. In this case, we chose to use the **Counter** class for cosmetic reasons: we wanted to make it look a bit more interesting. Once you implement score counting in this scenario, you will see that this counter not only has a more interesting look, but also includes an animation effect (counting up the numbers) when you add to the count.

Exercise 9.69 Fix the score counting. You have seen that there already is a score counter, but it is not being used yet. The counter is defined in class **Counter**, and a counter object is being created in the **Space** class.

To make the scoring work, you will have to do roughly the following: Add a method to the **Space** class named something like **countScore**. This method should add a score to the score counter. Call this new method from the **Asteroid** class whenever an asteroid gets hit (you may want to have different scores for splitting the asteroid and removing the last little piece).

Exercise 9.70 Add new asteroids when all have been cleared. Maybe the game should start with just two asteroids, and every time they are cleared away, new ones appear, one more every time. So in the second round, there are three asteroids, in the third round four, and so on.

Exercise 9.71 Add a level counter. Every time the asteroids are cleared, you go up a level. Maybe you get higher scores in later levels.

Exercise 9.72 Add an end-of-level sound. This should be played every time a level is completed.

Exercise 9.73 Add an indicator showing the load state for the proton wave, so that the player can see when it is ready to be used again. This could be a counter, or some sort of graphical representation.

Exercise 9.74 Add a shield. When the shield is deployed, it stays there for a short fixed time. While the shield is up, it can be seen on screen, and colliding asteroids do no damage.

There are, of course, countless more possible extensions. Invent some of your own, implement them, and submit your results to the Greenfoot website.

Summary of programming techniques

In this chapter we have worked on completing an asteroids game that was initially half-written. In doing this, we have encountered several important constructs again, including loops, lists, and collision detection.

We have seen one new style of loop—the *for* loop—and we have used it to paint the stars and to generate the proton wave images. We have also revisited the *for-each* loop when we implemented the proton wave functionality.

Two different collision detection methods were used: `getOneIntersectingObject` and `getObjectsInRange`. Both have their advantages in certain situations. The second one of those returned a list of actors to us, so we had to deal with lists again.

The more practice you get with lists and loops, the easier it becomes to use them. After using them for a while, you will be surprised that you found them so difficult at first.

Concept summary

- The **for loop** is one of Java's loop constructs. It is especially useful for iterating a fixed number of times.

- Greenfoot provides several methods for **collision detection**. They are in the `Actor` class.

- The **bounding box** of an image is the enclosing rectangle of that image.

- Objects can be of **more than one type**: the type of their own class and the type of its superclass.

- **Casting** is the technique of specifying a more precise type for our object than the one the compiler knows about.

Drill and practice

This time we will do some practice with for loops, and a little bit more with strings. For this we will use a separate scenario called *loop-practice* (you will find it in your Chapter 9 folder).

Open this scenario and open the editor for the `ChalkBoard` class. You will find a method called `practice`. For the following exercises, you will write all your code in this method.

The method initially has a single method call in it to write out the number 7. This is to show you how to write something on the board. It is easy—you just call the `write` method with either an `int`, a `char`, or a `String` parameter.

All the following exercises expect you to call the write method to write out some numbers or text.

Exercise 9.75 In the `practice` method, delete the method call that is present. Write a for loop that writes out the letter "a" 10 times.

Exercise 9.76 Write a for loop that writes out the numbers 0 to 19.

Exercise 9.77 Write a for loop that writes out the text snippets "a0," "a1," "a2," and so on, up until "a16" (without the quotes).

Exercise 9.78 Write a for loop that writes out all even numbers from 0 to 24.

Exercise 9.79 Write a for loop that writes out all multiples of five from 15 to 75.

Exercise 9.80 Write a loop that writes the square of all numbers from 1 to 12.

Exercise 9.81 Declare a local `String` variable and assign your name to it. Write out this variable.

Exercise 9.82 Instead of writing out the variable as a whole, write a loop that writes out each character from this string, one by one. Consult the documentation of class `String` to find out the length of a string, and how to access each character individually.

Exercise 9.83 Write a loop that writes out each character of your name twice. So if you name is "Jane," it should write J J a a n n e e.

Exercise 9.84 Write a loop that writes every second character of your name.

Exercise 9.85 Write a loop that writes every character of your name backward.

Exercise 9.86 Assign the word "Greenfoot" to your string variable instead of your name. Write a loop that writes every character of this string, except the characters "r" and "o." When it encounters these characters, it simply ignores them.

Exercise 9.87 Write a loop that writes every character of this string, but swaps every "o" for an "e," and every "e" for an "o."

The next three exercises are for the curious. You will have to do some research yourself. You will have to find out about the modulo operator (do a Web search if you cannot ask someone directly). It is written in Java as a percent symbol (%). You will need to use this modulo operator to check whether one number is a multiple of another.

Exercise 9.88 Write a for loop that writes out the numbers from 0 to 30 except, for every multiple of five, it writes the letter "X" instead of the number.

Exercise 9.89 Modify the loop from the previous exercise so that it also replaces multiples of three with the letter "O."

Exercise 9.90 Add another detail to the loop from the previous exercise: If the number is a multiple of three and five, write the letter "Z."

We will take a little time out for a second interlude—a break in the chapter sequence to do something a little different. This time, we will look at "Greeps"—a programming competition.

The Greeps are alien creatures. And they've come to Earth! One of the important things to know about Greeps is that they like tomatoes. They have landed with their spaceship and are swarming out to find and collect tomatoes (Figure I2.1).

The challenge in this programming competition will be to program your Greeps so that they find and collect tomatoes as quickly as possible. You will have limited time, and every tomato you manage to bring back to the spaceship scores a point.

You can do this project as a competition against a friend who programs their own Greeps, or you can do it as a contest for a whole group of programmers, such as a school class. If you are on your own, you could post your entry to the Greenfoot website and

Figure I2.1

Two Greeps hunt-
ing for tomatoes

see how you compare to other people there.[1] Or you could do it on your own just for the fun of it—either way, it should be an interesting challenge.

I2.1   How to get started

To start with, open the *greeps* scenario from your scenarios folder. Run it.

You will see that a spaceship lands in an area with sand and water. The Greeps will leave the spaceship and start searching for tomato piles (which happen to be found in various places in this area). Greeps are land animals—they cannot and will not walk into the water. (In fact, they are so sensitive to water that they dissolve very quickly in it, so don't try.)

When you try out the scenario, you will quickly see that the Greeps do not behave very intelligently. They head out in a random direction from the ship, but when they reach the edge of the water, they will just stay there, because they cannot go forward.

Your task will be to program the Greeps to use a more intelligent strategy, so that they find the tomatoes and bring them back to the ship.

There are some facts about the Greeps that you need to know:

- There are 20 Greeps in the spaceship. They will come out after landing to start their work. You cannot get any more of them.

- Greeps can carry a tomato on their back, but they cannot load tomatoes onto their own back. They can only load a tomato *onto another Greep's* back! This means that two of them have to be at the tomato pile at the same time to pick up a tomato.

- Greeps cannot talk or communicate verbally in any way. They can, however, spit paint onto the ground. And they can spit in three different colors (Figure I2.2)! There are rumors that there once was a tribe of Greeps who used this to convey information to each other.

- Greeps are very short sighted. They can only see the ground at their immediate location and cannot look any further.

- Greeps have a good memory—they never forget what they know. However, unfortunately, their memory is very limited. They can only remember a few things at a time.

Armed with this extensive background knowledge, we can now get ready to program our Greeps.

---

[1] If you submit the Greeps scenario to the Greenfoot website, please do not include source code. We want to keep this project as a challenge to future programmers and don't want to make it too easy to find solutions of others.

Figure 12.2

A tribe of Greeps using paint drops

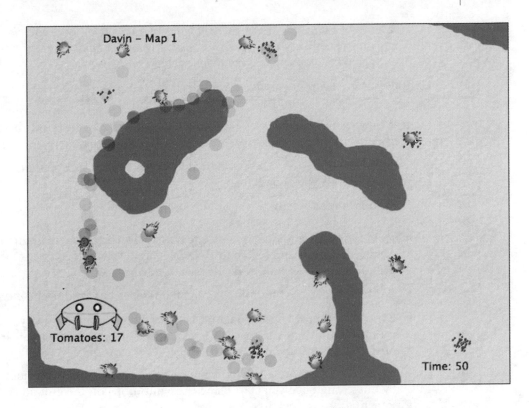

12.2 Programming your Greeps

To program your Greeps to collect as many tomatoes as possible, you should improve their behavior. The Greep class, which is included in the scenario, already includes some behavior that you can look at to get started.

We can see that Greep is a subclass of Creature. Class Creature provides a number of very useful methods that we can use.

There are, however, a number of rules that you must follow:

Rule 1: *Only change the class "Greep." No other classes may be modified or created.*

Rule 2: *You cannot extend the Greeps' memory. That is, you are not allowed to add fields (other than final fields) to the class. Some general purpose memory (one int and two booleans) is provided.*

Rule 3: *You cannot move more than once per "act" round.*

Rule 4: *Greeps do not communicate directly. They do not call each other's methods or access each other's fields.*

Rule 5: *No long vision. You are allowed to look at the world only at the immediate location of the Greep. Greeps are almost blind and cannot look any further.*

Rule 6: *No creation of objects. You are not allowed to create any scenario objects (instances of user-defined classes, such as Greep or Paint). Greeps have no magic powers—they cannot create things out of nothing.*

Rule 7: *No teleporting. Methods from Actor that cheat normal movement (such as setLocation) may not be used.*

It is important to follow these rules. It is technically easy to break them, but that is considered cheating.

To program your Greeps, you work mainly in the Greeps' `act` method (and any other private methods you choose to create).

Some tips to get started:

■ Read the documentation of class `Creature`. (The best way to do this is to open the class in the editor and switch to Documentation view.) These are some of the most useful methods for your work. Know what is there.

■ Work in small steps. Start making small improvements and see how it goes.

■ Some first improvements could be as follows: turn around when you are at water, wait if you find a tomato pile (and try to load tomatoes), turn if you are at the edge of the world, and so on.

You will soon figure out many more improvements you could implement. It gets especially interesting once you start using the paint drops on the ground to make marks for other Greeps to find.

12.3 Running the competition

It helps to have a judge who runs the competition. In a school, this might be your teacher. If you run this with friends, it could be a selected person (who then cannot take part as a normal contestant in the competition).

To make the competition interesting, there should be two versions of the Greeps scenario. One gets handed out to all contestants. (This is the one included in the book scenarios.) This scenario includes three different maps. The Greeps land and forage on each of the three maps in turn. (So the challenge for contestants is to develop movement algorithms that are flexible enough to work on different maps, not just a known one.)

The judge should have a different scenario that includes more maps. We recommend running the competition with 10 different maps. Contestants do not get access to the last seven maps—they can only test on the first three. Then they hand in their Greeps for scoring, and the judge then runs the contestants' Greeps on all 10 maps (maybe on a large display screen) to reach the official score.

The competition is best run over several days (or maybe a week or two), with repeated chances for contestants to submit their work for scoring, so that they can slowly improve.

12.4 Technicalities

For submission of an entry to the judge, the easiest mechanism is that contestants submit only the *Greeps.java* file. The judge then copies that file into his full (10-map) scenario, recompiles, and runs it. This ensures that no other classes are modified in the process.

Some artwork (to make flyers or posters for the competition) is available at

```
http://www.greenfoot.org/competition/greeps/
```

Instructors can also find instructions there for obtaining a version of the Greeps scenario with 10 maps. Alternatively, instructors can make more maps themselves fairly easily. An image of an empty map is provided in the *images* folder of the Greeps scenario. Water can just be painted onto the map, and map data (location of tomato piles, etc.) can be specified in the Earth class.

CHAPTER

10 Creating images and sound

topics:	creating sounds, creating images, dynamic image changes, handling mouse input
concepts:	sound formats, sound quality parameters, image file formats, RGBA color model, transparency

Many of the scenarios we have encountered previously were interesting not only because of the program code that defined their behavior, but also because they made effective use of sound and images. So far, we have not discussed the production of these media files much and have often relied on existing pictures and sounds.

In this chapter, we will learn about some aspects of creating and managing these media files. We will start with some background about sound in computer programs, followed by various techniques to create and handle images.

As a side effect, we will also encounter dealing with mouse input.

10.1 Preparation

In contrast to previous chapters, we will not build a complete scenario here but work through various smaller exercises that illustrate separate techniques that can then be incorporated into a wide variety of different scenarios. The first sequence of exercises guides us through creating a scenario that plays a sound—which we create ourselves—when the user clicks on an actor.

For these exercises, we shall not use a prepared, partly implemented starting scenario but create a new one from scratch.

> **Exercise 10.1** As a preparation for the exercises in this chapter, create a new scenario. You can call it anything you like.

You will see that the new scenario automatically includes the `World` and `Actor` super-classes, but no other classes.

> **Exercise 10.2** Create a subclass of `World`. Call it `MyWorld`. You can give it any background image you like. Compile.
>
> **Exercise 10.3** Change the size and resolution of the world so that it has a cell size of one pixel, and a size of 400 cells width and 300 cells height.
>
> **Exercise 10.4** Create an `Actor` subclass in your scenario. At this stage, it does not matter much what it is. You may like to look through the available library images shown in the *New class* dialog, and choose one that looks interesting. Name your class appropriately. (Remember: Class names should start with a capital letter.)
>
> **Exercise 10.5** Add code to your `MyWorld` class that automatically places an instance of your actor into the world.
>
> **Exercise 10.6** Write code into your actor's `act` method that moves the actor 10 pixels to the right every time it acts.

You should now have a scenario with an actor that moves to the right when you run it. Movement, however, is not our main goal here. We added movement only to have an initial visual effect to experiment with.

The next step in our preparation will be to make the actor react to mouse clicks.

Concept

We can use the **mouseClicked** method to check whether the user clicked on a given object.

> **Exercise 10.7** In class `Greenfoot`, there are several methods that can handle mouse input. What are they? Look them up in the *Greenfoot Class Documentation* and write them down.
>
> **Exercise 10.8** What is the difference between `mouseClicked` and `mousePressed`?

When we want to react to mouse clicks, we can use the `mouseClicked` method from the `Greenfoot` class. This method returns a boolean and can be used as a condition in an if-statement.

The parameter to the `mouseClicked` method can specify an object that we wish to check, and the method will return true if it was clicked on. We can pass `null` as the parameter if we do not care where the mouse was when it was clicked—the method will then return true if the mouse was clicked anywhere.

Exercise 10.9 Modify the code in your **Actor** class so that it only moves to the right in reaction to a mouse click. The mouse click can be anywhere in the world.

Exercise 10.10 Now modify your code so that the actor only moves when the user clicks on the actor. To do this, you have to pass the actor itself (instead of **null**) as a parameter to the **mouseClicked** method. Remember, you can use the keyword **this** to refer to the current object.

Exercise 10.11 Test your code: place multiple instances of your actor into the world and make sure that only the one you click on moves.

You should now have a scenario with an actor that can react to mouse clicks. This is a good starting point for our following experiments with sound and images. (If you had trouble creating this, there is a scenario called *soundtest* in the book scenarios for this chapter that implements this starting point.)

10.2 Working with sound

As we have seen earlier, the Greenfoot class has a playSound method that we can use to play a sound file. To be playable, the sound file must be located in the *sounds* folder inside the scenario folder.

As a start, let us play an existing sound file.

Exercise 10.12 Select a sound file from one of your other Greenfoot scenarios and copy it into the *sounds* folder of your current scenario. Then modify your actor so that it plays the sound (instead of moving) when you click on it.

Pitfall

Some operating systems (most notably Microsoft Windows) are configured so that file name suffixes (extensions) are not displayed. A file that is fully named *mysound.wav* would then be displayed only as *mysound*. This is a problem because we need to use the full name, including the suffix, from our Java code.

Writing Greenfoot.playSound("mysound"); would fail, because the file would not be found. However, without seeing the suffix, we have no idea what it is.

The solution is to change the operating system's settings so that suffixes are always displayed. Windows, for example, has a checkbox titled *Hide extensions for known file types*, and you should make sure that this is not checked. In Windows 8, you can find this checkbox by looking at your folder's contents and going through the menus *View / Options / Change Folder and Search Options / View*. In other Windows systems, the menu names may vary, but the checkbox will be there as well.

We can easily play an existing sound file. The more interesting task now is to make sound files ourselves.

10.3 Sound recording in Greenfoot

There are various options for obtaining sound files. We can copy sounds from other Greenfoot projects, or download them from free sound libraries on the Internet. If you copy sounds from the Internet, pay attention to copyright notices: Not everything that is on the Internet is free—respect other people's copyright! The easiest option to obtain sound files is to record them ourselves.

To do this, we need a microphone (many laptops have microphones built in, and often computer headsets have microphones attached). If you do not have a microphone available right now, you may want to skip this section.

In Chapter 3, we have already briefly seen Greenfoot's in-built sound recorder. It allows us to record a sound, trim it to remove unwanted parts at the beginning and end, and save it.

Exercise 10.13 Use Greenfoot's sound recorder (available from the *Controls* menu) to record a new sound for your sample scenario. Make your actor play that new sound when clicked.

Exercise 10.14 Introduce a second kind of actor. Place at least one instance of this class into the world. Make this actor produce a different sound when clicked.

Exercise 10.15 Use a digital camera or webcam to take a picture of one or more friends of yours. Create actors representing these friends. Record your friends saying something, and make the actors speak these recordings when you click on them.

10.4 External sound recording and editing

Using Greenfoot's sound recorder is quick and easy, and in many cases it will be sufficient. However, if we want to get more professional, we may want to record specific sound effects that are hard to produce with this simple recorder. If we care about the exact details of the sound, separate sound recording software may be useful.

Many sound recording programs are available; several of them are free. We will use *Audacity*[1] here for the sample screenshots. Audacity is a good choice because it is powerful, runs on different operating systems, and is free and fairly easy to use. There are many other sound recording programs, however, so feel free to use one of your own choice.

---

[1] Audacity is available from http://audacity.sourceforge.net

Figure 10.1

A sound recording
and editing program
(Audacity)

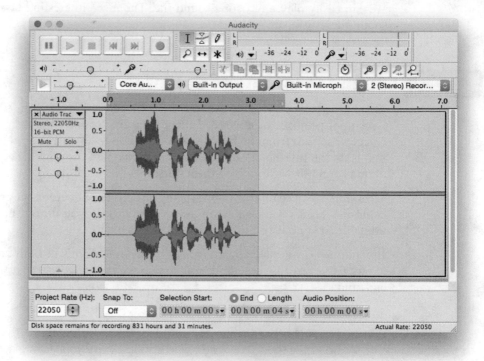

Figure 10.1 shows a typical interface of a sound recording program. You have controls for recording, playback, and so on, and a wave form display of the recorded sound (the blue graph).

Recording the sound is pretty straightforward—you can usually figure this out by playing with the program for a little while.

> **Exercise 10.16** Open a sound recording program and record a sound. Play it back. Does it come out as you expected? If not, delete it and try again.

As with Greenfoot's sound recorder, we will often have a delay or noise at the beginning and the end of our recording that we do not want. In Figure 10.1, for example, we can see a time of silence at the beginning and the end of the sound file (the straight horizontal lines on the left and right end of the graph). If we save the sound file as it is, the effect would be that the sound seems delayed when we play it (since the first part of the sound that gets played is half a second of silence).

As in the Greenfoot sound recorder, you should trim the sound file: cut off the unwanted bits at the beginning and end. However, in good sound editing programs you can do much more: you can cut segments from the middle, copy and paste to repeat a sound effect multiple times, reorder parts of the sound, and so on.

Exercise 10.17 Edit your sound file so that it includes only the exact sound you want. Remove any noise or silence at the beginning or end, or any parts in the middle that are not needed.

One of the most interesting capabilities of sound editing programs, however, is the use of *filters* or *effects*. Filters allow us to modify the sound or to generate entirely new sound elements. This way, many different sound effects can be generated.

By applying filters, such as amplification, echoes, reverting, speed changes, and others, to simple recorded sounds (such as speaking, clapping, whistling, shouting), we can create a wide variety of effects.

Exercise 10.18 If your sound program supports filters (sometimes called *effects*), apply some of them to your recorded sound. Select three of your favorite filters and describe, in writing, what they do. Give an example where you might use this effect.

Exercise 10.19 Produce the following sounds: a rabbit chewing a carrot; an explosion; a sound of two hard objects colliding; a "Game Over" sound where the player has lost the game; an "end of game" sound used when the player has won; a robot voice; and a "'jumping" sound (used when a game character jumps).

When the editing of the sound is complete, we are ready to save it to a file.

10.5 Sound file formats and file sizes

Sound files can be saved in many different formats and in different encodings, and this can get quite confusing very quickly.

Greenfoot can play sounds saved in WAV, AIFF, AU, and MP3 formats. Some of these formats, however, are what is known as "envelope formats"—they can contain different encodings, and Greenfoot can read only some of them. As a result, Greenfoot cannot, for example, play all WAV files.

Concept

Sounds can be saved in a variety of different **formats** and **encodings**. Not all programs can play all sound formats. For Greenfoot, we usually use the **WAV** format.

When you save your own recorded sounds, you should save them as a "signed 16 bit PCM WAV" file. This is the safest format to ensure playback. In many sound recording programs, this is achieved by using an "Export" function, rather than the standard "Save" function. Make sure to save in this format.

When you come across sound files that Greenfoot cannot play (maybe downloaded from the Internet), you can usually open them in your sound editing program and convert them to this format.

WAV is a good format to use for short sound effects. MP3, another popular format, is used mainly for music and other long recordings. It is a proprietary format (writing a program that produces it requires paying license fees), so many free sound editors do not support it. In Greenfoot, you can play MP3s (you could build your own MP3 player!), but it is not a useful format for saving our self-made sound effects.

When saving your sound file, you also have to make sure that your Greenfoot scenario can find it. To be accessible from your code, the sound file must be in the *sounds* folder inside your scenario folder. The Greenfoot sound recorder knows this, and saves files automatically to this location. When using an external sound editor, you have to ensure yourself that the file is stored in the right location.

Exercise 10.20 Save your recorded sound in an appropriate format for Greenfoot. Move the sound file into the *sounds* folder of your scenario. Modify the code of your `Actor` class so that it plays your sound when it is clicked.

Exercise 10.21 Modify your code so that it plays one sound effect when clicked with the left mouse button, and another sound effect when clicked with the right mouse button. To do this, you need to get information about the mouse click that tells you which button was pressed. Greenfoot has methods to achieve this—study the Greenfoot class documentation to find out how this can be done.

Exercise 10.22 Modify your code so that the actor, when it is clicked, plays a sound effect and moves to a new random location.

Concept

The **sample format, sample rate**, and **stereo/mono** setting of a sound recording determine file size and sound quality.

Sound files can quickly become very large. This is not a major problem as long as the scenario is only used locally, but if the scenario is exported, for instance, to the Greenfoot website, then the size can make a big difference. Sound and image files are usually the largest parts of a Greenfoot scenario, and the sound file sizes will affect the download time of a scenario.

To avoid overly large sound files we should pay attention to encoding details. When we record and save sounds we can make trade-offs between sound quality and file size. We can record and save the sound either in very high quality, leading to large files, or in lower quality, leading to smaller files. The settings we can vary are mainly:

- The sample format (usually 16-bit, 24-bit, or 32-bit).

- The sample rate, measured in Hertz (Hz), varying usually from around 8,000 Hz to 96,000 Hz.

- Stereo versus mono recording. (Stereo records two separate tracks and thus produces twice the amount of data.)

If you look carefully at Figure 10.1, you can see that the sound in that screenshot was recorded in 16 bit, 22,050 Hz, stereo.

Sometimes the default setting for sound recording programs are even higher (for example 32 bit, and a higher sample rate), and this is much higher quality than what is needed for simple sound effects. (We might want this quality for listening to music that we like, but we don't need it for a short *Bang!* sound effect.) In general, you should consider saving your sounds in lower quality, unless you feel you really need more quality.

Exercise 10.23 Search your sound recording program for settings for sample format, sample rate, and stereo/mono recording. In some programs you can convert existing sounds. In other programs you can specify these settings only for new recordings. Make a sound recording with different sample formats, with different sample rates, and in stereo and mono. Save these as different files and compare the file sizes. Make a table with file sizes for different settings. Which change has the largest benefit for the file size?

Exercise 10.24 Listen to the sounds produced in the previous exercise. Can you hear a difference? How much can you reduce the quality (and the file size) while still achieving acceptable quality?

10.6 More control: the GreenfootSound class

So far our interaction with sound was very simple: we played a sound file. This is sufficient for short sound effects, and the Greenfoot playSound method is an easy way to do this.

Sometimes, however, we need more control over sound. When we have background music, or if we want to create an MP3 player, we need the ability to start and stop sounds, to change the volume, and so forth. Greenfoot has a separate class to support this: the GreenfootSound class.

Exercise 10.25 Find the documentation for the GreenfootSound class in the Greenfoot class documentation. Study it. What is the range of accepted values for setting the volume?

Exercise 10.26 Modify your code so that it uses a GreenfootSound object for the sound. This sound object should be created in your actor's constructor, and stored in an instance variable. Then, when you click on the actor, it should play this sound.

Exercise 10.27 Modify your code again, so that it starts playing your sound effect in a loop when you click on your actor, and pauses the sound when you click again. You can then play and pause the sound repeatedly by clicking on the actor several times.

Some more exercises using the sound class are at the end of this chapter in the *Drill and practice* section.

10.7 Working with images

As discussed briefly in previous chapters (for example, when we produced the asteroids background in Chapter 9), managing images for actors and world backgrounds can be achieved in two different ways: We can use prepared images from files, or we can draw an image on the fly in our program.

We shall discuss both methods in a little more detail here.

10.8 Image files and file formats

There are various ways to acquire images for our scenarios. The easiest is, of course, to use images from the Greenfoot image library. These are presented automatically when we create new classes. There are also several good libraries of free icons and images available on the Internet. (Make sure, however, that the images you want to use are really meant for free public use—not everything is free or in the public domain just because it is on the Internet. Respect other people's copyright and license terms.)

The most interesting alternative, however, if we want to make our scenarios unique and give them their own atmosphere, is to make images ourselves.

There are several graphics programs available that we can use to produce images. *Photoshop* is maybe the best known commercial program, and is certainly a very good one to use if you happen to have it. However, there are also free and open source programs that provide similar functionality. *Gimp*[2] is an excellent free program with many sophisticated features, and it is worth installing. There are also many simpler paint programs that could be used.

Producing good looking graphics takes some time to learn, and cannot be discussed in detail in this book. Play and practice, and you will figure out many techniques and tricks. Here we shall concentrate on the technicalities of using the images.

One of the important questions is what file formats to use when saving images. As with sounds, there is a trade-off to be made between quality and file size. Image files have the potential to be very large (much larger than the code files in our scenarios), so they can easily dominate the overall download size of our project. Again, this is particularly important if we want to export our scenario to a web server, such as the Greenfoot website. Different image formats can lead to different file sizes by a factor of 10 or more, meaning that the scenario will download 10 times as fast (because it is only a tenth of the size) if we choose formats well.

---

[2] http://www.gimp.org

Concept

The **JPEG** image format compresses large images very well. This is often the best choice for backgrounds.

Greenfoot can read images in JPEG, PNG, GIF, BMP, and TIFF formats. Of these, JPEG and PNG are the two best formats for most uses.

JPEG images have the advantage that they compress very well. This means that they can be saved with very small file sizes. This is particularly true for full color images, such as photos and backgrounds (which is why many digital cameras use this format). When saving JPEG images, many graphics programs allow us to choose how much we want to compress the file. The more we compress, the smaller the file gets, but quality is also reduced. Gimp, for example, presents a "Quality" slider when we save an image in JPEG format. Reducing the quality creates smaller files. The loss in quality is most apparent if we have sharp edges with high contrast, such a written text or line drawings.

Concept

Pixels in images have a **transparency** value that determines whether we can see through them. Pixels may be partly transparent. If they are fully transparent, they are invisible.

Exercise 10.28 Create an image in your graphics program and save it as a JPEG file. Save it with at least four different quality settings. Then open the different files and view them side by side. Also compare the file sizes. Which quality setting is a good compromise between picture quality and file size for your image?

Exercise 10.29 In your graphics program, make a new background for your scenario that you created for the earlier sections of this chapter. Save it as a JPEG file. Use it in your scenario. Which size (height and width) should the image be? What happens if it is too big? What happens if it is too small?

Exercise 10.30 How do you think the JPEG algorithm manages to make files smaller? How could this work? Try to come up with a few theories and guesses as to how this could be done.

Exercise 10.31 How does JPEG actually compress files? Do some research on the Internet to find out and answer in writing.

The second image format that is very useful to us is PNG.

Concept

The **PNG** image format is often the best choice for actor images since it can handle transparency and compresses fairly well.

PNG images have the advantage that they can handle transparency very well. Any individual pixel can be partly or completely transparent. This allows us to create non-rectangular images. (As discussed in Chapter 9, all images are rectangular, but having transparent parts creates the appearance of arbitrary shapes.)

This ability to handle transparency, combined with good compression, makes PNG an ideal format for actor images. (JPEG images cannot have transparent pixels, so they cannot be used here, unless the actor happens to be rectangular. For backgrounds, this is generally not a problem, because we do not usually have transparency in backgrounds.)

There is rarely a need to use BMP, TIFF, or GIF images. BMP does not compress as well as other formats and does not support transparent pixels. TIFF images can preserve quality very well, but create larger file sizes. GIF is a proprietary format that has effectively been replaced by the better—and free—PNG format.

Exercise 10.32 Make two new images for your actor (the actor will switch between these two images). Save them in PNG format. Make one of these images the default image for your actor class.

Exercise 10.33 Modify your actor code so that it toggles between your two images every time the actor is clicked with the mouse.

Exercise 10.34 Modify your actor code again so that it displays the second actor image only while the mouse is pressed. In other words, the actor starts off with a default image; when the mouse is pressed on the actor, it displays a different image, and as soon as the mouse is released, it reverts to its original image.

10.9 Drawing images

The second method to obtain images for our actors and backgrounds is to draw them programmatically. We have seen examples of this in some of the scenarios in earlier chapters, for example when we painted the stars in the asteroids program.

Every pixel in an image is defined by two values: its color value and its transparency value (also called the *alpha value*).

The color value is again split into three components: the red, green, and blue component.[3] Colors represented this way are usually referred to as RGB colors.

This means that we can represent a pixel (with color and transparency) in four numbers. The order usually is as follows:

(R, G, B, A)

That is, the first three values define the red, green, and blue components (in this order), and the last is the alpha value.

In Java, all of these values are in the range [0...255] (zero to 255 inclusive). A color component value of 0 indicates no color in this component, while 255 is full strength. An alpha value of 0 is fully transparent (invisible), while 255 is opaque (solid).

Figure 10.2 shows a table of some of the possible colors, all with no transparency (alpha = 255). The table in Figure 10.2 was produced with the Greenfoot scenario *color-chart*, which is in the *chapter10* folder in the book scenarios.

Exercise 10.35 What do pixels look like which have a color/alpha value of (255, 0, 0, 255)? What about (0, 0, 255, 128)? And what is (255, 0, 255, 230)?

---

[3] This is just one possible model to represent color. There are others in use in computer graphics and in print. However, this is the one most commonly used in Java programming, so we will concentrate on this model here.

Figure 10.2
RGB color table

0,0,0	0,0,51	0,0,102	0,0,153	0,0,204	0,0,255
0,51,0	0,51,51	0,51,102	0,51,153	0,51,204	0,51,255
0,102,0	0,102,51	0,102,102	0,102,153	0,102,204	0,102,255
0,153,0	0,153,51	0,153,102	0,153,153	0,153,204	0,153,255
0,204,0	0,204,51	0,204,102	0,204,153	0,204,204	0,204,255
0,255,0	0,255,51	0,255,102	0,255,153	0,255,204	0,255,255
51,0,0	51,0,51	51,0,102	51,0,153	51,0,204	51,0,255
51,51,0	51,51,51	51,51,102	51,51,153	51,51,204	51,51,255
51,102,0	51,102,51	51,102,102	51,102,153	51,102,204	51,102,255
51,153,0	51,153,51	51,153,102	51,153,153	51,153,204	51,153,255
51,204,0	51,204,51	51,204,102	51,204,153	51,204,204	51,204,255
51,255,0	51,255,51	51,255,102	51,255,153	51,255,204	51,255,255
102,0,0	102,0,51	102,0,102	102,0,153	102,0,204	102,0,255
102,51,0	102,51,51	102,51,102	102,51,153	102,51,204	102,51,255
102,102,0	102,102,51	102,102,102	102,102,153	102,102,204	102,102,255
102,153,0	102,153,51	102,153,102	102,153,153	102,153,204	102,153,255
102,204,0	102,204,51	102,204,102	102,204,153	102,204,204	102,204,255
102,255,0	102,255,51	102,255,102	102,255,153	102,255,204	102,255,255
153,0,0	153,0,51	153,0,102	153,0,153	153,0,204	153,0,255
153,51,0	153,51,51	153,51,102	153,51,153	153,51,204	153,51,255
153,102,0	153,102,51	153,102,102	153,102,153	153,102,204	153,102,255
153,153,0	153,153,51	153,153,102	153,153,153	153,153,204	153,153,255
153,204,0	153,204,51	153,204,102	153,204,153	153,204,204	153,204,255
153,255,0	153,255,51	153,255,102	153,255,153	153,255,204	153,255,255
204,0,0	204,0,51	204,0,102	204,0,153	204,0,204	204,0,255
204,51,0	204,51,51	204,51,102	204,51,153	204,51,204	204,51,255
204,102,0	204,102,51	204,102,102	204,102,153	204,102,204	204,102,255
204,153,0	204,153,51	204,153,102	204,153,153	204,153,204	204,153,255
204,204,0	204,204,51	204,204,102	204,204,153	204,204,204	204,204,255
204,255,0	204,255,51	204,255,102	204,255,153	204,255,204	204,255,255
255,0,0	255,0,51	255,0,102	255,0,153	255,0,204	255,0,255
255,51,0	255,51,51	255,51,102	255,51,153	255,51,204	255,51,255
255,102,0	255,102,51	255,102,102	255,102,153	255,102,204	255,102,255
255,153,0	255,153,51	255,153,102	255,153,153	255,153,204	255,153,255
255,204,0	255,204,51	255,204,102	255,204,153	255,204,204	255,204,255
255,255,0	255,255,51	255,255,102	255,255,153	255,255,204	255,255,255

In Greenfoot, colors are represented by objects of the `Color` class from the `java.awt` package. After importing that class, we can create color objects either with just RGB values:

```
Color mycol = new Color (255, 12, 34);
```

or with RGB values and an alpha value:

```
Color mycol = new Color (255, 12, 34, 128);
```

If we do not specify an alpha value, the color will be fully opaque.

> **Exercise 10.36** Create a new Greenfoot scenario called *color-test*. In it, create a world with a background that displays a pattern. Create an **Actor** subclass called **ColorPatch**. Program the **ColorPatch** class so that it generates a new **GreenfootImage** of a fixed size, filled with a fixed color. Use this image as the actor's image. Experiment with different color and alpha values.
>
> **Exercise 10.37** Modify your code so that the color patch, when created, gets an image of a random size filled with a random color, and random transparency.
>
> **Exercise 10.38** Modify your code again so that the image is not filled, but instead has 100 small colored dots painted into it, at random locations within the actor's image.

10.10 Combining image files and dynamic drawing

Some of the most interesting visual effects are achieved when we combine static images from files with dynamic changes made by our program. We can, for example, start with a static image file, and then paint onto it with different colors, or scale it up or down, or let it fade by changing its transparency.

To try this out, we shall create a smoke effect. In our next scenario, we make a ball move across the screen, leaving a trail of smoke behind (see Figure 10.3).

> **Exercise 10.39** Create a new scenario called *smoke*. Make a nice looking, fairly neutral background image for it.
>
> **Exercise 10.40** Create a ball that moves across the screen at constant speed. When it hits the edge of the screen, it bounces off. (The screen is, in effect, a box, and the ball bounces within it.)

Figure 10.3

The smoke trail effect

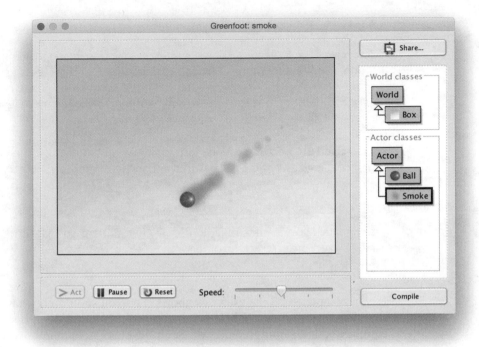

Figure 10.4

An image of a puff
of smoke

Now we will work on the smoke effect. First, create an image showing a puff of smoke
(Figure 10.4).

Note that the checkered background is not part of the image—it is shown here only to
demonstrate that the smoke puff image is semitransparent (we can see the background
behind it).

Your smoke does not have to be green—you can make it any color you like—but it
should be transparent. You can achieve this in a good graphics program by simply
drawing a dot with a large, soft, semitransparent paint brush. If you have trouble producing this image, you can use the prepared image file *smoke.png* from the *chapter10*
folder in the book scenarios.

Exercise 10.41 Create the smoke image as described above.

Exercise 10.42 Create a **Smoke** actor class in your scenario. When inserted into the world, a **Smoke** actor should fairly quickly fade away. That is, in every act cycle, the image of the actor should become smaller and more transparent. (The `GreenfootImage` class has methods to adjust the size and transparency.) When they are fully transparent or very small, they should remove themselves from the world.

Exercise 10.43 Modify your ball so that it leaves puffs of smoke behind. Producing a puff of smoke every time the ball moves may be a little too much: try creating a new smoke puff only in every second step of the ball. Test.

Exercise 10.44 Modify your smoke so that it does not always fade at exactly the same rate. Make the rate of fading somewhat random, so that some puffs of smoke fade away more quickly than others.

If you completed all the exercises above, then you should now have a good looking smoke trail behind your ball. If you had trouble with these exercises, or if you want to compare your solution to ours, you can have a look at the *smoke* scenario in the book projects. This implements the task described here.

Summary

Being able to produce sounds and images is a very valuable skill for producing good looking games, simulations, and other graphical applications. Knowing about sound and image file formats is important to make good choices about trade-offs between file size and quality.

Sounds can be recorded directly in Greenfoot, or recorded and edited with a variety of sound recording programs. Various parameters determine the sound quality and file size. For Greenfoot scenarios, we usually use WAV format with fairly low quality.

Images can also be saved in a variety of different formats. Different formats vary in how well they compress files, how well they preserve image quality, and how they handle transparency. JPEG and PNG are the formats most often used for Greenfoot scenarios.

By combining images from a file with dynamic image operations, such as scaling and transparency changes, we can achieve attractive visual effects in our scenarios.

Concept summary

- We can use the **mouseClicked** method to check whether the user clicked on a given object.

- Sounds can be saved in a variety of different **formats** and **encodings**. Not all programs can play all sound formats. For Greenfoot, we usually use **WAV** format.

- The **sample format**, **sample rate**, and **stereo/mono** setting of a sound recording determine file size and sound quality.

- The **JPEG** image format compresses large images very well. This is often the best choice for backgrounds.

- Pixels in images have a **transparency** value that determines whether we can see through them. Pixels may be partly transparent. If they are fully transparent, they are invisible.

- The **PNG** image format is often the best choice for actor images since it can handle transparency and compresses fairly well.

Drill and practice

Below are some exercises to practice your skills with sound and image manipulation.

Playing music

Exercise 10.45 Make a new scenario for a (very simple) MP3 player. Create an actor for a start button. Place an MP3 file into the scenario's sound folder. Program it so that clicking the button starts playing the MP3 file. Clicking it while it is playing stops playing the file.

Exercise 10.46 Make sure the button image changes: It should be the typical "play" triangle while the sound is not playing, and change to the usual "pause" symbol (double vertical bars) when it is playing.

Exercise 10.47 Add a stop button. This button should stop the sound. When you then press play again, the sound starts from the beginning (not from the point where it was stopped). Make sure the play button's image changes appropriately when the sound is stopped.

Exercise 10.48 Add two buttons to change the volume up and down.

Exercise 10.49 Add a display that shows the current volume.

Exercise 10.50 Add three buttons to select three different songs (which you must place in your sounds folder).

Manipulating images

Exercise 10.51 Make a copy of your *fatcat* scenario from Chapter 2 and open it. Change the constructor of **MyCat** so that the cat has a random size (with the current full size the maximum). Do this by scaling down the cat's image by a random amount in its constructor. Test by placing a few cats into the world.

Exercise 10.52 Rewrite the act method so that the cat slowly fades away when you run the scenario (like the Cheshire Cat in *Alice In Wonderland*).

Exercise 10.53 Change your cat so that it only starts fading away after you click on it.

For the following exercises, open the scenario *path-follower* from the *chapter10* folder. This scenario shows a creature (a *Greep*) that should follow a path. It does this by looking at the color of the ground: If the ground is brownish, it is a path, otherwise it is not.

At the moment, this scenario is incomplete. (Try it out!) Most of the code has been implemented, but the last few bits dealing with color are missing. You will now write them.

We will create the path-following behavior by getting the color from the world background at the position of each of the Greep's eyes. If we see green with the left eye, we turn a little to the right, and if we see green with the right eye, we turn left. This way, we will stay on the path.

There are three methods that have code missing; all are in the Greep class. They are `leftEyeColor`, `rightEyeColor` and `isPath`. Everything else is complete.

Let us start with the `leftEyeColor` method. This method should return the color of the world background at the position of the left eye (as an object of type `Color`).

Find the method. You will see that it already finds the coordinates of the left eye. They are stored in an object of class `Point`, and we can get the x- and y-coordinates of the eye by calling methods of that `Point` object.

You need to do the following:

- Get the world.
- From the world, get the world's background image.
- From the point object, get the eye's x- and y-coordinates.
- Get the color from the background image at the location of the eye.
- Return this color.

You may need to refer to the documentation of `World` and `GreenfootImage` to find out the names of the methods to do these tasks.

Reading color

Exercise 10.54 Complete the code of the `leftEyeColor` method so that it returns the color under the left eye.

Exercise 10.55 Complete the code of the `rightEyeColor` method so that it returns the color under the right eye.

Exercise 10.56 Complete the code of the `isPath` method so that it returns true only if the given color is that of the path, not grass. You can do this by checking the red component of the color: If the component value for red is greater than 160, you can assume that we are looking at path, not at grass. Refer to the documentation of class Color to find out how to retrieve the color's red component.

topics: simulations

concepts: emergent behavior, experimentation

In this chapter, we will discuss one type of software application in a little more detail: simulations.

Simulations are fascinating examples of computing because they are highly experimental and potentially allow us to predict the future. Many types of simulations can be (and have been) developed for computers: traffic simulations, weather forecasting systems, economics simulations (simulations of stock markets), simulations of chemical reactions, nuclear explosions, environmental simulations, and many more.

We have seen one simple simulation in Chapter 8, in which we simulated part of a solar system. That simulation was a little too simplistic to accurately forecast trajectories of real planets, but there are some aspects of astrophysics which that simulation may help us understand.

In general, simulations may serve two different purposes: they can be used to study and understand the system they are simulating, or they can be used for forecasting.

In the first case, the modeling of a system (such as the modeling of the stars and planets) may help us understand some aspects of how it behaves. In the second case, if we have an accurate simulation, we can play through "what if" scenarios. For example, we might have a traffic simulation for a city, and we observe that every morning a traffic jam develops at a certain intersection in the real city. How can we improve the situation? Should we build a new roundabout? Or change the traffic light signal patterns? Or perhaps we should build a bypass?

The effects of any of these interventions are often hard to predict. We cannot try out all these options in real life to see which is best, since that would be too disruptive and expensive. But we can simulate them. In our traffic simulation, we can try out each option and see how it improves traffic.

Concept

A **simulation** is a computer program that simulates some phenomena from the real world. If simulations are accurate enough, we can learn interesting things about the real world from observing them.

If the simulation is accurate, then the result we observe in the simulation will also be true in real life. But this is a big "if": Developing a simulation that is accurate enough is not easy, and it is a lot of work. But for many systems, it is possible to a useful degree.

Weather forecasting simulations are now accurate enough that a one-day forecast is fairly reliable. A seven-day forecast, however, is about as good as rolling dice: the simulations are just not good enough.

When we use simulations, it is important to be aware of the limitations: Firstly, simulations always have a degree of inaccuracy because we are not modeling the behaviors of the actors completely realistically, and because we may not know the exact state of the starting system.

In addition, simulations necessarily model only part of reality, and we must be aware that parts outside of our simulation might actually be relevant.

In the example of our traffic jam, for instance, maybe the best solution is neither of the options mentioned above, but to provide better public transport or bicycle lanes to get some cars off the road. If our simulation does not include that aspect, we would never find out just by using the simulation, no matter how accurate it is.

Despite these limitations, however, even very simple simulations are fascinating to play with, and good simulations are incredibly useful. They are so useful, in fact, that almost all of the world's fastest computers run simulations most, or at least a substantial part, of their time.

Side note: Supercomputers

A list of the fastest supercomputers in the world is regularly published on the Internet at *http://www.top500.org*. Most of these are described there in some detail, and for many of them, the list includes links to websites that describe their purpose and the kind of work they are used for.

Reading through this material, you can see that many are run by large research institutions or the military and that almost all are used to run simulations, often physics simulations. The military use these, for example, to test nuclear explosions in simulations, and research institutions conduct many different science experiments this way.

Simulations also have a special place in the history of object-oriented programming: Object orientation was invented explicitly to run simulations.

The very first object-oriented programming language, named *Simula*, was designed in the 1960s by Kristen Nygaard and Ole-Johan Dahl at the Norwegian Computer Center in Oslo. As the name suggests, its purpose was to build simulations. All object-oriented programming languages today can be traced back to that language. Dahl and Nygaard received the 2001 Turing Award—computer science's equivalent of the Nobel Prize—for this work.

Enough introduction—let's get our hands on the keyboard again and try out some things.

In this chapter, we will look at one simulation fairly briefly and then work on writing another one in more detail. We have now reached a stage where more work will be up to you to complete: We will discuss the outline of the tasks to implement, but you will have to work out the details yourself.

11.1 Foxes and rabbits

The first simulation we investigate is called *foxes-and-rabbits* (Figure 11.1). It is a typical example of a class of simulations called *predator-prey-simulations*—a type of simulation in which one creature chases (and eats) another. In our case, the predator is a fox and the prey is a rabbit.

The idea here is as follows: The scenario shows a field that contains populations of foxes and rabbits. Foxes are represented by blue squares, and rabbits are shown as yellow squares.

Both species have fairly simple behavior: Rabbits move around and—if they are old enough—may produce offspring. There is a set probability at each act step for rabbits to reproduce. There are two ways in which rabbits may die: They may die of old age or they may be eaten by a fox.

Foxes move and breed in a manner similar to rabbits (although they breed less frequently and have fewer young ones). One additional thing, however, that they do

Figure 11.1

The foxes-and-rabbits simulation

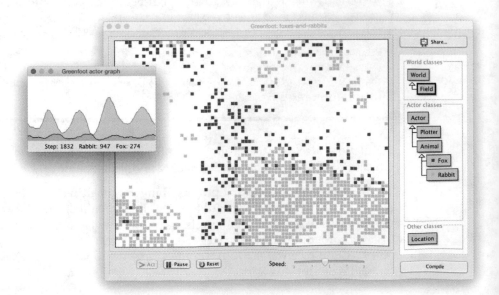

is hunt. If they are hungry and they see a rabbit sitting next to them, they will move to eat the rabbit.

Foxes can also die in two different ways: They can die of old age and they can starve. If they do not find a rabbit to eat for some time, they will die. (Rabbits are assumed to always find sufficient amounts of food.)

> **Exercise 11.1** Open the *foxes-and-rabbits* scenario. Run it. Explain the patterns of populations and movement you see emerging in the field.

> **Exercise 11.2** You will notice that this scenario shows a second small window with a population graph. One curve shows the number of foxes, the other the number of rabbits. Explain the shape of these graphs.

As we can see, the simulation is highly simplistic in many ways: Animals do not have to meet mates to reproduce (they can do that all on their own), food sources for rabbits are not included in the simulation, other factors of death (such as diseases) are ignored, and so on. However, the parameters that we do simulate are already fairly interesting, and we can do some experiments with them.

> **Exercise 11.3** Are the current populations stable? That is, do they always continue to run without one of the species dying out? If species become extinct, what is the average time they survive?

Does the size of the field matter? For example, imagine we have a national park with an endangered species. And someone wants to build a freeway through the middle of it that the animals cannot cross, essentially dividing the park into two parks of half the size each. The proponents of the freeway might argue that this does not matter because the total size of parkland is about the same as before. The park authority might argue that this is bad because it halves the size of each park. Who is right? Does the size of a park matter? Do some experiments.

> **Exercise 11.4** The `Field` class has definitions of constants toward the top of its source code for its width and height. Modify these constants to change the size of the field. Does the size of the field affect the stability of the populations? Do species die out more easily if the field is smaller or larger? Or does it make no difference? Try with very small and larger fields.

Other parameters with which we can experiment are defined in constants at the top of the `Rabbit` and `Fox` classes. Rabbits have definitions for their maximum age, the age from which they can breed, the frequency of breeding (defined as a probability for each step), and the maximum size of their litter when they do breed. Foxes have the same parameters and an additional one: the nutritional value of a rabbit when it is eaten (expressed as the number of steps that the fox can survive after eating the rabbit). The food level of a fox decreases by one in every step and increases when eating a rabbit. If it reaches zero, the fox dies.

Exercise 11.5 Choose a field size in which the populations are almost stable but occasionally die out. Then make changes to the **Rabbit** parameters to try to increase the chances of the populations' survival. Can you find settings that make the populations more stable? Do some settings make them less stable? Are the observed effects as you expected, or did some differ from your expectations?

Exercise 11.6 When the fox population is in danger of becoming extinct occasionally, we could speculate that we could improve the chances of foxes' survival by increasing the food value of rabbits. If foxes can live longer on eating a single rabbit, they should starve less often. Investigate this hypothesis. Double the amount of the **RABBIT_FOOD_VALUE** constant and test the scenario. Does the fox population survive longer? Explain the result.

Exercise 11.7 Make other changes to the **Fox** parameters. Can you make the populations more stable?

The exercises show that we can experiment with this simulation by changing some parameters and observing their effects. In this chapter, however, we shall not be content with experimenting with an existing simulation; we also want to develop our own. We will do that in the next section with a different scenario: *ants*.

11.2 Ants

The *ants* scenario (Figure 11.2) simulates the food collecting behavior of ant colonies. Or, to be more precise, we would like it to simulate this behavior, but it does not do it yet. We will develop it to do so. In its current state, the scenario has been prepared to some extent: The graphics exist and some of the implementation has been completed. The main functionality, however, is missing, and we will work on completing it.

Exercise 11.8 Open the scenario called *ants* from the *chapter11* folder of the book scenarios. Create an ant hill in the world and run the scenario. What do you observe?

Exercise 11.9 Examine the source code of the **Ant** class. What does it currently do?

Exercise 11.10 **Ant** is a subclass of class **Creature**. What functionality does a creature have?

Exercise 11.11 Examine the source code of class **AntHill**. What does this class do? How many ants are in an ant hill?

Figure 11.2
The ants simulation

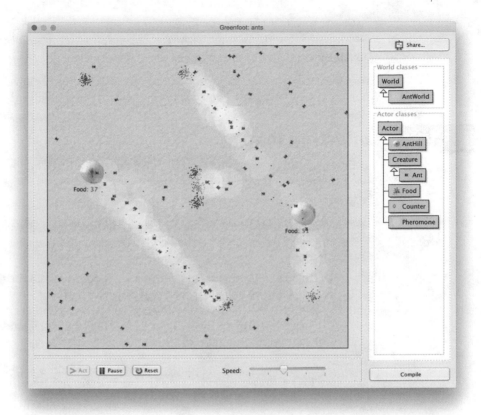

The first thing we notice is that the ants do not move. They are created in the middle of the ant hill, but since they do not move, after a short while they will all sit there on top of each other. So, the first thing for us to do is to make ants move.

> **Exercise 11.12** In the **Ant**'s **act** method, add a line of code to make the ant move. Do not use the **Actor**'s move method, but inherited methods from class **Creature**. Consult the documentation of class **Creature** to find out about the methods to use.

We will now go step by step through a series of improvements to this scenario:

- We will introduce some food to the scenario, so that the ants have something to collect.

- We will improve the ants, so that they can find the food and carry some of it home.

- Next we will add a **Pheromone** class. Pheromones are chemical substances that some animals produce to leave messages for other animals of their species.

■ We will improve the ants to make use of pheromones. They will leave drops of pheromones on the ground when they have found food, and other ants can then smell these pheromones and adjust where they are going.

These steps together roughly simulate the food collecting behavior of ant colonies. When complete, we can do some experiments with the simulation.

11.3 Collecting food

Our first task is to create some food in our scenario and to let ants collect it and carry it back to the ant hill.

> **Exercise 11.13** Create a new class called **Food**. The class does not need a fixed image. We will draw the image from within the class.

Each object of class **Food** represents a pile of food crumbs. Our plan is to create a new, dynamically drawn image for the **Food** object and draw a small dot on it for every crumb in the pile. A pile may start with, say, 100 crumbs, and every time an ant finds the pile, it takes a few crumbs away. That means that the image must be redrawn with fewer crumbs every time an ant takes some food.

> **Exercise 11.14** In class **Food**, create a field for the number of crumbs currently in the pile. Initialize it to 100.

> **Exercise 11.15** Create a new private method called **updateImage**, which creates an image of a fixed size and draws a dot on it at a random location for each crumb currently in the pile. Choose a size for the image of the pile that you think looks good. Call this method from the constructor.

If you completed the exercise above, and you placed food crumbs at a random location within the **Food** image (using the **Greenfoot.getRandomNumber** method to obtain the coordinates), then you will have noticed that the pile of crumbs had a somewhat squarish shape (Figure 11.3a). This is because the image itself is square, and the crumbs are evenly distributed over the image.

Figure 11.3

Placement of food crumbs with different randomizer algorithms

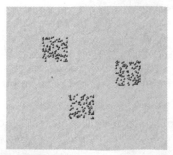
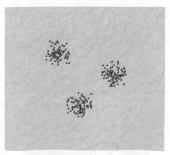

a) crumbs with even distribution   b) crumbs with Gaussian distribution

If we want to change this to look more like a pile (with most crumbs toward the middle, and other crumbs in a rough circle-shape around it, Figure 11.3b), then we can use another random number method to place the crumbs differently. We shall do this with Exercises 11.16 and 11.17. Note that these are more advanced exercises and they are purely cosmetic: they merely change the look of the food pile and none of its functionality, so they could safely be skipped.

Exercise 11.16 Consult the API documentation for the standard Java class library. Find the documentation for class `Random` from the `java.util` package. Objects of this class are *random number generators* that are more flexible than Greenfoot's `getRandomNumber` method. The method of interest to us is the one that returns random numbers in a Gaussian distribution (also called a "normal distribution"). What is the method's name, and what does it do?

Exercise 11.17 In your **Food** class, change your placement of food crumbs in the image to make use of the Gaussian distribution of random numbers. For this, you have to use a `java.util.Random` object to create the random numbers, instead of `Greenfoot.getRandomNumber`.

Side note: Random distributions

If we need random behavior in our programs, it is sometimes important to think about what kind of random distribution we need. Many random functions, such as the `Greenfoot.getRandomNumber` method, produce a *uniform distribution*. In this, the chance of every possible result occurring is the same. The Gaussian random number function gives us a *normal distribution*. This is one in which the average results are more likely to occur, and more extreme results are rarer.

If we, for example, program a dice game, we need a uniform distribution. Each side of the die is evenly likely to come up. On the other hand, if we model the speed of cars in a traffic simulation, a normal distribution would be better. Most cars are driving somewhere close to the average speed, and only few cars are very slow or very fast.

Next we need to add functionality to remove some crumbs from the food pile, so that ants can take some food.

Exercise 11.18 Add a public method to class **Food** that removes a few crumbs from the pile. Make sure that the image is redrawn with the correct number of remaining crumbs. When the crumbs are all gone, the **Food** object should remove itself from the world. Test this method interactively.

Now that we have a pile of food available in our scenario, we can make our ants collect it. Ants will now switch between two different behaviors:

- If they are not carrying food, they search for food.

- If they are currently carrying food, they walk toward home.

Ants switch between these two behaviors when they reach either a food pile or the home ant hill. If they are searching for food, and they run into a food pile, they pick up some food and switch from the first to the second behavior. If they then reach the ant hill, they drop the food there and switch back to the first behavior pattern.

We shall now implement this in our `Ant` class. Written in pseudo code, the `act` method might look somewhat like this:

```
if (carrying food) {
    walk towards home;
    check whether we are home;
}
else {
    search for food;
}
```

We implement this now one step at a time.

Exercise 11.19 In the `Ant` class, implement a `searchForFood` method. This method should initially just do a random walk and check whether we have run into a food pile. If we find a food pile, stop execution. (This is just to test whether we have correctly detected the food.)

Exercise 11.20 Add functionality to pick up some food when we find a food pile (instead of stopping execution). We need to remove some crumbs from the food pile (we should already have a method for this), note that we are now carrying food (we probably need a field for this), and change the ant's image. There is already an image prepared in the scenario, named *ant-with-food.png*, that you can use.

Exercise 11.21 Ensure that the ant walks toward home when carrying food.

Exercise 11.22 Implement a method that checks whether an ant has reached the home hill. If it has, it should drop its food. Dropping the food consists of noting that it is not carrying food anymore (including changing the image back) and calling the `AntHill`'s `countFood` method to record that it has collected this food crumb.

Concept

Using **short methods** with a specific purpose leads to better **code quality**.

Pay attention to the quality of your code: Use short methods with distinct purposes and make sure to comment your methods well. Do not write too much code into a single method.

You can find an implementation of the functionality discussed so far in the scenario *ants-2*. After completing your implementation (or when you get stuck), you might like to compare your solution with ours.

11.4 Setting up the world

Before we go on to add pheromones to our scenario, let us first add some initialization code that creates some ant hills and food for us automatically, so that we do not have to repeat this manually every time we wish to test.

> **Exercise 11.23** Add code to class `AntWorld`, so that it automatically creates two ant hills and a few piles of food in the world. You can do that by writing the code manually, or by using the *Save The World* function in Greenfoot's interface.

11.5 Adding pheromones

Now that we have a good start setup, we are ready to add pheromones. Each pheromone object is a small drop of a chemical substance that the ants leave on the ground. This drop will evaporate fairly quickly and then disappear.

Ants drop pheromones while they are walking back home from a food source. When other ants smell the drop of pheromone, they can then turn away from their home hill and walk in the direction toward the food.

> **Exercise 11.24** Create a class `Pheromone`. This class does not need an image—we shall draw the image programmatically.
>
> **Exercise 11.25** Implement an `updateImage` method in the `Pheromone` class. Initially, this method should create an image with a white circle drawn onto it and set this as the actor's image. The white circle should be partly transparent. Call this method from the constructor.
>
> **Exercise 11.26** Give the pheromones an *intensity* attribute. (That is, add an `intensity` field.) The intensity of a pheromone object should start out at a defined maximum intensity and decrease in every act cycle. When the intensity reaches zero, remove the pheromone object from the world. A drop of pheromone should evaporate in about 180 act cycles.
>
> **Exercise 11.27** Modify your `updateImage` method, so that it makes use of the pheromone's intensity. As the intensity decreases, the white circle representing it on screen should become smaller and more transparent. Make sure `updateImage` is called from the `act` method so that we see the image change on screen.
>
> **Exercise 11.28** Test your pheromones by placing them into the world manually and running your simulation.

We now have a `Pheromone` class available that our ants can use. Now we only have to get the ants to use it. The first half of using the pheromone is placing it into the world. The second half is noticing it and changing direction as a result. Let us do the first half first.

Exercise 11.29 Add a method to your ant that places a drop of pheromone into the world. Call this method repeatedly while the ant is walking home.

If, in the previous exercise, you placed a drop at every act cycle, you will notice that this places too much pheromone into the world. Ants cannot produce unlimited amounts; after placing a drop, they need some time to regenerate more pheromone.

Exercise 11.30 Modify the ant so that it can leave a drop of pheromone at most every 18 steps. To achieve this, you will need a field that stores the current pheromone level of an ant. When the ant places a pheromone drop, the pheromone level (remaining pheromones in the ant's body) goes down to zero, and then it slowly rises again until the ant is ready to leave another drop.

Figure 11.4 shows a trail of pheromones left by our ant at this point.[1] The drops are spaced out (the ant needs some time to regenerate pheromones), and the older pheromone drops are partly evaporated—they are smaller and more transparent.

Figure 11.4

An ant leaving a trail of pheromones

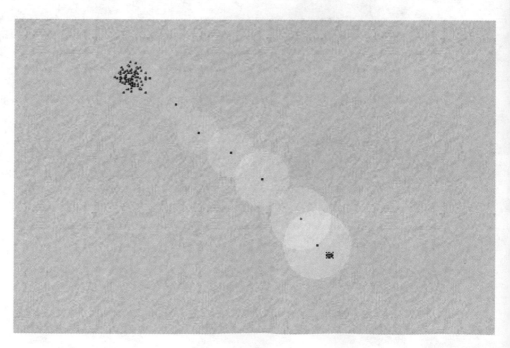

---

[1] If you look closely, you will notice that I have modified my pheromone image to have a small dark dot in the middle. This is so that pheromones can be seen better even when they are quite transparent.

The final thing to add is for ants to smell the pheromones, and change their direction of movement when they do.

If an ant smells a drop of pheromone, it should walk away from its home hill for some limited time. If it does not find food or smell a new drop of pheromone after some time, then it should revert to random walking. Our algorithm for searching for food might look something like this:

```
if (we recently found a drop of pheromone) {
    walk away from home;
}
else if (we smell pheromone now) {
    walk towards the center of the pheromone drop;
    if (we are at the pheromone drop center) {
        note that we found pheromone;
    }
}
else {
    walk randomly;
}
check for food;
```

When implementing this in your own scenario, remember to create a separate method for each distinct subtask. That way, your code will remain well structured, easy to understand, and easy to modify.

> **Exercise 11.31** Implement the functionality discussed above in your own scenario: When ants smell pheromones, they walk away from their home hill for the next 30 steps, before reverting to their default behavior.

If you completed this exercise, then your ant simulation is more or less complete (as much as any software application is ever complete). If you run your scenario now, you should see ants forming paths to the food sources.

11.6   Path forming

One interesting aspect of this scenario is that there is no code anywhere in the project that talks about forming paths. The behavior of the individual ants is quite simple: "If you have food, go home; if you smell pheromones, go away; otherwise go anywhere." However, together, the ants display some fairly sophisticated behavior: They form stable paths, refreshing the pheromones as they evaporate, and efficiently transport food back to their ant hill.

This is known as *emergent behavior*. It is behavior that is not programmed into any individual actor, but system behavior that emerges from the interactions of many (fairly simple) actors.

Most complex systems display some sort of emergent system behavior, whether they are traffic systems in cities, networks of computers, or crowds of people. Predicting these effects is very difficult, and computer simulations can help in understanding such systems.

Exercise 11.32 How realistic is our simulation of the use of pheromones by ants? Do some research into the actual use of pheromones by ant colonies and write down which aspects of our simulation are realistic, and where we have made simplifications.

Exercise 11.33 Assume pollution has introduced a toxic substance into the ants' environment. The effect is that their production of pheromones is reduced to a quarter of the previous amount. (The time between leaving drops of pheromones is four times as long.) Will they still be able to form paths? Test.

Exercise 11.34 Assume another pollutant has decreased the ants' ability to remember that they recently smelled a pheromone to a third. Instead of 30 steps, they can only remember the pheromone for 10 steps. What is the effect of this on their behavior?

There are many more experiments you can do. The most obvious is to try out different placements of ant hills and food sources and different values for the attributes that determine the ants' behavior.

The scenario *ants-3* in the *chapter11* folder shows an implementation of the tasks discussed above. It includes three different setup methods in the world class that can be called interactively from the world's pop-up menu.

Summary

In this chapter, we have seen two examples of simulations. This served two purposes. Firstly, this was a chance to practice many of the programming techniques we have discussed in earlier chapters and we had to use most of the Java constructs previously introduced. Secondly, simulations are an interesting kind of application to experiment with. Many simulations are used in real life for many purposes, such as weather forecasting, traffic planning, environmental impact studies, physics research, and many more.

If you managed to solve all the exercises in this chapter, then you have understood a great deal of what this book tried to teach you, and you are competent at basic programming.

Concept summary

■ A **simulation** is a computer program that simulates some phenomena from the real world. If simulations are accurate enough, we can learn interesting things about the real world from observing them.

■ Using **short methods** with a specific purpose leads to better **code quality**.

■ Simulations of systems often display **emergent behavior**. This is behavior not programmed into single actors, but emerging as a result of the sum of all behaviors.

CHAPTER

12

Greenfoot and the Kinect

topics: programming with the Microsoft Kinect

concepts: body tracking

We have learned to use many different and useful programming constructs by now, and now we are ready to apply them to another context. In this chapter, we will not introduce new programming concepts or Java constructs, but instead use our programming skills to play with an exciting and interesting toy: the Microsoft Kinect.

The Microsoft Kinect is a sensor board that includes a color camera, an infrared projector, and an infrared camera (Figure 12.1). The infrared projection and camera enable it to sense depth of the image in front of it, so it can "see" in three dimensions.

To do the exercises in this chapter, you need to have a Microsoft Kinect available. If you do not own one, you can safely skip this chapter. If you consider buying a Kinect for use with Greenfoot, make sure to read the notes on *Purchasing a Kinect* on the Greenfoot website.[1] Not all models of the Kinect work with Greenfoot.

Figure 12.1

The Microsoft
Kinect[2]

---

[1] See http://www.greenfoot.org/doc/kinect#purchase for notes on which model of the Microsoft Kinect to purchase for use with Greenfoot.

[2] Image source: Official Windows Magazine/Getty Images

In this chapter, we shall look at a sequence of scenarios that make use of the Kinect. We will first study some ready-made scenarios to see how things work, and then write some code of our own.

12.1 What the Kinect can do

The Kinect can detect people and their movement in front of its camera. Through Greenfoot and the Kinect, we can get information about the number of people in front of it, their position, and their body movements. This allows us to write programs that are controlled by moving our body in front of our computers.

Camera image

The first and most simple thing the Kinect does is give us an image from its camera. This is just like any other normal webcam image, and we can use this image in Greenfoot.

Depth image

In addition to the normal color image, we can get depth information. "Depth" is the distance from the camera of any point in front of it. Figure 12.2 shows the depth as a gray-scale image: the lightness of each pixel shows its distance from the camera.

Figure 12.2

The depth image

Body outlines

The Kinect can recognize people in its view, and reasonably reliably determine their outline in the camera image (Figure 12.3). It can distinguish between different people and give us the information about the location of a human body separately for every person it can see.

Skeleton tracking

The most useful thing the Kinect can do is *skeleton tracking*: It can identify the location, in all three dimensions, of various points of our body (Figure 12.4). It can give us the location of our hands, shoulders, feet, hips, head, and so on. This makes it very easy to write programs that are controlled by body movements. We can, for example, write a scenario where something happens when we touch a Greenfoot actor with our right hand or when our left foot is raised above our right knee. It does not need much imagination to come up with ideas how we can use this input to write interesting scenarios that are fun to play with.

Figure 12.3
Recognizing body outlines

Figure 12.4
Skeleton tracking

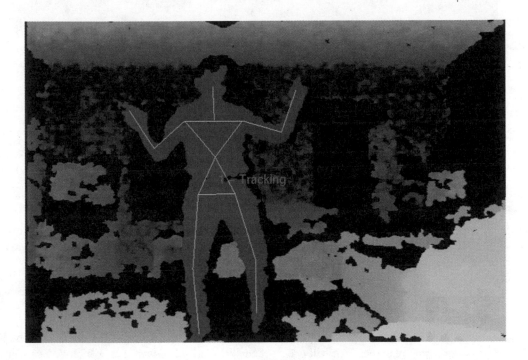

12.2 Installing the software

Before you can use the Microsoft Kinect with Greenfoot, you have to install some driver software. The driver software manages the communication with the hardware and provides a software interface to control the device.

When Greenfoot Kinect scenarios are running, we need the *Greenfoot Kinect Server* to run in the background to facilitate the communication between our Greenfoot scenario and the Kinect hardware. The Greenfoot Kinect Server, in turn, uses a library called *OpenNI*. Figure 12.5 shows the levels of communication between your Kinect scenario and the Kinect hardware.

Detailed installation instructions for these software components are on the Greenfoot website at http://www.greenfoot.org/doc/kinect.

Instructions are available for Windows, Linux (Ubuntu), and Mac OS X. Follow these instructions carefully before you start working with the following examples.

Running the Greenfoot Kinect server

When we want to run our Greenfoot Kinect scenarios, we first have to start the Greenfoot Kinect Server. It will run continuously in the background, and we have to keep it running as long as we are working with Greenfoot and the Kinect.

Figure 12.5
Layers of communication between Greenfoot and the Kinect

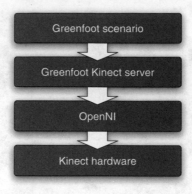

The installation instructions mentioned above provide details about how to start this server. (If you are running it from a terminal, you will see a lot of warning messages printed. Do not worry about this—it is normal.)

12.3 Getting started

To get started, we will first look at a very simple example: displaying the camera image on screen. We will use a scenario called *simple-camera*, which you can find in the book scenarios.

> **Exercise 12.1** Connect your Kinect to your computer. Start your Greenfoot Kinect Server. Then start Greenfoot and open the *simple-camera* example. Run it.

If your installation has worked, you should now see the image from the Kinect's camera in your world.

In the class diagram in the scenario, you see a number of classes. The `KinectWorld`, `Joint`, `KinectClient`, `Point3D`, and `UserData` classes are part of the Greenfoot Kinect infrastructure—they will always be present in scenarios using the Kinect. The only class specific to this scenario, holding our user code, is `MyWorld`.

Before trying our own code, let us have a quick look at the standard Greenfoot Kinect classes.

KinectWorld

This class should be used as the superclass for all your own world classes in Kinect scenarios. It provides the fundamental communication with the Kinect, giving you access to the data (camera image and user data) that we can receive from the Kinect. You should, at some stage, have a look at its methods. You may want to switch the editor to *Documentation view* to look at its methods—the implementation is not important at the moment.

KinectClient

This class is used internally by the `KinectWorld`—you should not need to use this directly.

UserData

This is a class that defines objects which are holding information about a user being tracked by the Kinect. You can get one object per user that the Kinect can see. You can receive `UserData` objects by using methods from your `KinectWorld`.

Joint

The `UserData` object, in turn, can give you access to information about each joint of the user (such as the right hand, the elbow, the knee). You receive this information in the form of objects of class `Joint`.

Point3D

Lastly, part of the joint information is the joint's location (in three dimensions). This is provided as a `Point3D` object.

The book scenarios folder contains a scenario called *kinect-start* that contains just these classes, and can be used as a starting scenario for your own projects.

12.4 The simple camera

The only scenario-specific code in the *simple-camera* scenario is contained in the `MyWorld` class (Code 12.1). Let us have a look at what it does.

The constructor of `MyWorld` simply calls the default constructor of `KinectWorld`.

The Kinect hardware gives us, by default, an image of 640 by 480 pixels, and the `KinectWorld`'s default constructor will create a world of the same size to match this. (Using different constructors, we can also create worlds of other sizes and scale the Kinect input, but this is not necessary now.)

The interesting code in this class is in the `act` method. First, it includes a call to the superclass's `act` method. This is important: The `KinectWorld`'s act method manages the communication with the server and you must always call it regularly. It's not difficult—just do not delete this line.

The last two lines are where things actually happen: we call the `getThumbnail-Unscaled` method, which gives us the camera image of the Kinect in its default size, as a `GreenfootImage`. The last line then sets this image as our world background.

Code 12.1

The World
class of the
simple-camera
scenario

```java
import greenfoot.*;

/**
 * This is a very simple demo world using the Kinect: This world shows the image from the
 * Kinect camera as the world background.
 *
 * @author Michael Kölling
 * @version 1.0
 */
public class MyWorld extends KinectWorld
{
    /**
     * Constructor for our world. Nothing to do.
     */
    public MyWorld()
    {
        super();
    }

    /**
     * In every act cycle, get the image from the Kinect and use it as our background image.
     * (Don't forget: The superclass act method must be called in all Kinect scenarios.)
     */
    public void act()
    {
        super.act();

        GreenfootImage cameraImage = getThumbnailUnscaled();
        setBackground(cameraImage);
    }
}
```

Exercise 12.2 Have a look at the methods of the `KinectWorld` class. All these methods are available for you to call in your own world classes. Which of these methods give you a camera image? What is the difference between them? Answer in writing.

Exercise 12.3 What are the methods to get user data? What is the difference between them?

12.5 The next step: greenscreen

Getting the camera image is a nice first step, but we could have done this with any webcam. Let us now look at the first of the abilities of the Kinect: identifying users.

A "greenscreen" is a technique long used in film and TV production to place actors in front of backgrounds that are not actually there. (Do a Web search to find out more!) It is usually done by placing actors in front of a green background, and then filtering out and replacing all green color in the resulting recording. Using the Kinect, we can easily do something similar, because the Kinect can distinguish between human and non-human objects and background in its view.

Exercise 12.4 Open the *greenscreen* scenario. Run it. What does it do?

Compared to the simple-camera example before, we have made two changes:

- We have moved the code to display the image to an actor, instead of displaying it as the world background. Now we place a single actor in the middle of the world, and the actor uses the Kinect image as its actor image. The effect is similar to before: The image is the same size as the world and will be displayed covering the whole world area.

- We have replaced the call to the `getThumbnailUnscaled` method with a call to `getCombinedUserImage`. This method also gives us the camera image, but filters out the background and provides us with an image of just the visible users.

As we can see, showing the users without the background is very easy, since the Kinect does all the difficult work for us. Since the user image is displayed as an actor, we can now put our own background in.

> **Exercise 12.5** Set a background image for the world. You can do this by using the *Set Image . . .* function from **MyWorld**'s pop-up menu. The scenario provides an image called *weather-map.png* that you can use.
>
> **Exercise 12.6** Try the scenario with various other background images of your own.

Both these examples—*simple-camera* and *greenscreen*—used just the image of the user as either the world background or an actor image. This is an interesting first step, but if we want to interact with other objects on the screen, we need to go one step further: We need to analyze the user image to find out where on screen the user is. Luckily, the Kinect helps us with that as well.

12.6 Stick-figure: tracking users

The *stick-figure* scenario in the book folder shows a first example of tracking users. This time, we will not show the camera image of the user, but use the coordinates of the joints of the user in the image to draw.

> **Exercise 12.7** Open the stick-figure scenario. Run it. Stand in front of your Kinect and see what happens.

When testing this scenario, you can see that it tracks the user in front of the camera and draws a stick figure (Figure 12.6). You may also notice that it is sometimes difficult to know whether you are in view of the Kinect camera, and where exactly to stand so that you can be tracked. To solve this problem, we will first insert a *thumbnail image* into this scenario, before we investigate how the stick figure is drawn.

Figure 12.6

The stick-figure
example scenario

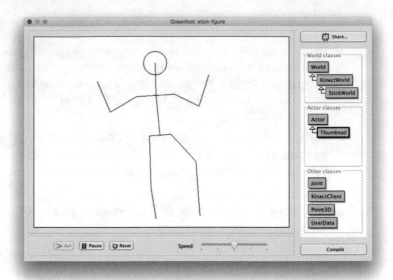

A thumbnail image is a small image which helps us gain a quick overview. It is called "thumbnail" because of its small size; we do not use it to see detail, but just to get the essential information. We will see that the use of a thumbnail to help us place ourselves in front of the camera is useful in many Kinect scenarios.

In the stick-figure scenario, you can see a class called `Thumbnail`.

Exercise 12.8 Run your stick-figure scenario. Interactively create an object of class `Thumbnail` and place it into the world. What do you see?

Exercise 12.9 Add code to your `StickWorld` class that creates and adds a `Thumbnail` object automatically. Place it at any location of your choice.

Exercise 12.10 Change the location of your thumbnail picture so that it is shown in the bottom right corner of the screen.

The implementation of the `Thumbnail` class is quite simple. It contains only these two lines of code in its `act` method:

```
KinectWorld world = (KinectWorld)getWorld();
setImage(world.getThumbnailUnscaled());
```

We can see that the thumbnail actor just gets the thumbnail image from the `KinectWorld` and sets it as its own image.

There is a second part to this, and it is in the constructor of the `StickWorld` class:

```
public StickWorld()
{
    super(THUMBNAIL_WIDTH, THUMBNAIL_HEIGHT, 1.0, false);
}
```

We can see that the `StickWorld` calls a different `KinectWorld` constructor, one that has four parameters. The first two parameters (using constants in this case) specify the size of the thumbnail image we wish to receive from the `KinectWorld` when we ask for it. This is how we define the exact size we want our thumbnail to be.

Exercise 12.11 What is the exact size of the thumbnail used in this example?

Exercise 12.12 Double the size of the thumbnail image.

Exercise 12.13 What is the meaning of the other two parameters of the `KinectWorld`'s constructor that is called in the **super** call?

Now that we have a thumbnail displayed, it is easier to place ourselves in front of the camera and know where to stand. We can now examine how this scenario manages to draw the stick figure.

The relevant code is in the `StickWorld` class (see Code 12.2).

Code 12.2

Drawing stick figures of tracked users

```
/**
 * Act: show users as stick figures.
 */
public void act()
{
    super.act();
    UserData[] trackedUsers = getTrackedUsers();
    paintStickFigures(trackedUsers);
}
```

```
/**
 * Paint stick figures on the world background for every user we can see.
 */
private void paintStickFigures(UserData[] trackedUsers)
{
    eraseBackground();

    for (UserData user: trackedUsers)
    {
        user.drawStickFigure(getBackground(), 60);
    }
}
```

```
/**
 * Erase the world backgorund.
 */
private void eraseBackground()
{
    getBackground().setColor(Color.WHITE);
    getBackground().fill();
}
```

Studying the code, we can see that drawing the stick figures is easy, because the `UserData` class provides a method called `drawStickFigure`. So all we need to do is the following:

- In every act cycle, we get an array of all tracked users, using the `getTrackedUsers` method. We pass this array to our own `paintStickFigures` method.

- We then erase the world background (to erase previously drawn stick figures) and draw new stick figures by calling the `drawStickFigure` method for every user in our array.

We can see that drawing the stick figure for a user is well supported. This will be useful in various different Kinect scenarios. We also see that our code should be able to process stick figures for multiple users at the same time.

> **Exercise 12.14** Look up the `drawStickFigure` method in the `UserData` class. What are its two parameters?
>
> **Exercise 12.15** Run the scenario again and place more than one person in front of the camera. Does the scenario correctly track each one?
>
> **Exercise 12.16** How many people can be tracked at the same time? Can you find a limit? Try by placing as many people as you can in front of the camera.

Figure 12.7
Painting with your hands

Figure 12.8
Multiple canvases layered in front of the world background

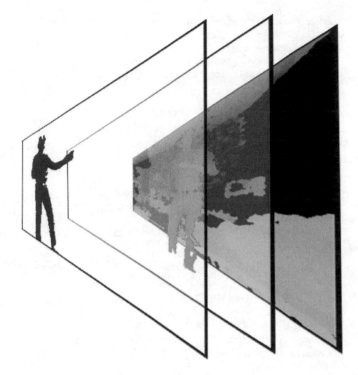

12.7 Painting with your hands

The examples we have seen so far were mostly ready when we opened them, and we have used them to study some basic techniques. There was not much for us to do.

Now that we have a basic understanding of the Kinect's interface, we can start by writing some code of our own. Our next goal is to write a scenario that lets us paint on the screen using our hands and feet (Figure 12.7).

> **Exercise 12.17** Open the *body-paint-start* scenario. Run it. Try out what it does.

Concept

Tracked users are those currently recognized and analyzed by the Kinect hardware.

Again, as usual, we begin by using a starting scenario, *body-paint-start*, that contains some rudimentary code. Trying it out, we can see that it currently behaves very similar to the *stick-figure* example.

The first visible difference is that there is a new class: Canvas.

The scenario is set up so that a separate canvas object is created for every user that is currently being tracked. Each canvas object has a transparent image the size of the full screen. Since the image is initially empty (fully transparent) it is invisible, but this essentially gives every user a separate transparent layer to draw on (see Figure 12.8).

Code 12.3 shows how this is achieved. A new (empty) GreenfootImage is created and set as the actor's image. We can see that the image's paint color is initialized to a random color, so that future drawing operations start off with (probably) different colors for different users.

Code 12.3

The Canvas
constructor

```
public Canvas(int width, int height, UserData user)
{
    this.user = user;
    setImage(new GreenfootImage(width, height));
    getImage().setColor(randomColor());
}
```

The only other thing that the constructor does is to store an object of type `UserData` in a field called `user`. This object holds information about the user that is associated with this canvas, and we can use it to access details of the user's pose.

Exercise 12.18 The constructor shown in Code 12.3 makes use of a method called `randomColor`. This method is implemented in the same class. Investigate this method and explain, in writing, how it selects a random color. How many different possible colors can it return? Can you add another possible color?

We can now start painting by writing code in our `act` method.

Paint with your hand

The first thing we want to do is to put some paint onto our canvas at the position of the user's right hand. We can put paint on the canvas by drawing a medium-sized circle onto our actor's image:

```
getImage().fillOval(x, y, 20, 20);
```

In this example, the two parameters of 20 are the width and height of the oval drawn, creating a circle of diameter 20. The parameters x and y have to be replaced by the position of the user's hand. So the only thing to work out now is how to find out about the screen location of the user's hand.

Figure 12.9

Retrieving informa-
tion about users

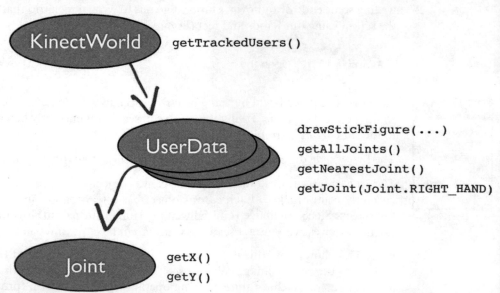

In general, we get information about users by starting with the `getTrackedUsers` method from the `KinectWorld` class (Figure 12.9). This will give us an array of `UserData` objects with an entry for every user that is being tracked. We can then use various methods of the `UserData` object (only some are shown in Figure 12.9) to get detailed information about each user. For us, the `getJoint` method is the most interesting at the moment.

`getJoint` will give us an object of type `Joint`, which we can then use to retrieve the joint's *x*- and *y*-coordinates.

Exercise 12.19 The `getJoint` method expects a parameter specifying which joint we are interested in. We usually use constants here that are defined in the `Joint` class (see Figure 12.9). Check the documentation of class `Joint` to see what constants are available to specify joints. How many different joints can we find out about?

In the `act` method in our `Canvas` class, the `UserData` object has already been retrieved and stored in the field called `user`. We can therefore proceed directly to retrieve the joint for the right hand from it:

```
Joint rightHand = user.getJoint(Joint.RIGHT_HAND);
```

Once we have the right hand joint, we can now extract its *x*- and *y*-coordinates and use these to paint our circle on screen:

```
getImage().fillOval(rightHand.getX(), rightHand.getY(), 20, 20);
```

This is all that needs to be done in order to paint with your hand. Try it out!

Exercise 12.20 Insert the code discussed above into your own `Canvas act` method. You need only those two lines as shown here. Test!

You should see that we are now painting (continuously) at the location of the right hand.

Stop painting

To make our painting a bit more controllable, it would be nice if we could also move our right hand without painting. To do this, we want to change our code so that it only paints when the right hand is the nearest joint to the camera. That way, we can paint by holding our hand forward, and stop by pulling it back.

The `UserData` class has a method called `getNearestJoint` that we can use to achieve this. Try this yourself at first without reading on (we will discuss it after the exercise).

> **Exercise 12.21** Change your code so that it only paints when the right hand is the nearest joint to the camera. Do this by getting the nearest joint and checking whether it is the right hand.

If you worked out this exercise on your own, you will have seen that we can simply add an if-statement to compare the nearest joint with the constant for the right hand. If the right hand is not nearest, we do nothing; otherwise we paint.

```
Joint rightHand = user.getJoint(Joint.RIGHT_HAND);
if (user.getNearestJoint() == Joint.RIGHT_HAND)
{
    getImage().fillOval(rightHand.getX(), rightHand.getY(), 20, 20);
}
```

Let us do two more improvements—but this time you have to write the code yourself.

Erase your painting

When we have painted something, but we are not quite happy with it or we want to start over, it would be nice to be able to erase the screen. Erasing the screen (effectively erasing the actor's image) can easily be achieved by using the **GreenfootImage**'s **clear** method:

```
getImage().clear();
```

We now want to add functionality that lets users erase the screen by raising their left hand over their head. The principle is quite easy: We can get the *y*-coordinates of both the left hand and the head and check which one is larger.

> **Exercise 12.22** Add code to your **act** method that erases the screen when the user raises the left hand over the head.

Changing color

The next improvement is quite similar in its structure: change the color of the paint when the user raises the right foot. (You can detect this by checking whether the right foot is above the left knee.) The existing **randomColor** method helps you to select a new (random) color.

> **Exercise 12.23** Add some code to change the paint color to a different random color when the user raises the right foot.

You can probably think of several other things to do with this scenario. There are many ideas to try. The code for the exercises discussed here is available in the book scenarios as *body-paint*, in case you want to compare your own code to ours.

The only code in this scenario that we have not discussed is code in the `PaintWorld` class that manages the creation and removal of canvases from the world. The most complicated aspect of this is to keep track of new users appearing, and existing users leaving, while the program is running, and to create and delete canvases accordingly. We will not analyze this here but instead discuss this issue in the next example.

12.8   A simple Kinect game: Pong

The last project that we will discuss in this chapter is a very simple game: *Pong*. Pong is a well-known, simple game where we play a kind of tennis with paddles on screen. In our case, we will have two paddles, one controlled by each of our hands, and we will play against the computer which has one paddle (Figure 12.10).

As so often, we have two versions of the scenario in our *book-scenarios* folder; one as the starting point for our exercises, and one with the finished solution.

> **Exercise 12.24** Open the *kinect-pong-start* scenario. Run it. Find out how to play.

Figure 12.10

A simple Kinect game

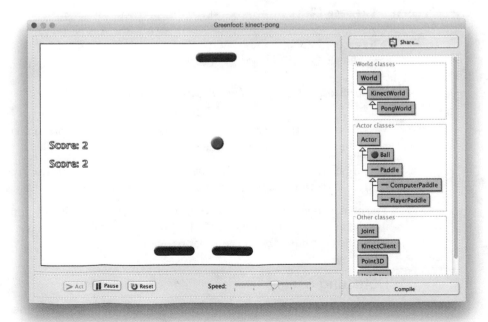

When you try the starting scenario, you will see that it implements a very simple pong-style game that can be played with the keyboard. You play one player, the computer plays the other. (You can find out which keys to use by reading the source code or just trying it out.)

There is nothing new in this scenario that we should not be able to easily understand at this point. Let us do some quick code reading exercises to familiarize ourselves with the existing project. Answer the following questions in writing.

Exercise 12.25 Which keys control the player's paddle?

Exercise 12.26 What are the methods that are inherited from `Paddle` by both the player's paddle and the computer's paddle?

Exercise 12.27 When the paddle moves right or left, by how many steps does it move in each act cycle?

Exercise 12.28 What does the computer paddle do when there is no ball on screen? (You can check your answer by removing the ball interactively and then running the scenario.)

Exercise 12.29 What strategy does the computer paddle use to decide where to move?

Exercise 12.30 How many objects are inserted into the world when the scenario is initialized? What are they?

Exercise 12.31 Which class keeps the score?

Exercise 12.32 There is a delay between the scenario being started and the ball starting to move. How long is that delay?

Exercise 12.33 Explain how this delay is implemented.

We can see that this scenario is a very straightforward simple implementation. We will now change it to make use of the Kinect to control our paddles.

This time, we will start with the part that we left out of our discussion in the previous section: detecting when a user enters the view of the camera.

The goal is this: The game should be in an idle state (waiting) as long as no user is visible. When a user enters the view, the game starts. When there is no user in view (i.e., when the user has left), the game stops again.

Detecting users

We have seen previously that we can get an array of all users currently being tracked by using the `getTrackedUsers` method:

```
UserData[] users = getTrackedUsers();
```

We can then check whether any users are present by checking whether the length of this array is zero:

```
if (users.length > 0)
{
    ...
}
```

(Remember that length for an array is really a public field, not a method. There are no parentheses after the word length. This looks unusual, but this is how Java defines it.)

Exercise 12.34 In PongWorld, create a new private method called startGame. This method needs no parameters. Move the creation of the player paddle and the ball into this method, so that the player's paddle and the ball are created only when the game starts.

Exercise 12.35 Test the game. If you run your scenario now, the visible effect should just be that you do not see a player paddle or a ball (because we do not call the start-Game method yet).

Exercise 12.36 In your act method, check for tracked users. If there are any users, start the game. Check by running your scenario and standing in front of the camera. The game should start.

Exercise 12.37 In a naïve implementation (if you just call startGame when the length of the tracked user array is greater than zero), you will get many paddles and balls. This is because startGame would be called in every act cycle, creating more and more balls and paddles. Make sure only one player paddle and one ball is created. For this purpose, a boolean called idle is already provided. When the game is idle and you see a tracked user, you should start the game and record that the game is now not idle.

If you managed to do the exercises so far, the game should now be in an idle state at the beginning (the computer paddle moves slowly while it waits), and the player paddle and ball are created when you enter the screen.

Before finishing the game play, let us deal with players leaving the game as well.

Exercise 12.38 Add another private method called stopGame. In it, remove the player paddle and the ball from the world.

Exercise 12.39 Extend your act method so that it calls stopGame when the game is not idle, but no players are detected. The game should then enter the idle state again.

Your game should now be in a state that it starts as players enter, and stops when they leave. You will notice that it will only stop several seconds after the player has left, not immediately. When the Kinect loses track of players, it keeps trying to detect them again for a while before giving up and deciding they really have left.

Controlling the paddle

The next thing to do is to implement the actual game play. For the player paddle to be controlled by the human, the user data must be passed to the paddle. Since this is a single player game, we can just work with the first user data object of our tracked user array. If multiple users are visible, we just ignore the others.

So, if we want to pass the user data of the first visible user to our `startGame` method, we can write:

```
startGame(users[0]);
```

Exercise 12.40 Add a parameter of type `UserData` to your `startGame` method and pass the user data of the first visible user into this method when the game starts.

Exercise 12.41 Add a similar parameter to the constructor of class `PlayerPaddle`, and pass the parameter that `startGame` receives on to the `PlayerPaddle` constructor.

Exercise 12.42 In class `PlayerPaddle`, store the `UserData` received by the constructor in a field called `user`.

Your scenario should now be in a state where it compiles again, but our work so far has no visible effect.

All that remains for us to do now is to set the position of the paddle according to the user data. You can call the `getJoint` method from the user object to obtain the joint for the right hand. Then you can use `setLocation` for the paddle with the hand's x-coordinate and the paddle's own y-coordinate as the parameters.

Exercise 12.43 Remove the code from the `PlayerPaddle`'s `act` method. Instead insert new code that gets the user's right hand joint, and then sets the paddle's location using the hand's x-coordinate (leaving its y-coordinate unchanged).

Now we can play!

Making use of the player's hand's location is in the end quite easy. Your `act` method should only be two or three lines long.

Before we finish, let us make one further extension: playing with both hands.

Exercise 12.44 In class `PlayerPaddle`, make the hand to be used variable. Create a field of type `int` called HAND. Initialize this field in the constructor, using a new additional constructor parameter. In your `act` method, use this variable instead of `Joint.RIGHT_HAND` to specify the joint to watch.

Exercise 12.45 In class `PongWorld`, where the player paddle is created, add `Joint.RIGHT_HAND` as the second constructor parameter.

Now we are back where we started: We have one paddle controlled by our right hand. But now we can easily specify which hand we want to use, allowing us to create another paddle for the left hand.

> **Exercise 12.46** Where the player paddle is created, add the creation of a second paddle for the left hand.

That's it! We can now play with both hands. As always, if you are not sure about some of your code, check the *kinect-pong* scenario in the book scenarios folder.

Summary

In this chapter, we have connected Greenfoot to the Microsoft Kinect. Apart from giving us a chance to create a number of really interesting examples, we have seen that programming with hardware devices does not look so different from what we encountered before. We use the same programming techniques—method calls, variables, parameters, types—as in earlier chapters.

When we program with external devices, we are usually given an *API*—a programming interface—consisting of a number of classes and methods to access the device. Learning to use the device then is a matter of studying that API and understanding what it lets us do. After that, all we need are our general Java and programming skills to write some programs.

Concept summary

- **Skeleton tracking** is the identification and tracking of some known points on a body, such as hands, elbows, head, feet, and so on.

- Communication with hardware components is typically arranged through some **driver software**.

- **Tracked users** are those currently recognized and analyzed by the Kinect hardware.

Drill and practice

Here are some more exercises you can do with our last example, *kinect-pong*. Of course, you can extend any of the other examples as well, but we will leave it up to you to come up with ideas for those.

Exercise 12.47 In your Kinect pong game, add some sound effects. Add at least the following: a sound when the ball hits the paddle, a sound when the ball goes out, and a sound when the game starts.

Exercise 12.48 Change the background.

Exercise 12.49 Declare a winner (with message and sound) when one player reaches eight points.

Exercise 12.50 Make the top paddle controllable by a second player.

Exercise 12.51 Give the second player two paddles as well.

Exercise 12.52 Introduce a barrier: each player can block off their whole side for a few seconds by raising their left foot. They can do that only three times in a game.

Exercise 12.53 If any player raises both hands above their head, the speed of the ball increases.

The book examples folder contains one more scenario, intended mainly as a demo to show you how to draw a cartoon character instead of the stick figure. Our character is called *Fred* and the scenario is called *fred-with-radio*.

We will not discuss this scenario here, but leave you to play with it yourself. One thing you might want to do is to replace the two sound files with songs of your choice—then you can play your favorite two songs by touching the radio with your right or left hand.

CHAPTER

13

Additional scenario ideas

topics:	ideas for more scenarios
concepts:	(no new concepts introduced)

This is the last chapter of this book. It is different from the other chapters in that it does not try to teach you any new concepts or techniques of programming. Instead it briefly presents a number of additional scenarios to give you some ideas for other things you might like to investigate and work on.

All scenarios described here are also available as Greenfoot projects with source code in the book scenarios. However, most of them are not complete implementations of the idea they represent.

Some scenarios are almost complete, and you may like to study them to learn further techniques and see how certain effects were achieved. Others are beginnings, partial implementations of an idea, which you could take as a starting point for your own project. Still others are illustrations of a single concept or idea that might provide inspiration for something you could incorporate into one of your own scenarios.

In short, view these as a collection of ideas for future projects, and study them for a small glimpse into what else is possible for a competent programmer to achieve.

13.1 Marbles

The marbles scenario (Figure 13.1) implements a game in which you roll a golden ball over a board with the aim of clearing the board of all silver balls within a limited number of moves. The game is reasonably complete.

Several things are worth observing about this scenario. The first thing that stands out is that it looks rather attractive. This has very little to do with Java or Greenfoot programming and is mostly due to the use of good looking graphics. Using nicely designed graphics and sounds can make a big difference in the attractiveness of a game.

Figure 13.1

The Marbles game

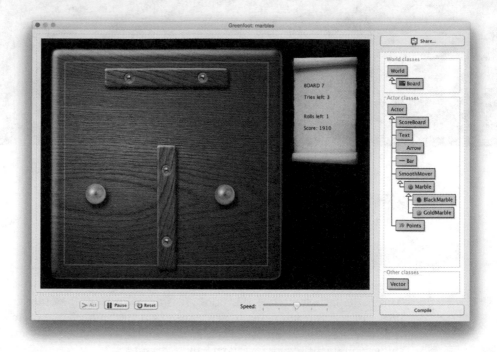

Marbles uses a nice-looking background image (the game board and scroll for the text display) and actors with semitransparent drop shadows (the marbles and the obstacles).

The other interesting aspect to examine is the collision detection. The marbles do not use any of the built-in Greenfoot collision detection methods since these all work on the rectangular actor images. The marbles, on the other hand, are round, and we need precise collision for this.

Luckily, when the actors are round, this is not very difficult. Two marbles collide if their distance (measured from their center points) is less than their diameter. We know the diameter, and the distance is fairly easy to compute (using the Pythagoras theorem).

The next interesting thing is the way the new movement direction of a colliding marble is computed. There is a little trigonometry involved here, but if you are familiar with that, then it is not too hard.

Collisions with the fixed obstacles are easier, since they are always horizontally or vertically oriented rectangles. Therefore, a marble hitting one of these obstacles simply reverses its direction along one of the axes (x or y).

You could reuse the marble collision logic for all sorts of other games that involve round objects colliding.

Figure 13.2
A (partial) lift simulation

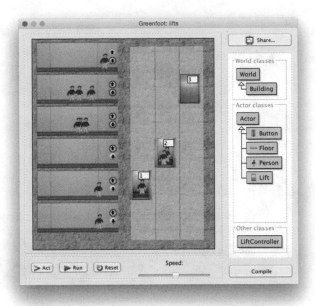

13.2 Lifts

The *lifts* scenario shows a simple lift (or elevator) simulation (Figure 13.2). It shows several floors of a multistory building and three lifts moving up and down. People appear on the floors and press the call buttons and enter the lifts when they come.

This is actually a very rudimentary, unfinished implementation. Much of what we see on the screen is fake: It does not properly simulate what is going on, and is just written for show.

For example, the people do not properly enter the lifts (they are just erased when a lift reaches a floor). The number of people shown in a lift is just a random number. Lifts also do not react to call buttons—they just move up and down randomly. There is no control algorithm implemented for the lifts.

So this is just a quick demo that presents the idea and the graphics. To finish the project, the movement of people would have to be properly modeled (in and out of the elevators). And then we could experiment with implementing and testing different lift control algorithms.

13.3 Boids

The *boids* example shows a simulation of flocking behavior of birds (Figure 13.3).

Figure 13.3

Boids: a simulation of flocking behavior

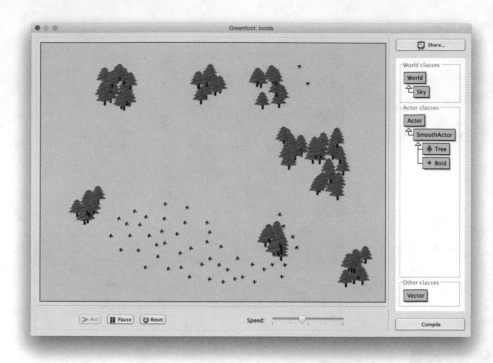

The term "boids" comes from a program developed in 1986 by Craig Reynolds that first implemented this flocking algorithm. In it, each bird flies according to three rules:

- Separation: steer away from other birds if getting too close.

- Alignment: steer toward the average heading of other birds in the vicinity.

- Cohesion: steer to move toward the average position of other birds in the vicinity.

With this algorithm, the birds develop movement that is pleasant to watch. Included in this scenario is also obstacle avoidance: trying not to fly into trees.

A version of this algorithm was used, for example, in Tim Burton's 1992 film *Batman Returns* to create animation for computer-generated swarms of bats and penguin flocks, and in the *Lord of the Rings* films to create the movement of the Orc armies.

The version for this book was written by Poul Henriksen.

You can find out much more about this by searching the Web for "boids." And while this scenario currently does nothing other than show the movement, one feels that there has to be a game in it somewhere.

Figure 13.4

An explosion effect

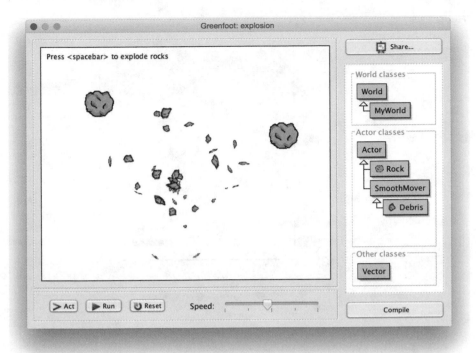

13.4   Explosion

The *explosion* scenario (Figure 13.4) demonstrates how we can implement a more spectacular looking explosion effect. The object that explodes is, in this case, a simple rock that we have encountered in other scenarios before. (It played, for example, the role of the asteroid in the *asteroids* scenario.) But we could really explode anything we like.

To achieve this effect, we have a `Debris` class that represents a part of the rock. When the rock explodes, we remove it from the world and place 40 pieces of debris in its place.

Each piece of debris is randomly stretched and rotated to make it look unique and initially has a movement vector in a random direction. At every step, we add a bit of downward movement to simulate gravity, and the result is the explosion you see when you run this scenario.

A tutorial video explaining this scenario in more detail is available on the Greenfoot YouTube channel at *https://www.youtube.com/user/18km.*

13.5   Breakout

Breakout is a classic computer game in which the player controls a paddle at the bottom of the screen to bounce a ball upwards to remove some blocks. If you do not know the game, do a Web search.

Figure 13.5

The beginning of a
Breakout game

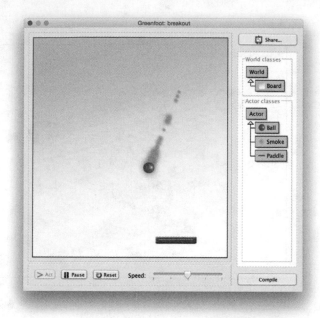

The *breakout* scenario (Figure 13.5) is a partial implementation of this game. It uses the ball with the smoke effect that we discussed in Chapter 10 and adds a paddle for the player to control the ball. It has, however, no blocks to aim for, so in its current form it is not very interesting.

Many variations of Breakout have been created over time. Many use different patterns of layout for the blocks at different levels. Most also have some "power-ups"—goodies hidden behind some blocks that float down when the block is removed. Catching them typically makes something interesting happen in the game (extra balls, increased speed, larger or smaller paddles, etc.)

Completing this game in an interesting way can make a good project. It could also be modified to have two paddles, one on either side, essentially turning it into the classic Pong game.

13.6 Platform jumper

A very common style of game is a "platform" game. The player typically controls a game character that has to move from one area on the screen to another, while over-coming various obstacles. One such obstacle may be a gap in the ground the character is walking on, with some means of getting across it.

The *pengu* scenario implements a small segment of such a game (Figure 13.6). There are two pieces of ground on either side of the screen, and the penguin can get across by jumping onto a moving cloud.

Figure 13.6

The start of a simple platform jumper game

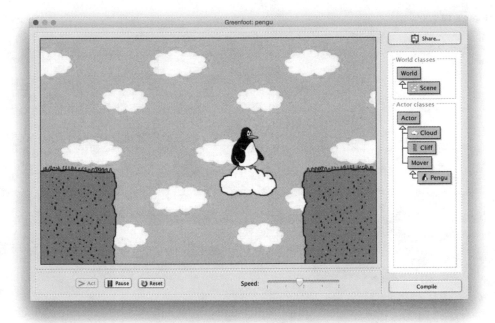

This scenario is included here to demonstrate how an actor can move along the top of another (the penguin on top of the ground), and how jumping and falling might be implemented.

A tutorial video discussing this in more detail is available on the Greenfoot YouTube channel at *https://www.youtube.com/user/18km*, under the name "Running, jumping and falling."

13.7 Wave

The next scenario is called *wave* (Figure 13.7). It is a simple simulation of the propagation of a wave on a piece of string. Play around with it for a little while, and you will discover what it does.

One of the fascinating aspects of this example is how a fairly simple implementation—in each act round, each bead simply moves toward the middle of its two neighbors—achieves a quite sophisticated simulation of various aspects of wave propagation.

This example is included here to illustrate that, with a bit of thought and preparation, various behaviors from other disciplines could be simulated. In this case, it is a simple physical effect. Equally, one could simulate chemical reactions, biological interactions, interactions of subatomic particles, and much more. With some careful planning, we can learn something about other application areas, as well as learning about programming.

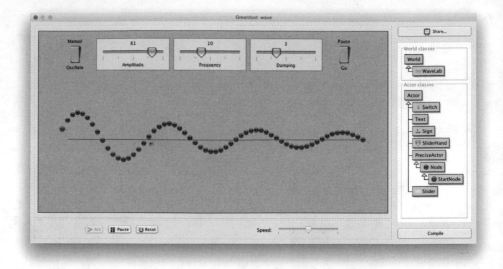

This scenario also implements slider and switch controls, which may be useful in other projects.

13.8 Map

The last scenario we present here is called *maps* (Figure 13.8). It displays a map on the world background and has buttons to zoom in and out.

The interesting aspect of this class is that it uses live data accessed via the Internet (in this case, the map data). The map image is not fixed; it is not built into this scenario but is retrieved at runtime from the Google maps online service. (This also means, of course, that this scenario will only work on a computer connected to the Internet.)

In its current form, the map is centered on the University of Kent in England, but this is easy to change. Look into the `MapViewer` class and you will find, in comments, various examples of other locations you can try. You can, in general, use any sufficiently distinct textual name of a location, be that the name of a country, a city, or a landmark, or you can use latitude and longitude coordinates.

The implementation is quite simple because it makes use of a ready-made `Map` helper class, and this is where the hard work is hidden.

The map helper class is one of the classes provided with Greenfoot: You can access it via the *Import Class…* function in the *Edit* menu of Greenfoot's main window.

In general, accessing live data from the Internet can make for some really interesting examples. From the same menu (*Import Class…*) you can also import another helper class called `Weather`, which gives you live, real-time weather data retrieved from an online service.

Figure 13.8

A Greenfoot scenario with live map access

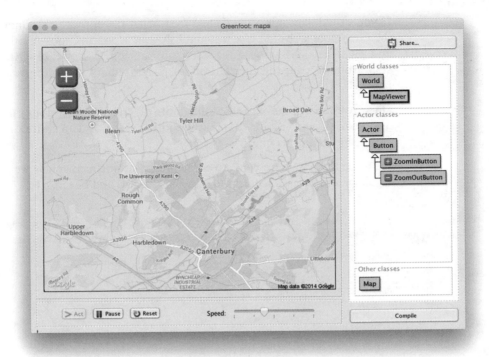

Try this to program your own live weather display. Or combine it with the map to create a live weather map.

Summary

In this concluding chapter of our book, we have tried to show that there are many more directions you can follow, beyond the examples we have discussed in more detail throughout this book.

As you become more experienced, you will become more confident and more able to turn your ideas into reality as you develop your programs. As a programmer, an infinite world of creative endeavor lies in front of you, both within Greenfoot and without, using other development environments.

When you program in other environments, outside of Greenfoot, you will have to learn new skills and techniques, but everything you have learned using Greenfoot will be useful and applicable.

If you have followed this book all the way through to this point, you have learned a great deal about programming in Java, and indeed programming in an object-oriented language in general. In learning to program, the beginning is always the hardest part, and you have that behind you.

If you would like support and ideas for further Greenfoot programming, make use of the Greenfoot website.[1] Use it to publish your scenarios, look at other people's work, and get some ideas. Look at the video tutorials for tips and tricks. And join the discussion group to chat to other Greenfoot programmers, get and give help, and discuss new ideas.

Once you feel you have reached the limits of Greenfoot, you may like to look at our next environment: BlueJ.[2] But that is another story, and an entirely new book, thicker and deeper than this one, awaits you...

We hope that you have come to enjoy programming as much as we do. If you have, a whole new world lies before you. Program, enjoy, and be creative!

---

[1] www.greenfoot.org
[2] www.bluej.org

Installing Greenfoot

This appendix will tell you where to find the Greenfoot software and the scenarios used with this book, and how to install them.

To work with the sample projects in this book, you will need to install two things: the Greenfoot software and the book scenarios.

A.1 Installing Greenfoot

Download Greenfoot from http://www.greenfoot.org, and follow the installation instructions.

On Windows and Mac OS, the Greenfoot download includes a Java system (JDK), so you do not need to install this separately. On Linux, the JDK will be automatically downloaded as part of the installation process if not already present.

A.2 Installing the book scenarios

Download the book scenarios from http://www.greenfoot.org/book. You will receive a file named *book-scenarios.zip*. This is a compressed *zip* file that must be extracted. On Windows systems, this can usually be achieved by right-clicking and selecting *Extract All* from the menu. On Mac OS and Linux systems, you can double-click the file to extract it.

After extracting this file, you will have a folder named *book-scenarios* stored in your file system. Remember where you saved it—you will need to open the projects from this folder while you work through the book.

The Greenfoot API consists of five classes:

Actor	Actor methods are available to all actor subclasses.	MouseInfo	Provide information about the last mouse event.
World	World methods are available to the world.	GreenfootImage	For image presentation and manipulation.
Greenfoot	Used to communicate with the Greenfoot environment itself.	GreenfootSound	For sound playback.
		UserInfo	To save user data on a server (only when running on Greenfoot website).

The API shown here is for Greenfoot version 2.4.0. If you use a newer version of Greenfoot, please check the documentation online.

Class World

`World(int worldWidth, int worldHeight, int cellSize)`	Construct a new world.
`World(int worldWidth, int worldHeight, int cellSize, boolean bounded)`	Construct a new world (possible unbounded).
`void act()`	Act method for the world. Called once per act cycle.
`void addObject(Actor object, int x, int y)`	Add an Actor to the world.
`GreenfootImage getBackground()`	Return the world's background image.
`int getCellSize()`	Return the size of a cell (in pixels).
`Color getColorAt(int x, int y)`	Return the color at the center of the cell.
`int getHeight()`	Return the height of the world (in number of cells).

(continued)

Class World (continued)

List **getObjects**(Class cls)	Get all the objects in the world.
List **getObjectsAt**(int x, int y, Class cls)	Return all objects at a given cell.
int **getWidth**()	Return the width of the world (in number of cells).
int **numberOfObjects**()	Get the number of actors currently in the world.
void **removeObject**(Actor object)	Remove an object from the world.
void **removeObjects**(Collection objects)	Remove a list of objects from the world.
void **repaint**()	Repaint the world.
void **setActOrder**(Class... classes)	Set the act order of objects in the world.
void **setBackground**(GreenfootImage image)	Set a background image for the world.
void **setBackground**(String filename)	Set a background image for the world from an image file.
void **setPaintOrder**(Class... classes)	Set the paint order of objects in the world.
void **showText**(String text, int x, int y)	Show some text centered at the given position in the world.
void **started**()	Called by the Greenfoot system when execution has started.
void **stopped**()	Called by the Greenfoot system when execution has stopped.

Class Actor

Actor()	Construct an Actor.
void **act**()	The act method is called by the Greenfoot framework to give objects a chance to perform some action.
protected void **addedToWorld**(World world)	This method is called by the Greenfoot system when the object has been inserted into the world.
GreenfootImage **getImage**()	Return the image used to represent this Actor.
protected List **getIntersectingObjects** (Class cls)	Return all the objects that intersect this object.
protected List **getNeighbours**(int distance, boolean diagonal, Class cls)	Return the neighbours to this object within a given distance.
protected List **getObjectsAtOffset** (int dx, int dy, Class cls)	Return all objects that intersect the given location (relative to this object's location).
protected List **getObjectsInRange** (int r, Class cls)	Return all objects within range "r" around this object.
protected Actor **getOneIntersectingObject**(Class cls)	Return an object that intersects this object.

(continued)

Class Actor (continued)

`protected Actor getOneObjectAtOffset (int dx, int dy, Class cls)`	Return one object that is located at the specified cell (relative to this objects location).
`int getRotation()`	Return the current rotation of the object.
`World getWorld()`	Return the world that this object lives in.
`int getX()`	Return the x-coordinate of the object's current location.
`int getY()`	Return the y-coordinate of the object's current location.
`protected boolean intersects (Actor other)`	Check whether this object intersects another given object.
`boolean isAtEdge()`	Detect whether the actor has reached the edge of the world.
`protected boolean isTouching(Class cls)`	Check whether this actor is touching any other objects of the given class.
`void move(int distance)`	Move this actor the specified distance in the direction it is currently facing.
`protected void removeTouching (Class cls)`	Remove one object of the given class that this actor is currently touching (if any exist).
`void setImage(GreenfootImage image)`	Set the image for this object to the specified image.
`void setImage(String filename)`	Set an image for this object from an image file.
`void setLocation(int x, int y)`	Assign a new location for this object.
`void setRotation(int rotation)`	Set the rotation of the object.
`void turn(int amount)`	Turn this actor by the specified amount (in degrees).
`void turnTowards(int x, int y)`	Turn this actor to face towards a certain location.

Class Greenfoot

`Greenfoot()`	Constructor.
`static void delay(int time)`	Delay execution by a number of time steps. The size of one time step is defined by the speed slider.
`static String getKey()`	Get the most recently pressed key since the last time this method was called.
`static int getMicLevel()`	Get the microphone input level.
`static MouseInfo getMouseInfo()`	Return a mouse info object with information about the state of the mouse.

(continued)

Class Greenfoot (continued)

`static int getRandomNumber (int limit)`	Return a random number between 0 (inclusive) and limit (exclusive).
`static boolean isKeyDown (String keyName)`	Check whether a given key is currently pressed down.
`static boolean mouseClicked(Object obj)`	*True* if the mouse has been clicked on the given object.
`static boolean mouseDragEnded (Object obj)`	*True* if a mouse drag has ended.
`static boolean mouseDragged(Object obj)`	*True* if the mouse has been dragged on the given object.
`static boolean mouseMoved(Object obj)`	*True* if the mouse has been moved on the given object.
`static boolean mousePressed(Object obj)`	*True* the mouse has been pressed on the given object.
`static void playSound(String soundFile)`	Play sound from a file.
`static void setSpeed(int speed)`	Set the speed of the simulation execution.
`static void setWorld(World world)`	Set the World to run to the one given.
`static void start()`	Run (or resume) the simulation.
`static void stop()`	Stop the simulation.

Class MouseInfo

`Actor getActor()`	Return the actor (if any) that the current mouse behaviour is related to.
`int getButton()`	The number of the pressed or clicked button (if any).
`int getClickCount()`	The number of mouse clicks of this mouse event.
`int getX()`	The current x position of the mouse cursor.
`int getY()`	The current y position of the mouse cursor.
`String toString()`	Return a string representation of this mouse event info.

Class GreenfootImage

`GreenfootImage(GreenfootImage image)`	Create a GreenfootImage from another GreenfootImage.
`GreenfootImage(int width, int height)`	Create an empty (transparent) image with the specified size.
`GreenfootImage(String filename)`	Create an image from an image file.

(continued)

Class GreenfootImage (continued)

GreenfootImage(String string, int size, Color foreground, Color background)	Create an image with the given string drawn as text using the given font size, with the given foreground color on the given background color.
GreenfootImage(String string, int size, Color foreground, Color background, Color outline)	Create an image with the given string drawn as text using the given font size, the given foreground color on the given background color with an outline.
void **clear**()	Clear the image.
void **drawImage**(GreenfootImage image, int x, int y)	Draw the given Image onto this image.
void **drawLine**(int x1, int y1, int x2, int y2)	Draw a line, using the current drawing color, between the points (x1, y1) and (x2, y2).
void **drawOval**(int x, int y, int width, int height)	Draw an oval bounded by the specified rectangle with the current drawing color.
void **drawPolygon**(int[ ] xPoints, int[ ] yPoints, int nPoints)	Draw a closed polygon defined by arrays of x and y coordinates.
void **drawRect**(int x, int y, int width, int height)	Draw the outline of the specified rectangle.
void **drawShape**(Shape shape)	Draw a shape directly on the image.
void **drawString(**String string, int x, int y)	Draw the text given by the specified string, using the current font and color.
void **fill**()	Fill the entire image with the current drawing color.
void **fillOval**(int x, int y, int width, int height)	Fill an oval bounded by the specified rectangle with the current drawing color.
void **fillPolygon**(int[ ] xPoints, int[ ] yPoints, int nPoints)	Fill a closed polygon defined by arrays of x and y coordinates.
void **fillRect**(int x, int y, int width, int height)	Fill the specified rectangle.
void **fillShape**(Shape shape)	Draw a filled shape directly on the image.
BufferedImage **getAwtImage**()	Return the BufferedImage that backs this GreenfootImage.
Color **getColor**()	Return the current drawing color.
Color **getColorAt**(int x, int y)	Return the color at the given pixel.
Font **getFont**()	Get the current font.
int **getHeight**()	Return the height of the image.
int **getTransparency**()	Return the transparency of the image (range 0 to 255).

(continued)

Class GreenfootImage (continued)

int **getWidth**()	Return the width of the image.
void **mirrorHorizontally**()	Mirror the image horizontally (flip around the x-axis).
void **mirrorVertically**()	Mirror the image vertically (flip around the y-axis).
void **rotate**(int degrees)	Rotate this image around the center.
void **scale**(int width, int height)	Scale this image to a new size.
void **setColor**(Color color)	Set the current drawing color.
void **setColorAt**(int x, int y, Color color)	Set the color at the given pixel to the given color.
void **setFont**(Font f)	Set the current font.
void **setTransparency**(int t)	Set the transparency of the image (range 0 to 255).
String **toString**()	Return a string representation of this image.

Class GreenfootSound

GreenfootSound(String filename)	Create a new sound from the given file.
int **getVolume**()	Get the current volume of the sound, between 0 (off) and 100 (loudest).
boolean **isPlaying**()	True if the sound is currently playing.
void **pause**()	Pause the sound if it is currently playing.
void **play**()	Start playing this sound.
void **playLoop**()	Play this sound repeatedly in a loop.
void **setVolume**(int level)	Set the current volume of the sound between 0 (off) and 100 (loudest).
void **stop**()	Stop playing this sound if it is currently playing.
String **toString**()	Return a string representation of this mouse event info.

Class UserInfo

static int **NUM_INTS**	The number of integers that can be stored.
static int **NUM_STRINGS**	The number of Strings that can be stored.
static int **STRING_LENGTH_LIMIT**	The maximum number of characters that can be stored in each String.
int **getInt**(int index)	Get the value of the int at the given index (0 to NUM_INTS-1, inclusive).
static UserInfo **getMyInfo**()	Get the data stored for the current user.

(continued)

Class UserInfo (continued)

`static List getNearby(int maxAmount)`	Return a string representation of this mouse event info.
`int getRank()`	Get the users overall rank for this scenario.
`int getScore()`	Get the user's score.
`String getString(int index)`	Get the value of the String at the given index (0 to NUM_STRINGS-1, inclusive).
`static List getTop(int maxAmount)`	Get a sorted list of the UserInfo items for this scenario, starting at the top.
`GreenfootImage getUserImage()`	Return an image of the user.
`String getUserName()`	Get the username of the user that this storage belongs to.
`static boolean isStorageAvailable()`	Indicate whether storage is available.
`void setInt(int index, int value)`	Set the value of the int at the given index (0 to NUM_INTS-1, inclusive).
`void setScore(int score)`	Set the user's score.
`void setString(int index, String value)`	Set the value of the String at the given index (0 to NUM_STRINGS-1, inclusive).
`boolean store()`	Store the data to the server.

C

Collision detection

In this book, various collision detection methods are used in different situations. Below is a summary of the collision detection methods available for Greenfoot actors, and a short explanation of their purpose, and when to use them.

C.1 Method summary

Greenfoot's collision detection methods can be found in the **Actor** class. There are seven relevant methods. They are as follows:

```
boolean isTouching(Class cls)
```
Check whether this actor is touching any objects of the given class.

```
List getIntersectingObjects(Class cls)
```
Return all the objects that intersect this object.

```
Actor getOneIntersectingObject(Class cls)
```
Return an object that intersects this object.

```
List getObjectsAtOffset(int dx, int dy, Class cls)
```
Return all objects that intersect the given location (relative to this object's location).

```
Actor getOneObjectAtOffset(int dx, int dy, Class cls)
```
Return one object that is located at the specified cell (relative to this object's location).

```
List getNeighbours(int distance, boolean diagonal, Class cls)
```
Return the neighbours to this object within a given distance.

```
List getObjectsInRange(int r, Class cls)
```
Return all objects within range "r" around this object.

C.2 Convenience methods

Two of the methods, `getIntersectingObjects` and `getObjectsAtOffset`, have associated convenience methods, starting with `getOne...`

These convenience methods work in very similar ways to the method they are based on, but they return a single actor instead of a list of actors. In cases where multiple other actors could be found (for example, several other actors intersect with ours at the same time), the variant returning a list returns all the relevant actors. The variant returning a single actor randomly picks one of the intersecting actors and returns that one.

The purpose of these convenience methods is just to simplify code: Often we are only interested in a single intersecting actor. In those cases, the convenience method allows us to handle the actor without having to use a list.

C.3   Low versus high resolution

As we have seen throughout this book, the resolution (cell size) of Greenfoot worlds can vary. This is relevant for collision detection, as we will often use different methods, depending on the resolution.

We distinguish two cases: low-resolution worlds, where the entire actor image is completely contained within a single cell (Figure C.1a) and high-resolution worlds, where the image of an actor spans multiple cells (Figure C.1b).

Figure C.1

Examples of low and high resolution in Greenfoot worlds

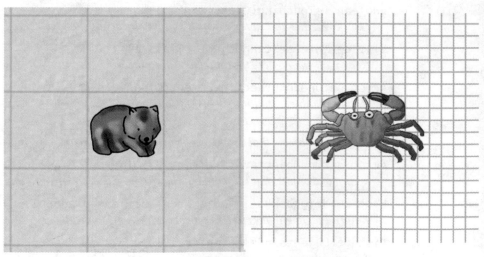

a) a low-resolution world   b) a high-resolution world

C.4   Intersecting objects

Methods:

```
List getIntersectingObjects(Class cls)
    Return all the objects that intersect this object.

Actor getOneIntersectingObject(Class cls)
    Return an object that intersects this object.
```

Figure C.2

Intersection of
actors using their
bounding boxes

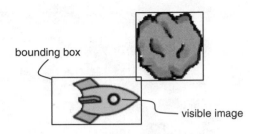

These methods return other actors whose image intersects with the calling actor's image. Images intersect when any part of one image touches any part of another image. These methods are most useful in high-resolution scenarios.

Intersection is computed using bounding boxes, so overlap of fully transparent parts of the images is also treated as intersection (Figure C.2).

The isTouching method uses the same type of test but returns a simple boolean rather than the actor:

> boolean isTouching(Class cls)
> *Check whether this actor is touching any objects of the given class.*

These methods are often used to check whether one actor has run into another kind of actor. The inaccuracy resulting from using bounding boxes (rather than the visible part of the image) can often be neglected.

The parameter can be used as a filter. If a class is specified as a parameter to these methods, only objects of that class are considered and all other objects are ignored. If null is used as a parameter, any intersecting object is returned.

C.5 Objects at offset

Methods:

> List getObjectsAtOffset(int dx, int dy, Class cls)
> *Return all objects that intersect the given location (relative to this object's location).*

> Actor getOneObjectAtOffset(int dx, int dy, Class cls)
> *Return one object that is located at the specified cell (relative to this object's location).*

These methods can be used to check for objects at a given offset from an actor's own current location. They are useful for both low- and high-resolution scenarios.

The *dx* and *dy* parameters specify the offset in a number of cells. Figure C.3 illustrates the location at offset (2,0) from the wombat (2 cells offset along the *x* coordinate and 0 cells offset along the *y* coordinate).

Figure C.3
Checking a given
offset from a loca-
tion (example here:
offset 2,0)

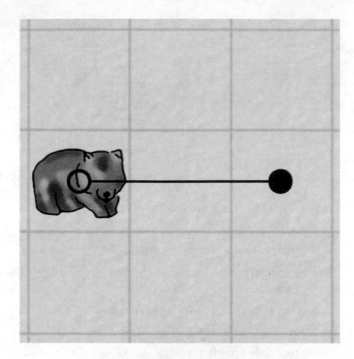

Another actor is considered to be at that offset if any part of that actor's image intersects with the center point of the specified cell. The `cls` parameter again provides the
option to filter the objects to be considered (see above).

These methods are often used to check an area in front of an actor (to test whether it
can move forward) or below an actor (to check whether it is standing on something).

C.6 Neighbors

Method:

```
List getNeighbours(int distance, boolean diagonal, Class cls)
```
Return the neighbours to this object within a given distance.

This method is used to retrieve objects from cells surrounding the current actor. It is
useful mainly in low-resolution scenarios.

Note the spelling of the method name: It really is **getNeighbours** (with British
spelling)—Greenfoot is not an American system.

The parameters specify the distance from the calling actor that should be considered
and whether or not diagonally positioned cells should be included. Figure C.4 illustrates the neighboring cells at distance 1, with and without diagonals included.

A distance of *N* is defined as all cells that can be reached in *N* steps from the actor's
own position. The **diagonal** parameter determines whether diagonal steps are
allowed in this algorithm.

Figure C.4

Example of the
getNeighbours
method

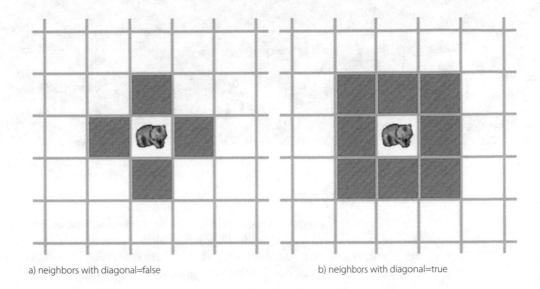

a) neighbors with diagonal=false   b) neighbors with diagonal=true

As with the previous methods, the `cls` parameter provides the option to consider only objects of a given class.

C.7   Objects in range

Method:

```
List getObjectsInRange(int r, Class cls)
```
Return all objects within range "r" around this object.

This method returns all objects within a given range of the calling actor. An object is in range if its location is a cell whose center point is at distance `r` or less from the calling actor (Figure C.5). The range `r` is measured in cells.

Figure C.5

The cells in a given
range around a
location

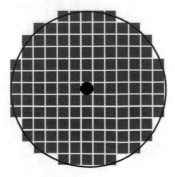

This method is mostly useful for high-resolution scenarios. As with the methods above, a class filter can be applied.

Some Java details

D.1 Java data types

Java knows two kinds of types: primitive types and object types. Primitive types are stored in variables directly, and they have value semantics (values are copied when assigned to another variable). Object types are stored by storing references to the object (not the object itself). When assigned to another variable, only the reference is copied, not the object.

D.1.1 Primitive types

The following table lists all the primitive types of the Java language:

Type name	Description	Example literals		
Integer numbers				
byte	byte-sized integer (8 bit)	24	−2	
short	short integer (16 bit)	137	−119	
int	integer (32 bit)	5409	−2003	
long	long integer (64 bit)	423266353L	55L	
Real numbers				
float	single-precision floating point	43.889F		
double	double-precision floating point	45.6324e5	0.4	
Other types				
char	a single character (16 bit)	'm'	'?'	'\u00F6'
boolean	a boolean value (true or false)	true	false	

Notes:

- A number without a decimal point is generally interpreted as an int, but cally converted to byte, short, or long types when assigned (if the value fi can declare a literal as long by putting an "L" after the number. (l—lower-case works as well but should be avoided because it can easily be mistaken for a one.)

- A number with a decimal point is of type double. You can specify a float literal by putting an "F" or "f" after the number.

- A character can be written as a single Unicode character in single quotes or as a four-digit Unicode value, preceded by "\u."

- The two boolean literals are true and false.

Because variables of the primitive types do not refer to objects, there are no methods associated with them. However, when used in a context requiring an object type, autoboxing might be used to convert a primitive value to a corresponding object.

The table below details minimum and maximum values available in the numerical types.

Type	Minimum	Maximum
byte	−128	127
short	−32768	32767
int	−2147483648	2147483647
long	−9223372036854775808	9223372036854775807
	Positive minimum	**Positive maximum**
float	1.4e–45	3.4028235e38
double	4.9e–324	1.7976931348623157e308

D.1.2 Object types

All types not listed in the *Primitive types* section are object types. These include class and interface types from the standard Java library (such as String) and user-defined types.

A variable of an object type holds a reference (or "pointer") to an object. Assignment and parameter passing have reference semantics (that is, the reference is copied, not the object). After assigning a variable to another one, both variables refer to the same object. The two variables are said to be aliases for the same object.

Classes are the templates for objects, defining the fields and methods that each instance possesses.

Arrays behave like object types—they also have reference semantics.

rators

ithmetic expressions

...has a considerable number of operators available for both arithmetic and logical ...ressions. Table D.1 shows everything that is classified as an operator, including ...perations such as type casting and parameter passing. Most of the operators are either binary operators (taking a left and a right operand) or unary operators (taking a single operand). The main binary arithmetic operations are:

+	*addition*
−	*subtraction*
*	*multiplication*
/	*division*
%	*modulo or remainder-after-division*

The results of both division and modulo operations depend on whether their operands are integers or floating point values. Between two integer values, division yields an integer result and discards any remainder, but between floating point values a floating point value is the result:

```
5 / 3 gives a result of 1
5.0 / 3 gives a result of 1.6666666666666667
```

(Note that only one of the operands needs to be of a floating point type to produce a floating point result.)

When more than one operator appears in an expression, then *rules of precedence* determine the order of application. In Table D.1 those operators having the highest precedence appear at the top, so we can see that multiplication, division, and modulo all take precedence over addition and subtraction, for instance. This means that both of the following examples give the result 100:

```
51 * 3 − 53
154 − 2 * 27
```

Binary operators with the same precedence level are evaluated from left to right and unary operators with the same precedence level are evaluated right to left.

When it is necessary to alter the normal order of evaluation, parentheses can be used. So both of the following examples give the result 100:

```
(205 − 5) / 2
2 * (47 + 3)
```

The main unary operators are −, !, ++, − − , [ ] and new. You will notice that ++ and − − appear in both of the top two rows in Table D.1. Those in the top row take a single operand on their left, while those in the second row take a single operand on their right.

Table D.1

Java operators, highest precedence at the top

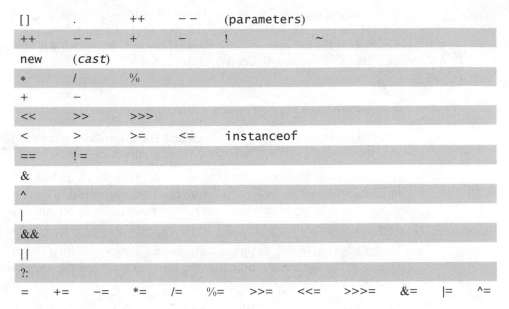

[]	.	++	– –	(parameters)	
++	– –	+	–	!	~
new	(*cast*)				
*	/	%			
+	–				
<<	>>	>>>			
<	>	>=	<=	instanceof	
==	!=				
&					
^					
|					
&&					
||					
?:					

=	+=	–=	*=	/=	%=	>>=	<<=	>>>=	&=	|=	^=

D.2.2 Boolean expressions

In boolean expressions, operators are used to combine operands to produce a value of either *true* or *false*. Such expressions are usually found in the test expressions of if-statements and loops.

The relational operators usually combine a pair of arithmetic operands, although the tests for equality and inequality are also used with object references. Java's relational operators are:

==	equal-to	!=	not-equal-to
<	less-than	<=	less-than-or-equal-to
>	greater-than	>=	greater-than-or-equal-to

The binary logical operators combine two boolean expressions to produce another boolean value. The operators are:

&&	and
||	or
^	exclusive-or

In addition,

!   not

takes a single boolean expression and changes it from `true` to `false`, and vice versa.

Both && and || are slightly unusual in the way they are applied. If the left operand of && is false then the value of the right operand is irrelevant and will not be evaluated. Similarly, if the left operand of || is true then the right operand is not evaluated. Thus, they are known as short-circuit operators.

D.3 Java control structures

Control structures affect the order in which statements are executed within the body of a method or constructor. There are two main categories: *selection statements* and *loops*.

A selection statement provides a decision point at which a choice is made to follow one route through the body of a method or constructor rather than another route. An *if-else* statement involves a decision between two different sets of statements, whereas a *switch* statement allows the selection of a single option from among several.

Loops offer the option to repeat statements, either a definite or an indefinite number of times. The former is typified by the *for-each* loop and *for* loop, while the latter is typified by the *while* loop and *do* loop.

In practice, it should be borne in mind that exceptions to the above characterizations are quite common. For instance, an if-else statement can be used to select from among several alternative sets of statements if the else part contains a nested if-else statement; and a for loop can be used to loop an indefinite number of times.

D.3.1 Selection statements

D.3.1.1 *if-else*

The *if-else* statement has two main forms, both of which are controlled by the evaluation of a boolean expression:

```
if (expression)
{
    statements
}

if (expression)
{
    statements
}
else
{
    statements
}
```

In the first form, the value of the boolean expression is used to decide whether to execute the statements or not. In the second form, the expression is used to choose between two alternative sets of statements, only one of which will be executed.

Examples:

```java
if (field.size() == 0)
{
    System.out.println("The field is empty.");
}

if (number < 0)
{
    reportError();
}
else
{
    processNumber(number);
}
```

It is very common to link if-else statements together by placing a second if-else in the else-part of the first. This can be continued any number of times. It is a good idea to always include a final else-part.

```java
if (n < 0)
{
    handleNegative();
}
else if (number == 0)
{
    handleZero();
}
else
{
    handlePositive();
}
```

D.3.1.2 *switch*

The *switch* statement switches on a single value to one of an arbitrary number of cases. Two possible use patterns are:

```
switch (expression)
{
    case value: statements;
        break;
    case value: statements;
        break;
    further cases omitted
    default: statements;
        break;
}
switch (expression)
{
    case value1:
    case value2:
    case value3:
        statements;
        break;
    case value4:
    case value5:
        statements;
        break;
    further cases omitted
    default:
        statements;
        break;
}
```

Notes:

- A switch statement can have any number of case labels.

- The `break` instruction after every case is needed, otherwise the execution "falls through" into the next label's statements. The second form above makes use of this. In this case, all three of the first values will execute the first statements section, whereas values four and five will execute the second statements section.

- The `default` case is optional. If no default is given, it may happen that no case is executed.

- The break instruction after the default (or the last case, if there is no default) is not needed but is considered good style.

Examples:

```java
switch(day)
{
    case 1: dayString = "Monday";
        break;
    case 2: dayString = "Tuesday";
        break;
    case 3: dayString = "Wednesday";
        break;
    case 4: dayString = "Thursday";
        break;
    case 5: dayString = "Friday";
        break;
    case 6: dayString = "Saturday";
        break;
    case 7: dayString = "Sunday";
        break;
    default: dayString = "invalid day";
        break;
}

switch(month)
{
    case 1:
    case 3:
    case 5:
    case 7:
    case 8:
    case 10:
    case 12:
        numberOfDays = 31;
        break;
    case 4:
    case 6:
    case 9:
    case 11:
        numberOfDays = 30;
        break;
    case 2:
        if(isLeapYear())
            numberOfDays = 29;
        else
            numberOfDays = 28;
        break;
}
```

D.3.2 Loops

Java has three loops: *while*, *do-while*, and *for*. The for loop has two forms. Except for the for-each loop, repetition is controlled in each with a boolean expression.

D.3.2.1 *while*

The while loop executes a block of statements as long as a given expression evaluates to *true*. The expression is tested before execution of the loop body, so the body may be executed zero times (that is, not at all). This capability is an important feature of the while loop.

```
while (expression)
{
    statements;
}
```

Examples:

```
System.out.print("Please enter a filename: ");
input = readInput();
while (input == null)
{
    System.out.print ("Please try again: ");
    input = readInput();
}

int index = 0;
boolean found = false;
while (!found && index < list.size())
{
    if (list.get(index).equals(item))
    {
        found = true;
    }
    else
    {
        index++;
    }
}
```

D.3.2.2. *do-while*

The do-while loop executes a block of statements as long as a given expression evaluates to *true*. The expression is tested after execution of the loop body, so the body always executes at least once. This is an important difference from the while loop.

```
do
{
    statements;
} while (expression);
```

Example:

```
do
{
    System.out.print("Please enter a filename: ");
    input = readInput();
} while (input == null);
```

D.3.2.3 *for*

The for loop has two different forms. The first form is also known as a *for-each loop*, and is used exclusively to iterate over elements of a collection. The loop variable is assigned the value of successive elements of the collection on each iteration of the loop.

```
for (variable-declaration : collection)
{
    statements;
}
```

Example:

```
for (String note : list)
{
    System.out.println(note);
}
```

The second form of for loop executes as long as a *condition* evaluates to *true*. Before the loop starts, an *initialization* statement is executed exactly once. The *condition* is evaluated before every execution of the loop body (so the loop may execute zero times). An *increment* statement is executed after each execution of the loop body.

```
for (initialization; condition; increment)
{
    statements;
}
```

Example:

```
for (int i = 0; i < text.size(); i++)
{
    System.out.println(text.get(i));
}
```

Both types of for loop are commonly used to execute the body of the loop a definite number of times—for instance, once for each element in a collection. A for-each loop cannot be used if the collection is to be modified while it is being iterated over.

Index